Gender and Japanese Management

JAPANESE SOCIETY SERIES
General Editor: Yoshio Sugimoto

Lives of Young Koreans in Japan
Yasunori Fukuoka

Globalization and Social Change in Contemporary Japan
J.S. Eades, Tom Gill and Harumi Befu

Coming Out in Japan: The Story of Satoru and Ryuta
Satoru Ito and Ryuta Yanase

Japan and Its Others:
Globalization, Difference and the Critique of Modernity
John Clammer

Hegemony of Homogeneity:
An Anthropological Analysis of Nihonjinron
Harumi Befu

Foreign Migrants in Contemporary Japan
Hiroshi Komai

A Social History of Science and Technology in
Contempory Japan, Volume 1
Shigeru Nakayama

Farewell to Nippon: Japanese Lifestyle Migrants in Australia
Machiko Sato

The Peripheral Centre:
Essays on Japanese History and Civilization
Johann P. Arnason

A Genealogy of 'Japanese' Self-images
Eiji Oguma

Class Structure in Contemporary Japan
Kenji Hashimoto

An Ecological View of History
Tadao Umesao

Nationalism and Gender
Chizuko Ueno

Native Anthropology: The Japanese Challenge
to Western Academic Hegemony
Takami Kuwayama

Youth Deviance in Japan: Class Reproduction of Non-Conformity
Robert Stuart Yoder

Japanese Companies: Theories and Realities
Masami Nomura and Yoshihiko Kamii

From Salvation to Spirituality: Popular Religious Movements in Modern Japan
Susumu Shimazono

The 'Big Bang' in Japanese Higher Education:
The 2004 Reforms and the Dynamics of Change
J.S. Eades, Roger Goodman and Yumiko Hada

Japanese Politics: An Introduction
Takashi Inoguchi

A Social History of Science and Technology in
Contempory Japan, Volume 2
Shigeru Nakayama

Gender and Japanese Management
Kimiko Kimoto

The Philosophy of Agricultural Science: Japan and Beyond
Osama Soda

Gender and Japanese Management

Kimiko Kimoto

Translated by
Teresa Castelvetere
with the assistance of
Ikuko Sorensen

Trans Pacific Press
Melbourne

First published in Japanese in 2003 by Keisō Shobō as *Josei rōdō to manejimento*

This English edition first published in 2005 by
Trans Pacific Press, PO Box 120, Rosanna, Melbourne, Victoria 3084, Australia
Telephone: +61 3 9459 3021 Fax: +61 3 9457 5923
Email: info@transpacificpress.com
Web: http://www.transpacificpress.com

Copyright © Trans Pacific Press 2005

Designed and set by digital environs Melbourne. enquiries@digitalenvirons.com

Printed by BPA Print Group, Burwood, Victoria, Australia

Distributors

Asia and the Pacific
Kinokuniya Company Ltd.

Head office:
38-1 Sakuragaoka 5-chome, Setagaya-ku, Tokyo
156-8691, Japan
Telephone: +81 (0)3 3439 0161
Fax: +81 (0)3 3439 0839
Email: bkimp@kinokuniya.co.jp
Web: www.kinokuniya.co.jp

Asia-Pacific office:
Kinokuniya Book Stores of Singapore Pte., Ltd.
391B Orchard Road #13-06/07/08
Ngee Ann City Tower B
Singapore 238874
Telephone: +65 6276 5558
Fax: +65 6276 5570
Email: SSO@kinokuniya.co.jp

Japan
Kyoto University Press
Kyodai Kaikan
15-9 Yoshida Kawara-cho
Sakyo-ku, Kyoto 606-8305
Telephone: (075) 761-6182
Fax: (075) 761-6190
Email: sales@kyoto-up.gr.jp
Web: http://www.kyoto-up.gr.jp

UK and Europe
Asian Studies Book Services
Franseweg 55B, 3921 DE Elst, Utrecht,
The Netherlands
Telephone: +31 318 470 030
Fax: +31 318 470 073
Email: info@asianstudiesbooks.com
Web: http://www.asianstudiesbooks.com

USA and Canada
International Specialized Book
Services (ISBS)
920 NE 58th Avenue, Suite 300
Portland, Oregon 97213-3786
USA
Telephone: (800) 944-6190
Fax: (503) 280-8832
Email: orders@isbs.com
Web: http://www.isbs.com

Australia and New Zealand
UNIREPS
University of New South Wales
Sydney, NSW 2052
Australia
Telephone: +61(0)2-9664-0999
Fax: +61(0)2-9664-5420
Email: info.press@unsw.edu.au
Web: http://www.unireps.com.au

All rights reserved. No production of any part of this book may take place without the written permission of Trans Pacific Press.

ISSN   1-443-9670 (Japanese Society Series)

ISBN   1-8768-4319-5 (Hardback)
ISBN   1-8768-4320-9 (Paperback)

Contents

Figures — vi
Tables — vii
Preface — ix
Acknowlegements — xiv

Part I

1 Labour Studies and a Gender Perspective: A Critical Summation of Women's Labour Studies — 3
2 Methodology and Subject — 33

Part II

3 Job Segregation Mechanisms: Excessive Work Duty Gendering — 67
4 Response-negotiation Relations in the Work Organisation: the Segregation Line between 'Them and Us' — 108
5 The Challenge of 'Creating Female Store Managers': Management Style and Gender — 160

Conclusion: Getting Closer to the Realities of the Work Organisation — 223

Notes — 233
References — 250
Postscript — 265
Index — 269

Figures

2.1:	Changing employee profile in the six largest department stores	57
2.2:	Changing employee profile in the five largest supermarkets	57
2.3:	Changes in the average age of regular employees	58
3.1:	Company A's status ranking system	71
3.2:	Distribution chart of personnel in survey shop	77
3.3:	Average annual income model by educational background (Company A)	90
4.1:	Changes in the number of employees	110
4.2:	Changes in average length of continuous service	111
4.3:	Schematic representation of distribution of in-store positions	115
4.4:	Numerical composition of positions by gender (regular employees in sales)	115
4.5:	Proportion of women in each department (National 1999)	117
4.6:	Qualifications of rank-and-file employees and chief clerks (Store A)	127
4.7:	Aspirations for promotion of rank-and-file employees and chief clerks (Store A)	127
4.8.1:	Work perceptions 1 (Store A)	143
4.8.2:	Work perceptions 2 (Store A)	143
4.8.3:	Work perceptions 3 (Store A)	145
4.9:	Occasions leading to a sense of reward and achievement (Area B Business Operations Department)	146
4.10:	Complaints and aspirations of part-timers (Store A)	153
4.11:	Part-timers' evaluation of their work performance (Store A)	153
5.2:	Changes in the number of stores (Company X)	185
5.3:	Store manager promotions (8 cases who joined the company in 1980)	190

Tables

2.1:	Changes in the number of stores by sales format	52
2.2:	Changes in annual sales volume and sales share by sales format (million yen)	53
2.3:	Changes in employee numbers by sales format (regular employees)	54
2.4:	Changes in the proportion of regular female employees by sales format	55
2.5:	A breakdown of regular employees by sales format (1999)	56
3.1:	The development of Company A's personnel management systems	70
3.2:	Changes in the number of employees by status grade level	74
3.3:	Number of women in managerial positions in the workplace	75
3.4:	Attributes of dispatched salespeople	99
4.1:	Status ranking system and corresponding positions in Company X	112
4.2:	Overview of interviewees (Store A)	119
4.3:	Number of employees by section in Store A	120
4.4:	Distribution of mobility paths selected (Store A)	125
4.5:	Years of service of female employees on the store-specific path (Store A)	125
5.1:	Career characteristics of female store managers	162
5.2:	Career characteristics of male store managers	162
5.3:	Number of years of store experience of female middle managers, excluding store managers (1998)	167
5.4:	Breakdown of daily work hours of store managers (Area C Operations Department)	175
5.5:	Store managers' experience outside the store	184
5.6:	Number of years taken to reach each occupational position, by store managers' years of entry	184
5.7:	Career development of store managers (8 cases taken from the 1980 intake into the company)	188
5.8:	Presence or absence of section head experience in sales	189

Preface

This book, based on a critical awareness of the need to open up new horizons in women's labour studies, arose from a series of interview surveys in actual work organisations. This problem consciousness is as set out below.

As is widely known, the Japanese employment practices of lifetime employment, seniority-based wages and company-based labour unions, established after the end of the Second World War, have applied to the long-term employment of men; women have not had these benefits. Women have been assigned the status of a short cycle labour force, repeatedly moving in and out of the labour market, and also that of providing the flexibility with which to alleviate the rigidity brought about by men's long-term employment security. This situation has continued to have a decisive impact on the enduring structures of the sexual division of labour in Japanese society. Men show an extreme inclination towards being 'company men' and women, because of the 'makeshift' nature of their employment, have become 'workplace flowers' – they have become locked into a scenario in which they aspire to the goal of rearing children and being re-employed as part-timers, after they have resigned to marry or to have children.

The relations between women and work are always, however, undergoing considerable change. Women are deepening their links with work: today, we are already witnessing a trend towards long-term continuous employment for women and, in addition to this, a process of women tackling a variety of careers. The factors behind these moves by women are a retreat from so-called 'marriage aspirations' and 'full-time housewife aspirations'. We can see this, in a sense, as the rise of 'work aspirations'. By shedding light on the experiences of these women we see that existing work practices as still restricting them.

These types of transformations undergone by women have led on the one hand to a different set of, and constantly higher, expectations being placed on women's labour. Women's labour is attracting more attention in terms of policy as the trend is increasingly towards having fewer children and living longer. A clear statement of this is found in the *The National Lifestyle White Paper* (*Kokumin Seikatsu Hakusho*) (1997), which for the first time featured 'A Society of Working Women'. Also, from the second half of the 1990s there was a general critical awareness of gender fairness, and a recognition of this at the state level as seen in the Revised Equal Employment Opportunity Law between Men and Women (1997) and the Basic Law for a Gender-Equal Society (1999) (*Danjo Kyōdō Sankaku Shakai Kihon Hō*). This was one of the chief factors which led to reforms to the existing framework, beginning with the social security system.

On the other hand, some companies enthusiastically grappling with attempts to 'make positive use of women' (*josei katsuyō*) have also begun appearing amongst Japanese companies, which have previously been indifferent to the issue of the treatment of women. The motivation for this is not necessarily an attempt to introduce a value standard of gender fairness; rather, it is part of an attempt to reform Japanese employment practices, in a manner appropriate to a period of 'extremely intense competition', and also an attempt to make better use of talented people. Whilst Japanese firms hold up making positive use of young people and women as one of the objectives of the reorganisation of Japanese employment practices, they tend also to regard the neglect of middle-aged and older men as natural. At the same time, the dynamics at work in undermining the vested interests of women, in the form of substituting part-time employees for female regular employees, are still at work in periods of prolonged recession.

In the above fashion, an overlapping set of complex conditions is appearing in present-day Japanese society and women's labour is ushering in a reform period. Neither an optimistic and bright picture nor a dark picture full of pessimism corresponds to reality in these circumstances. Searching for the main factors leading to new possibilities whilst scrutinising the complex realities before them is the task before researchers currently working in the area of women's labour. As we do this we ought to take a hard look at the various elements prescribing the state of the women concerned and realistic processes for transforming these. It will be by focussing our attention on these matters that we will be able to find the path along which gender fairness in the workplace can be realised.

With this particular problem consciousness in mind, this book looks at real cases in large-scale retail industries with a high level of reliance on women's labour and which, moreover, have achieved excellent actual results in 'making positive use of women'. Through intensive interview surveys inside work organisations, this book, firstly, attempts to make clear, in a multi-faceted way, the main reasons for the inability of women to reach the top levels of management, despite the existence of a single system of treatment for both men and women (the status ranking system) (*shokunō shikaku seido*). The points highlighted here are not limited to the cases dealt with in this book but are broadly issues of relevance to the organisational culture discernible to varying extents throughout Japanese work organisations. In that sense, this book has taken on the task of attempting to analyse the actual state of Japanese work organisations, which, because of their neglect of talented females, now lag considerably behind the international standard.

Secondly, this book attempts to grasp the special significance of the management styles being adopted by those women who have been able to ride the wave of their organisation's self-imposed challenge of trying to select women for middle manager positions, by exploring their career development processes and their management styles. In doing this I take particular note of the pride and resistance of female rank-and-file regular employees and part-timers at the very bottom of the work organisation. I also attempt to explain, from the standpoint of organisational reform, the connecting structures between what happens at the very bottom and management from above. Via the above analysis, this book attempts to question once again the relationships between 'management', which has until now been the domain of men, and 'women' in the work organisation. Finally, in addition to exploring the possibilities for women to act as innovators in existing work organisations, I attempt to indicate how androcentric organisational culture, incapable of rapid change, will change as a result of organisational challenges in pursuit of organisational efficiency.

The problem consciousness underpinning the research method used in this book attempts to bring a gender perspective truly to bear in labour analysis. Research into women's labour studies to date in Japan has poured its energy into establishing the premise that the conditions for labour market participation for women are, first and foremost, disadvantageous conditions of participation because women bear the responsibility for housework and child rearing. This research has then gone on to use this argument to explain the poor treatment and conditions, instability, low skill levels and the status of women as victims of discrimination. The result of this has been to place excessive emphasis on the specificity of women's labour, as distinct from male labour. This research approach has also been limited by its failure to extend its discussion to the processes forming and transforming gender relations inside the work organisation. It is, in reality, not only researchers in the field of women's labour who demonstrate this particular understanding of the issues. The people responsible for putting into practice personnel policies in work organisations also attempt to understand the presence of women, first and foremost, on the basis of their household and child rearing responsibilities. Applying this perspective invites the dual results of coming to view women's early resignation from work posts as 'natural' and a disregard for the various causes, found inside the organisation, which inevitably drove these women to resign. The exploration of organisational reform measures appropriate to modern-day conditions will be difficult unless we overcome this understanding of the situation, which is based on gender stereotypes, in both research and business practices.

The precise task before us now is to make clear, using an analysis of present conditions, how the gender norms are themselves constructed and how gender relations are conducted inside work organisations. In order for this to occur, we need to put to one side – momentarily – talk about the statistical fate of women in the labour market being a given because of their roles in childbirth, housework and child rearing and also arguments limited to complaints about disparities in treatment conditions. We need to seek instead a path for bringing to bear a gender perspective in analyses of work organisations based on social and cultural differences between the sexes. What this means precisely is highlighting the mechanisms which construct gender relations and gender norms right in the middle of workplaces. Historian John W. Scott's positing, in *Gender and the Politics of History* (1988), that 'gender is the social organisation of sexual difference' and that sexual difference is 'a variable social organization that itself must be explained' (Scott, 1988, 2) could serve as a path enabling the pursuit of these themes in labour analysis and also the identification of the major change factors in the present realities facing work organisations.

This book is organised along the following lines. Firstly, in Part I, I give a critical summary of the achievements of women's labour studies and make clear the need for case studies (Chapter 1). Then, as well as discussing the analytical method adopted in the case studies found in Part II, I also make clear the historical assumptions and characteristics of the department store and general merchandise supermarket, which are surveyed in this book, as well as the position of this book in existing research (Chapter 2). In Part II, I carry out an analysis of work organisations. Chapter 3 is an analysis of an actual case of a department store and Chapters 4 and 5 are an analysis of an actual general merchandise supermarket. These analyses include a consideration of the following keywords: job segregation by gender, segregation within work organisations, response-negotiation relations, organisational culture and management style.

The particular methodological characteristics permeating this book lie in its attempt to delve down to the deepest layers of the organisation and to approach the diverse relationships woven into these layers. This book does not limit itself to understanding how gender relationships are reproduced inside work organisations, it attempts to analyse how work organisations change, as they experience resistance and challenges from the people in them and from the organisations themselves. In other words, I attempt to consider the factors linked to organisational reform, whilst identifying and attaching meaning to the daily work practices of every individual in the work organisation. This is because I think that it will be via this very approach that we will be able to bring into relief the relationships between women and management.

Acknowledgements

The original research for this book was undertaken over a ten-year period. During this time, many people and organizations in one of Japan's largest department stores, Company A, and largest general merchandise supermarkets, Company X, assisted me and put me in contact with interviewees.

My main debt is to all the people I interviewed. They welcomed me into their workplaces and generously answered questions, spoke of their career histories and reminded me of numerous important points relating to their everyday world of work. I am sorry that the need to ensure confidentiality makes it impossible for me to thank them by name.

I must express my gratitude to Yuki Aritomi, an assistant in the Graduate School of Social Sciences of Hitotsubashi University for her help in organizing the substantial research data. I am also grateful to Miyoko Machida of Keisō Shobō publishers who launched the original publication of this book in Japanese.

The translation and publication of this book in English, two years after its original publication in Japanese, has been made possible with the assistance of a Grant-in-Aid for Publication of Scientific Research Results from the Japan Society for the Promotion of Science. I am grateful for the JSPS' generous financial support.

Finally, I would like to express my special thanks to Professor Yoshio Sugimoto, Professor of Sociology at La Trobe University and Director of Trans Pacific Press, for his constructive suggestions and warm encouragement. I am deeply grateful to my translator, Teresa Castelvetere, who made painstaking efforts with all the detailed work involved in producing this volume. I would also like to thank Atsuko Yokota for doing such a good job with the cover photo for this book.

This book is dedicated to my parents, Miyokichi Sakai and Toshiko Sakai, both of whom have provided me with emotional support for a very long time.

August 2005
Kimiko KIMOTO

Part I

1 Labour Studies and a Gender Perspective: A Critical Summation of Women's Labour Studies

The status of women's labour studies in Japan

Identifying the issues

This chapter aims to clarify the achievements of, and challenges facing, women's labour studies which have been conducted from a gender perspective in Japan. A fundamental problem has been the surprising failure of women's labour studies in the past to see an analysis of the changing features of women's paid work as being of central concern to their own work. This chapter will question why this has been the case and, after undertaking a critical summary of women's labour studies in Japan, will attempt to identify future tasks. In the course of this process I will elucidate the position of this book in terms of the history of women's labour studies and will also set out the methodological criteria applied in the case studies described in Section II.

Jumping ahead slightly, the conclusion of this book will be that women's labour studies in Japan have stressed the 'specificity' arising from women's domestic and child rearing roles and have operated from the premise that paid work can be understood along these lines. This was a methodological position which, either consciously or unconsciously, directly linked the status and role of women within the labour market to the division of labour between men and women in the family. This view could be referred to as 'gender-based division of family labour determinism'. Furthermore, this view inevitably displayed a strong tendency to concentrate discussion on women's labour alone and showed practically no interest in empirical studies, which by inquiring into the links with men's labour, could illuminate gender relations at work in the labour process. As a result, this view has not yet impressed upon the whole community of labour studies that a full-scale introduction of a gender perspective is indispensable.

This chapter will highlight future research tasks by looking back at the history of these studies and pointing out the problems encountered thus far.

To this end, I will set out the trends in women's labour studies both in Japan and in the West, with particular emphasis on comparisons between Japanese and British studies. The reason for this is the decisive influence on Japanese research of Marxist-Feminist-based research in Europe and also the continuing large-scale influx of these works into Japan.[1] This influence notwithstanding, for some reason important research trends in the West have been overlooked in Japan, with research here having remained at the level of women's labour theories lacking the theoretical or methodological momentum to point them towards an analysis of paid work. The pressing task is to move away from this level and advance on to a fuller analysis of paid work from a gender perspective – the aim of this book.

'Men's labour studies' in Japan

Before discussing women's labour studies, we need to look at existing labour studies. The research undertaken thus far has focused on men. This tendency is not peculiar to Japan but one also commonly found in other countries. In Japan, in particular, research has concentrated on looking at men only, especially those in large private companies, in order to shed light on the special character of labour relations. Although, admittedly, the absence of women as research subjects encouraged this situation, previous labour studies have, as a matter of course, generalised and discussed male workers as 'workers'. Meanwhile, although research into 'female labour', referred to as both *joshi rōdō* and *fujin rōdō* and dealing with the issues faced by women, was established as one research area, it would be fair to say that it had practically no impact in terms of dislodging the view of 'workers' contained in labour studies'. This resulted from the strong tendency for research into women's labour, invariably, to consider women, in comparison to men, as 'special' and 'peripheral' and to discuss their specificity in connection with the issues of inequality and discrimination.

One of the features of the labour relations that have underpinned Japan's company society is the acknowledgement by giant private companies that male regular employees are the core troops in their companies. Male regular employees enjoyed good working conditions – such as long-term employment, relatively high wages and generous in-company welfare – which maintained their high motivation and company loyalty and formed the basis on which employees as well as their family members were integrated into company society.[2] In contrast to the 'core' group of male regular employees in the giant companies, an enormous 'peripheral' group has developed, including employees in small and medium-sized companies, foreign and also female employees. It is therefore not without reason that labour studies have primarily focused on men.

Labour studies in the past have, however, shown a tendency to limit major research areas to large companies, without paying much attention to the smaller and medium-sized contracting companies that support large companies. Even though one may have found only men in large companies themselves, it should have been possible, had one looked, to identify the job segregation by gender that existed in the large body of small and medium-sized contracting companies surrounding and underpinning the large company.[3] Nonetheless, a portion of existing labour studies still have not come to terms with the fact that they have been lacking a gender perspective. Even in a recent publication giving an overview of the history of research in labour sociology in Japan, 'gender', as a key word, is not to be found and the discussion throughout is limited to male workers in manufacturing industry (Kawanishi, 2001). Although it is 'the ultimate goal' (Kawanishi, 2001, 108) of Japanese labour sociology to elucidate the 'images of workers', this discipline still lacks a gender perspective. Needless to say, the world of labour is one into which come a diverse range of individuals, with various differences (not only gender, but also class, social status, generation, educational background, ethnicity and the like), and also a world in which these differences are controlled in a most stringent manner. Is it possible then to grasp the 'images of workers' without paying attention to the way in which gender differences – the core difference amongst this varied array of differences – have been woven into the world of labour? In this book, I consciously identify and call this narrow view in traditional labour studies 'men's labour studies'.

The characteristics of women's labour studies in Japan

It is against this background that women's labour studies in Japan have been developing arguments with a gender perspective. This research has tried to elucidate the fundamentally different role of women who, compared to men – the core employees in company society, have no choice but to take up shorter-term employment. As well as making clear the issues specific to women, especially those issues facing women who bear the burden of domestic and child-rearing roles, this research has also analysed the role of women as low-paid or unskilled workers in the labour market (Hirota, 1979). The focus has been primarily to explore the theoretical position of women's labour in the process of capital accumulation. As women workers carry the responsibility for domestic and child-rearing roles under the prevalent division of labour by gender, they are compelled to enter and exit the labour market as a peripheral group. The task of theorising about the problems inherent in and arising from this situation– in terms of the structural relationship between capital accumulation and the family – has become the focal task.[4] In other words, 'female labour' or 'women's labour' has been considered, and theories constructed about it, in relation to matters not analysed in 'men's labour studies' – that is, the family and domestic labour. Research into men's and women's labour have developed as two separate areas which do not ever mingle with each other unless men and women are collectively discussed in issues such as unstable employment or low-paid workers.

In contrast to the neglect of the existence of women on the part of mainstream labour studies, this type of research into women's labour has adopted a perspective, which while focusing on women, always aims to refer to the mutually complementary relationship between men and women in company society. While the long-term and stable employment of men tends to make the company structure rigid, women workers are likely to avoid this tendency. In other words, women's labour studies have tried to clarify the unique role and position of women as the ones who avoid this rigidity. This made it possible to gain a bird's-eye view of the dual structures between the genders: men, on one hand, tending constantly towards being company beings and older women, on the other, moving increasingly into part-time work as a consequence of their short employment history (Kumazawa, 1993). Thus, the methodological characteristic of women's labour studies has been that it has subsumed both the sphere of labour and that of reproduction, including the family, and tried to connect these two.

The task of this chapter

What impact did this growing body of work in women's labour studies have on existing 'men's labour studies'? As will be discussed in detail later, since the late 1980s women's labour studies in Japan, stimulated by Marxist-Feminism in the West, have continuously renewed themselves by going beyond the traditional arguments. In the middle of the 1990s, however, one of the leading scholars in women's labour studies, Emiko Takenaka, was still commenting that, 'In Japan, women's labour studies is recognised as a special field of study, as opposed to a general research area, and finds it difficult to escape this view.' (1995, 29) 'General research', in this case, naturally means men's labour studies and is a frank admission of the fact that the growing body of women's labour studies has not been able to exercise much influence on existing labour studies. It is true that women's labour studies and men's labour studies often seem to be totally separate discussions, even though they both deal with 'labour'. In the early 1990s, however, even scholars of the main generation conducting 'men's labour studies' started reflecting that women's labour had been excluded from their work (Totsuka and Tokunaga, 1993, 17). Now that the 'feminisation of the labour force' (Fukasawa, 1993; Takenaka, 1994) is having a decisive impact on society as a whole, it is appropriate that this neglect of women's labour should be rectified. The quest now is for a methodology through which to introduce a gender perspective into labour studies, especially into its empirical studies.

This chapter will start with a critical summary of women's labour studies in Japan, identifying the problems that it has faced. Firstly, I will reassess women's labour via a discussion of the domestic labour debate, from a feminist perspective (mainly a European and United States perspective). Secondly, I will consider the impact of this debate on research into women's paid work in Japan.

The domestic labour debate and the 'special theory' of women's labour

The domestic labour debate in the West

The discovery of domestic labour

Margaret Benston (1969) initiated the domestic labour debate, which took place mainly in Europe and the United States, when she set out to illuminate the materialistic basis of the social oppression of women. Her argument included criticism of existing Marxist Economics, which had relegated domestic labour to a peripheral position, as if it did not exist. She argued that the inferior position of women stems from the fact that their domestic labour is not included in economic analyses because, despite being valuable labour, wages are not paid. Her contention was perceived as an important proposition in Marxist-Feminism and developed into a debate about the relationship between women's unpaid work within the family, the reproduction of labour and paid work. In Britain, for example, heated discussions have taken place since the mid-1970s looking for ways to build new theories incorporating domestic labour into their perspectives. The characteristics of domestic labour in the capitalist economic system were explained by comparing them with those of alienated labour. The main points of the debate surrounded questions such as whether women's labour market participation could form a definitive strategy for women's liberation and how domestic labour should be analysed. The debate about the role played by domestic labour in the capitalist economy has led to quite a vibrant discussion of the question of whether wages ought to be paid for domestic labour.[5]

The domestic labour debate was important in that it aimed to reassess the very concept of domestic labour, which had been excluded from discussions of the capitalist economic system, by questioning its significance and role. What emerged from this debate was confirmation that domestic labour is valuable labour for humans and produces use value but it does not produce surplus value (Beechey, 1987=1993, 7; Furuta, 1997, 330). This meant that 'housework', which had been 'an invisible presence' because of the line segregating market and family, was raised to the status of 'domestic labour' and was established as an object of study. This debate was significant in that it generated an interest in reassessing the economy and society as a whole by directly addressing the issue of the respective relations between market labour and non-market labour and also between productive labour and reproductive labour, which until then had been dealt with as dichotomies. It made clear that domestic labour was an indispensable premise for the existence and development of capitalism. However, as will be mentioned again later, as early as the late 1970s/early 1980s, this debate was regarded as one that had become too bogged down in economic terminology. Many feminists felt that the debate should not be restricted to the confines of narrowly based arguments attributing the cause of the social suppression of women to the non-remunerability of domestic labour.

The housewife debate in Japan

In Japan, a similar exchange took place long before the domestic labour debate occurred in the West. As is widely known, in 1955 Ayako Ishigaki wrote 'Housewife as a Secondary Occupation', in the journal

Fujin Kōron (*Women's Public Opinion*), arousing public opinion. This is known as 'the first housewife debate'. The main discussion concerned the question of whether or not women ought to take up a responsible primary occupation and not simply resign themselves to the role of being a housewife. This was not, however, a reassessment of the housewife role itself, which is borne by women. The publication by Fujiko Isono of 'Confusion in Theories of Women's Liberation', in the *Asahi Journal*, sparked a second housewife debate, which started in 1960 and made similar arguments to those seen during the earlier domestic labour debate in the West. Isono took up the very question of 'housewife labour' and asked whether 'a housewife produces value' in the capitalist economy. Her question was based on an awareness of the issues that surround the path to 'women's liberation'. She asked if the only way for women to gain independence was to participate in paid work and also questioned what women who are engaged in domestic labour ought to do in order to achieve social and economic independence. Without going into the details here, the debate ended with confirmation – based on the application of the prevailing Marxist Economics interpretation, as represented by the arguments of the Marxist economist, Tadao Takagi – that a housewife's labour does not produce economic value.[6]

It seems that the matters confirmed during the debates in Japan are not dissimilar to the case of debates in the United States and the United Kingdom, as discussed earlier. However, a significant difference was the force of the attempt to break the limitations of the theoretical framework of traditional Marxist Economics, which was only capable of regarding domestic labour as an 'invisible presence'. As will be discussed later in the book, we should not overlook the fact that feminists in the West recognised the limitations of the domestic labour debate, in that it had become bogged down in economic terminology and moved on to develop research to overcome this situation. In the case of Japan, the fact that the housewife debate appeared at a very early stage accounts for the nature of its conclusions. This debate appeared at a time when Japan had not yet experienced the second wave of the modern feminism movement, which started in the advanced countries in the 1960s and 1970s.

A negative summation of the domestic labour debate
Accordingly, following the 1980s, Japan had to 're-import' the domestic labour debate, which had taken place in western countries in the 1970s. The earliest introduction of this debate was by Yoshiko Kuba in 1979,

followed by Emiko Takenaka and Atsushi Shibuya in 1980 (Kuba, 1979; Shibuya, 1983; Takenaka, 1989a), but it was Chizuko Ueno who popularised the debate with her forceful presentation (1990).[7] Therefore, information regarding the domestic labour debate in the West was brought into Japan only after the 1980s, and as noted by Ueno, even by the end of the 1990s, 'we still have not seen the end of 'the domestic labour debate' (1995, 698). As is clear from her assertion, the debate about women's labour in Japan was developing in the 1990s, still being dragged along, as it were, by the discussions that started in the domestic labour debate. Many western thinkers, however, had already given a negative summation of the domestic labour debate and succeeded in breaking through its limitations in the late 1970s.

In the 1980s, one of the leading voices of Marxist-Feminism at the time, Michèle Barrett, gave a critique of the domestic labour debate saying that 'gender relations are reduced to an effect of the operation of capital (Barrett, 1980, 24) and refused to discuss the causes of the social suppression of women as an extension of the domestic labour debate (Barrett, 1980, 210). Lisa Vogel also pointed out that the debate 'took the form of rather intricate and dry elaborations of Marxist theory' and was regarded 'as an obscure exercise in Marxist pedantry' (Vogel, 1981, 204). According to Veronica Beechey's recollections in 1987, which will be discussed again later, she valued the debate, albeit reservedly, as an important opportunity for Marxist feminists to construct their theories. The debate conclusively demonstrated that domestic labour is labour rather than an act of love: that it performs an important economic function in the capitalist production system and that the bulk of what women do in the family is precisely labour. However, she is critical of the existence of a 'tendency to pay attention to the family rather than the labour market' saying that, 'it seems that the whole debate went up something of a blind alley'. This is because the conditions of housewives have been generalised to women as a whole and because women's paid work has been undervalued. She summarises the way in which the whole approach is 'excessively functionalist, economically reductionist and insufficiently historical'. Furthermore, she makes the scathing criticism that on the whole 'the result was that gender relations got lost' (Beechey, 1987=1993, 208–209, 6–9 in translation). She sounded the alarm, warning that the debate has fallen into the trap of overemphasising the 'specificity' of women who perform domestic labour and disregarding their paid work.

Many scholars in Japan seem to have failed to grasp the new developments and changes of direction in methodology that took place in the West following serious self-reflection regarding the domestic labour debate. This seems to be closely related to the stagnant state of research being conducted in women's labour studies, especially into women's paid work in Japan. This is due to the propensity for sweeping arguments that attempt to discuss women's paid work on the basis of the theory of women's domestic labour or to generalise in terms of 'the patriarchal system or capitalist system', with little attention being paid to building up a theory and methodology directed towards an analysis of the real situation. Now let us examine the development of discussions since the 1980s in Japan.

Japanese features of the domestic labour debate

An overview of 'the special theory' of women's labour

Emiko Takenaka was one of the first scholars to introduce the domestic labour debate to Japan. She offers an overview of 'the special theory' of women's labour while using this debate as the basis of her own arguments. She opened up the new plane on which women's labour theory in Japan now stands and the books on women's labour in Japan authored or co-authored by her (Takenaka, 1983; 1989a; 1991; Takenaka and Kuba, 1994) are essential reading, referred to by every researcher in the field of women's labour. The theory underlying her work reflects the strong influence of the domestic labour debate in the West. She tried to identify 'the specific conditions under which women enter the labour market' by applying the category of 'the system of commodification of the labour force that forms the material basis for the unification of the capitalist system and the division of labour by gender' (1989a, 6). She then attributed 'the ultimate cause of the division of labour by gender in employment' to 'a system of commodification of the labour force '. This stems from 'the fact that the very formation of the labour market is based on a system of commodification of the labour force and that this system, in itself, presupposes the family to be a direct productive unit of the labour force, which includes job segregation by gender in which the labour to reproduce labour is considered to be an exclusively female function' (1989a, 26).[8]

This is a formularisation that seeks a way of escaping the limitations of past Marxist women's labour theory in Japan by examining the reproductive mode of the modern family. Previous studies, represented by the work of Chitose Shimazu (1978), failed to comprehend that working class families are organised on the basis of modern monogamy

– that is, as a monogamous family based on the division of labour by gender – and incorporated into 'the system of the commodification of the labour force'. Shimazu's discussion is based on *The Origin of the Family, Private Property and the State* (1884) by Friedrich Engels and makes the distinction between bourgeois marriage and proletarian marriage in a modern society. While the former is 'built on in-house slavery, either explicitly or implicitly, accepted by the wife', for the latter the only motivation for marriage is sexual love. Furthermore, Shimazu considers the latter to be a family that connotes 'progressiveness' in the sense that it opens up the possibility of equality between men and women. The reason given for this is the lack of materialistic backing for a proletarian man to warrant his control and supremacy over women, but this is not historically substantiated. Rather, what historical studies show us is a process of acceptance and internalisation of the bourgeois family norm, including the division of labour by gender in modern society – 'men work outside and women keep house' – by the working class family. Therefore, the question of what prevents 'progressiveness' in a working class family from manifesting itself needs to be reversed. The question we must ask is how the working class family has come to internalise the modern family norm that was first established in the middle class with its different economic base.[9]

Takenaka's argument, which has incorporated the achievements of theories from the second wave of feminism, overcomes such limitations. First of all, it must be noted that her work surpasses traditional Japanese studies of women's labour in that it tackles directly the question of the division of labour by gender in the family and, therefore, its relationship to those who shoulder responsibility for domestic labour. Takenaka gave due consideration to the great impact made on the working class family by the 'modern family' model that includes the division of labour between men and women. By doing so, Takenaka freed those of us who were searching for the path to women's liberation using a simplistic argument which insists that for women to be liberated they should remain in their workplaces and keep working. This is indeed a remarkable achievement on her part.

A critique of 'the special theory' of women's labour
However, Takenaka's argument starts to reveal its weakness when she moves directly from this to a discussion of women's paid work. Takenaka begins her consideration of the cause of women's unequal position and lower wages in paid work by looking at the division of

domestic labour by gender and then moves on to consider 'the system of the commodification of the labour force'. The un-remunerated nature of domestic labour contributes to the profit making of capital by suppressing the value of such labour. This, at the same time, determines the positioning of women in the labour market. Takenaka argues that this means that women who bear the burden of domestic labour are 'utilised as cheap labour serving as a control valve for differing economic conditions' (1989a, 55). Thus, she gives an overview of 'the special theory' of women's labour while her argument carries over, as it were, the domestic labour debate. It is necessary to note that she clearly has the 'specificity' of women's labour in mind. In addition, Takenaka's theory, which may be referred to as 'gender-based division of family labour determinism' and which says that the division of labour on the basis of gender in the family determines the inferiority of women's labour in the labour market, forms the core of 'the special theory' of women's labour.[10]

Mari Ōsawa criticized Takenaka's argument saying that, 'the issues are structured on the assumption that women's labour is a special, peripheral area' (1993a, 20). This highlights the inadequacy of Takenaka's argument as an expository theory in that it tries to explain the wage differences between men and women in the labour market by looking at women as 'the gender that gives birth', which is itself a notion based on the division of labour by gender. This criticism is to the point. Ōsawa argues that it is not women's labour alone which should be considered special and that 'if there are specific conditions for women to enter labour market', then 'the male breadwinner who has transferred the responsibility of domestic labour to his wife', himself, ought to be regarded as no less 'special' than women (1993a, 18). Takenaka has accepted this criticism (1993, 117). Ōsawa's view that we must attach gender not only to women but also to men is an important one.

This alone, however, is not sufficient as a critique of Takenaka. Criticism must also be directed towards the problematic nature of the methodology with which she aims to explain the distribution, positions and conditions of labour within the labour market. She tries to explain these things by looking at the conditions of entry into the labour market, which originate from the gender-based division of labour in the family. The domestic labour debate, which has influenced Takenaka, was itself based on a 'gender-based division of family labour determinism' view, which attaches importance to the aspect of labour supply. Naturally, analysing factors that affect labour supply is an essential research area, but we cannot say that labour supply alone determines the labour process. Factors affecting the positioning of women's labour within the labour market are more complex than this and Takenaka's methodology, which attempts to proceed directly to an explanation of these factors from the theory of domestic labour, seems to be too hasty. It is therefore necessary to overcome the weaknesses of 'gender-based division of family labour determinism'.

A dual systems theory or a unified theory?
Let us now take a look at the domestic labour debate in Japan mentioned earlier and which was said to be still continuing in 1995. The debate was developed as an introduction and interpretation of Marxist-Feminism. Particularly Japanese features can be noted in its development process, however, with diverse western arguments being framed simply as evidence of 'capitalism', 'patriarchy' or of a 'capitalist patriarchy'. In other words, the discussion has been divided into two groups in Japan. The dual-systems theorists take the view that sees capitalism and patriarchy as two parallel systems, while, in opposition to them, the unified theorists see the two systems as one (Takenaka, 1989b; Ueno, 1990; Ida, 1995). Sylvia Walby and Heidi Hartmann have been repeatedly quoted by other scholars as representative theorists for the former group and Iris Young and Veronica Beechey for the latter. This debate in Japan mainly refers to studies from the 1970s, and some from the middle of the 1980s, in the West. There has been a steady introduction into Japan of works caught up in the middle of the controversy over the domestic labour debate and those influenced by it. This has resulted in any critical summation of the domestic labour debate and its acute significance having been almost entirely overlooked.

Silvia Walby (1986), for example, who has often been quoted, is certainly one of the proponents actively advocating the dual-systems theory. However, she supports the previous generation who gave an ultimately critical summation of the domestic labour debate and she clearly dismisses – as a traditional view – the argument that attributes one's positioning in paid work to the gender-based division of labour in the family. She argues that we must analyse the total domain of social life, including the labour market, not through the family and domestic labour, but by making full use of the ideas of patriarchy and capitalism as weapons with which to analyse British society in the twentieth century (1990). As will be mentioned later, Beechey as well as Hartmann clearly held the view that they must move beyond the domestic labour debate.

In Japan, on the other hand, the attention of scholars was almost entirely directed to discussions about whether 'a dual-systems theory or unified theory' was required. It can be argued that the 'importation' of this form of Marxist-Feminism, primarily concerned with the domestic labour debate, was a necessary step for Japan in order to understand the meaning of the discussions in the West which had been exposed to the second wave of feminism from the 1960s. Feminist researchers in the West redirected the focus of their studies after reflecting on the domestic labour debate. It seems that the big problem in Japan was that this type of redirection by western researchers was overlooked and the discussion developed into an abstract one – vague both in terms of nationality and age.

The lack of momentum towards an analysis of paid work

The inclination towards unpaid work

From the 1990s onwards, Takenaka has moved onto the discussion of social policy from a gender perspective. A considerable amount can be learned from her studies (Takenaka, 1998; 2001), which have incorporated the results of social policy studies in the 1990s in the West. Takenaka's work is based on the view that the gender approach to social policy 'has urged us to re-question existing studies in all areas of the family, companies and states'. However, when she discusses social policy as a whole, unexpectedly, there is little reference to the specific issues of paid work and labour policy. While she says that the initial task for any social policy that looks towards the twenty-first century is the realisation of 'the idea that entitlement to receive benefits is based on civil rights', Takenaka offers nothing more than a few words about 'solving part-time labour issues' being 'the strategic position' necessary for achieving this (Takenaka, 1998, 158). Takenaka is also critical of 'an immiseration of paid labour' -based on the ideas of Susan Himmelweit, who values highly the concept of labour that was developed under the domestic labour debate of the 1970s. Takenaka suggests as the second task, 'deliberately carving out a space for those activities which cannot be fitted into either pole of that dichotomy' (Himmelweit 1995, 16) (labour and non-labour)'. She lays great stress on 'the path that leads to the valuation of unpaid work, reserving time for unpaid work' (Takenaka 1998, 159).[11] Takenaka's research started with an analysis of paid work, but its importance is diminishing in her work and the focus of her discussion shows a growing tendency to shift to domestic labour and unpaid work.

Takenaka is not alone in this tendency. Mari Ōsawa, as mentioned earlier, has criticised Takenaka's 'special theory'. She criticises as sexism 'the neglect and slighting of domestic labour and labour carried out by family workers' in traditional studies of labour issues (referred to as 'men's labour studies' in this book) and suggests 'gendering work'. Gendering work, as used here, means 'to transcend the dichotomy of production and consumption and to restructure the concept of work that is overly centred on male employed workers' (Ōsawa, 1995, 103). She pays considerably more attention to the theoretical incorporation of unpaid work than to the task of analysing paid work itself. This seems to be a trait that she shares with Takenaka.

This tendency can be seen, in its more extreme form, in discussions by Chizuko Ueno. Ueno also suggests 'gendering the concept of "work"' in a similar sense to Ōsawa. She maintains that this is because 'it is obviously not possible to talk about "equality" at "the place of employment" in isolation and without first questioning the unbalanced distribution of "unpaid work" between the genders' (Ueno, 1995, 704). This recognition is premised on a sceptical, or rather negative, understanding of paid work in that the proponents 'will not take the naïve position that "working is liberation" while still accepting the current state of "paid work"'. Ueno points out that 'women's participation in the labour force' – rather than improving the status of women – resulted in women being treated as 'a second class labour force', and that 'the paradoxical "effect"' of the Equal Employment Opportunity Law between Men and Women was that the law only made it possible for a limited number of privileged women to "gain employment just like men" on the "major career path"' (Ueno, 1995, 700–702).

The tendency to attach little importance to paid work

The task of restructuring the concepts of work and non-work is an important one.[12] The use of extremely stereotypical images to discuss women's paid work makes it difficult to gain ready acceptance of the assertion that the focal point of research is not paid work but the incorporation of unpaid work. Arguments like Ueno's, which depict the lot of women's paid work as thoroughly miserable and which imply that women's paid work is not worth analysing in the search for factors to bring about change, are, at the very least, extremely problematic.

It is still important to continue the discussion about '"equality" in "the place of employment"', which Ueno views negatively. A small number of well-conducted studies that aim to open up new horizons for these discussions under current conditions have been published. An example of these is the work of Masumi Mori, Takeo Kinoshita, Shunko Ishiro and Michie Takashima who carried out a detailed analysis of the jobs performed in a trading company, *Pei Ekuiti Kenkyūkai* (Pay Equity Study Group), 1997. Furthermore, as the realities surrounding women's paid work have been changing, closely following and analysing the direction that this change is taking remains an important task. Ueno's understanding of women's paid work is premised on the theory of bipolarisation, but this does not seem to reflect reality. It is true that women's labour studies in the past have operated on the premise of the bipolarisation of women. The assumption then was that women were polarised into the 'elite group' of women on one hand, who have developed their careers like men, and the others, who left the labour market as they married and had children and returned to work as part-timers. The unsympathetic looks cast at 'the small number of privileged women', as Ueno puts it, was due to the fact that they belonged to an exclusive minority and that their status was maintained only by becoming completely absorbed into the world of men and working just like a man. Part-timers, on the other hand, were thought to be the majority of women and to share the same fate as women with domestic and child rearing roles. However, as studies by Wakana Shutō and Ikurō Takagi show, 37 per cent of all women employees belong to neither the 'elite' or 'part-timer' group and fall outside this type of bipolarisation (Shutō and Takagi, 1998, 36). Women, as a group, are becoming diversified and it is not possible to put them all together as a 'second-class labour force'. It is indeed the content of this diversification that needs analysis.[13] The task of restructuring the concept of work, to which Ueno and others attach importance, needs to be backed by an accurate analysis of reality.

Yoshiko Kuba began paying attention to unpaid work at an early stage and suggested that the measurement of such work is necessary. It should be noted that she has accurately pointed out that 'changes to gender relations in unpaid work presuppose the equality of women and men in employment, such as paid work' (*Josei no anpeido wāku kenkyūkai* (The Study Group for Women's Unpaid Work), 1995, 94). It is, understandably, not possible to measure unpaid work without examining the realities of paid work. In any case, the analysis of paid work and studies of unpaid work need to develop in a well-balanced manner. Any approach emphasising unpaid work as a means of gaining a better understanding of women's labour is one that, on the whole, undervalues the importance of the analysis of the mechanisms found within the labour process. The domestic labour debate had a problematic arrival in Japan – there was no serious appreciation of the significance of the negative summations that had accompanied its appearance in western countries. Many problems arose from the fact that this arrival process lacked both a theoretical and methodological momentum towards the analysis of paid work.

Why the domestic labour debate cannot be concluded

The realities which allow the premise: woman = housewife (1)

In 1995, according to Ueno, 'the domestic labour debate is not over yet' (Ueno, 1995, 698). As far as I can see, the domestic labour debate in Marxist-Feminism in the West, which was subsequently introduced to Japan, was largely concluded at the beginning of the 1980s, with the debate being given a negative summation. In Japan, however, the domestic labour debate is still going on and it is not thought that there is anything amiss in discussing women's labour mainly in relation to the entry conditions of women to the labour market. The following realities in Japan have helped to perpetuate this situation.

Firstly, there is the reality that hardly anyone has opposed the generalisation that women are the ones with the responsibility for domestic and child rearing roles. In truth, there are an increasing number of single women due to the fact that these days more women marry late or stay single. Also, there are women who do not have children. The fact that the norm of the modern family model has been firmly established in Japan in spite of this is closely linked to the reality that makes it possible to maintain the generalisation that it is women who play the role of housewife and child carer. The modern family model was accepted and established as the model applicable to the majority of people in Japan at the time when Japanese employment practices were formed and established in the 1960s. At the time when the centrality of the modern family model was beginning to be questioned in the West, amid the waves of the feminism movement, this model, conversely, acquired hegemony in Japan. This was a time when large companies began forging closer ties with their employees' families – as they began practising 'leaner management' in the wake of the oil shocks (Kimoto, 1995a; 2000b; 2002b). The Japanese-style modern family model is now firmly established because it has been supported by the material basis of generous in-company welfare and seniority-based wages that are available mainly in large companies. Therefore, the idea of 'the housewife', central to the modern family model, has been the focal point of discussion and the generalisation that the idea of 'the housewife' applies to all women has been accepted without much resistance. This generalisation of women as housewives met with sharp criticism from black feminists in Britain and in the United States but conditions in Japan did not prompt this type of criticism.[14] It was therefore difficult to find opportunities for rethinking a conscious women's labour studies methodology.

The realities that allow the premise: woman = housewife (2)

Secondly, the reality that Japanese companies did not pay attention to 'making positive use' of women employees also allowed the generalisation 'woman = housewife' to establish itself. The employment conditions under Japanese employment practices clearly show that there were certainly strong pressures to assign women perpetually to a peripheral labour force group. These employment conditions can be characterised as ones in which part-timers and full-timers are poles apart, the differences between male and female wages stand out as the biggest amongst the developed nations and women are trapped in an M-shaped employment cycle. It was against this backdrop that 'the special theory' had a realistic basis for offering an explanation. The issue of part-timers, in particular, arises because re-entry into the labour market, after having been a full-time housewife, is uniformly seen as a low career path. This is a typical example of entry conditions to the labour market determining one's position and conditions after employment.

The conditions of part-timers in Japan suggest that there is a 'caste' system in place in the labour market. This 'caste' system discriminates against a housewife on the grounds that her main role in life is to be a housewife. Furthermore, if we look at the details of circumstances that have been revealed in court cases concerning discrimination against women in the areas of promotion and advancement or wages, it is clear how unfairly large companies have been treating women, who are now working for longer periods than ever before. These examples clearly show that Japanese employment practices have presupposed the long-term employment of only men while women have been used as a cheap means of adjusting the excess labour force. In other words, employment practices themselves have regarded women as 'housewife' employees, who are working to supplement family finances, and unmarried women as short-term employees, acting as reserves for 'housewife' employees. These features also indicate that the modern family model is firmly embedded in employment practices. Given that this was the reality being faced, we can understand that it was difficult to have a critical awareness which questioned the ability of 'the special theory' to explain the situation.

The trap of gender stereotyping

It was therefore difficult, even as late as the1990s, to develop a critical awareness of the pressing need for a negative summation of the deficiencies of the domestic labour debate in order to move ahead.

As mentioned earlier, now that the ways of being a woman – including being a woman employee – have become more diverse, it is no longer possible to consider the category of housewife as one that represents all women. It is necessary, therefore, to get away from the current level of methodology which establishes, a priori, the disadvantageous entry conditions into the labour market of women employees, as dictated by their domestic and child rearing roles. These disadvantageous entry conditions, in turn, form the basis of what are thought to be satisfactory explanations for the inferior working conditions, instability and unskilled state of women. A cliché-ridden explanation, too often given for why the majority of women are found in certain types of work, is that this is because it is 'low-paid, unskilled work'. There is a perception behind this explanation that this is the only work that women can do because of their family responsibilities. Researchers engaged in analysis can, themselves, ill afford to fall into the trap of gender stereotyping. Is the work low-paid because women do this type of work? Or, do women take these jobs because they are lower grade jobs? Who has determined the job grading, anyway? These important questions are yet to be answered and it is not possible to explore the possibility of change without first attempting to find answers to them. It is now high time that we consciously left behind women's labour theory with its basis in the domestic labour debate in western countries in the 1970s. The essential task for us is to look for a methodology that can overcome the problems found in the domestic labour debate.[15]

The introduction of a gender perspective into the labour process

Overcoming the domestic labour debate

What direction did scholars in the West take after having reflected on and criticised the domestic labour debate? They overcame the weaknesses in the domestic labour debate and set about elucidating the gender relations in paid work. There were basically two approaches. One was to look to the ideology of a 'family wage' and the other to conduct empirical studies of women's paid work, which is the main theme of this book. Both approaches have been developed as part of the effort to expand the framework of Marx's labour process theory. The labour process debate got going particularly from the mid-1970s, especially following the publication of Harry Braverman's *Labor and Monopoly Capital* (Braverman, 1974=1978). The feminist scholars who had previously been disillusioned with the domestic labour debate participated in the labour process debate with a view to critiquing it.[16]

A rejection of domestic labour-based explanations and interpretations

One of the most noted scholars to have noticed the importance of a 'family wage' is Heidi Hartmann. Having realised that a satisfactory analysis of women's paid work is impossible using Marxist categories that neglect gender variables, she analysed historical cases of labour union structures and union history in the United States and the United Kingdom at the turn of the nineteenth century. She asserted that it was the very structures created primarily by men that played a decisive role in imposing restraint on women's participation in the labour market (Hartmann, 1976). She rejected the reductionist method that discusses the status of women in the labour market using domestic labour theory as a starting point. She aimed to illustrate the power relations at work between the genders in the labour market and how this is reflected in the family domain. Hartman persistently emphasised issues of patriarchy and sought their motivating factors in the male groups' efforts to protect their own interests. However, subsequent labour analyses by feminists have developed her ideas in a different manner. That is, they have searched for an analytical method capable of clarifying the connecting structures between gender relations and work, rather than incorporating the concept of patriarchy into labour analysis. With the place of work as their subject, feminists started to pay more attention to the role that gender and gender ideology play and to the social formation process behind this role.

This defines the first viewpoint, that is, the ideology of a 'family wage': the concept that the wage earned by a husband is sufficient to feed his whole family. This concept was established among working class families in advanced capitalist nations including the United Kingdom, in the period from the turn of the nineteenth century to the First World War. Scholars regarded this ideology as the dynamic link between the labour process and the family and noted how closely the working of this ideology is connected with the status of women in the labour market, especially with job segregation by gender. This viewpoint was applied in empirical studies of women's employment following the 1980s, which will be discussed later in the book. This stance is also linked to a critical awareness of the question of how gender relations affect and shape the organisation of labour. However, this application of the ideology resulted in a methodological perspective which, rather than leading one to a direct analysis of labour, encouraged an analysis of the relationships between the labour process and the family.[17]

The other path to overcoming the domestic labour debate lies in pursuing an analysis of the reality of women's employment. We will have a closer look at this next.

A gender analysis of the labour process

As mentioned earlier, Hartmann argues that job segregation by gender was the main tool ensuring the supremacy of men in the labour market (Hartmann, 1976). Her argument was significant in that it challenged the traditional view that directly connected the gender-based division of labour in the family and the status of women within the labour market. This encouraged many researchers to conduct studies on job segregation by gender. Those who understood Hartmann's argument to be a criticism of the traditional method, which only analysed women using the 'family responsibility model', looked for conscious ways of utilising a gender perspective as their methodology (Witz, 1993). Let us now take a look at the work of Veronica Beechey, the most noted scholar to adopt this approach.

Beechey was one of the Marxist feminists who from the late 1970s tried to reshape the existing theoretical structure by introducing a gender perspective, while also re-evaluating Marx's labour process theory, and by using concepts such as deskilling, an industrial reserve army and the dual labour market. The labour process debate opened up the path to empirical studies of the labour process in the West. Many feminists involved in the debate also started to conduct empirical studies.[18] It was in 1983 when quite important case studies of women's labour in specific industries, occupation types and workplaces started to appear that Beechey, through her critical reviews of these studies, propounded a methodology which would allow a thorough-going application of a gender perspective (1987=1993).

Beechey, starts off by criticising past general trends in the work of feminists, including herself, and constantly stresses the seriousness of the mistake of simply 'extrapolating' the status of women in occupation and job structures as being the result of the division of labour by gender inside the family. This is a serious error because researchers who do this are themselves accepting, as an inevitable premise, the prevailing gender ideology, which divides the public from the private domain and connects the former with men and the latter with women. Beechey maintains that it is necessary to adhere to a perspective that sees the labour process as the place where gender is shaped and reshaped, and consistently 'to analyse the construction of gender within the labour process itself (Beechey, 1987=1993, 179).

Beechey's proposition can be understood as an attempt to analyse thoroughly the processes intrinsic to the labour process itself through which gender relations are built. In doing this she puts aside, temporarily, the various conditions and norms that are brought into the labour process from outside. These steps are part of the task of explaining the division of occupations between the genders – why are women employed in particular types of occupations and men in others? An analysis of various factors is essential to this task. Sometimes, 'women's jobs', care work for example, may assume the appearance of a 'natural' division, an extension of the domestic role played by women. However, whenever a woman is placed in an unskilled and low-paid job, management strategies – including labour cost strategies or labour union practices that are centred on male skilled workers – are invariably at play. In spite of this, mechanisms, which are an extension of the gender-based division of labour in the family, lead to job segregation by gender in the workplace being seen as a 'natural' premise. It is these mechanisms that need to be investigated. Accordingly, what is required is an analysis of the various factors affecting the dynamics between the genders and the ideologies that operate in the labour process. This, in turn, requires the greatest possible elimination of fixed ideas and the building up of empirical analyses of specific industries, occupation types and workplaces, including analyses of historical and current situations.

A critique of the masculine conception of 'workers' and 'work'
Beechey's methodological proposition does not mean that we can neglect the family. Her proposition reflects on past studies that too often discussed the place of work as an analogy for the family, extrapolating

from the division of labour by gender within the family. She then suggests consciously separating the labour process from the family. Beechey's reason for this was her thinking that these studies could not advance any further without an analysis of the labour process on its own. Additional efforts would be required to fill the gap between analyses of the family and the labour process.

After proposing this perspective, Beechey, inevitably, goes on to criticise past labour studies. She criticises these studies for their dependence on a 'familial' model (or a family responsibility model), which ignores the labour process and workplace relations when dealing with women's labour. As a natural next step she then directed her criticism towards the bias in those labour studies in the past that took men as their subject. Beechey declared that the 'worker' model that was used in these studies while masquerading as unisex, in effect depended on a 'masculine concept of workers'. She observed that the 'workplace' model has been used as a matter of course and that in this model 'men have not been regarded as gendered subjects' and 'workplaces are seen as discrete entities, working lives considered separately from families and communities' (1987=1993, 206–207, 230). It is imperative to use the same analytical framework for both men and women and to remember that men too are gendered subjects, in order to overcome the conditions found in past studies. Beechey's proposition, therefore, seeks methodological reform of not only women's labour studies but effectively also of the whole of labour studies by introducing a gender perspective into the labour process.

The accumulation of case studies

This section will list some of the major representative research works drawn from case studies that have been conducted using a gender perspective. While numerous monographs have been published, only three works of substance are selected and discussed here. These works have had a significant impact on later studies and are very frequently cited.[19]

An analysis of gender relations in the printing sector
Cynthia Cockburn's work is both the most pioneering and the most representative. She turned her attention to the effect of technological innovation on job segregation by gender, conducting detailed case studies in the printing divisions of four newspaper companies in London (Cockburn, 1983). Cockburn emphasises the importance

of case studies to her view that in order to explain the forces that enable job segregation by gender to continue to exist, it is necessary to 'look at small-scale, local mechanisms within the workplace itself and in particular at the relationship between women and men in the workforce' (Cockburn, 1988, 32). At the base of Cockburn's critical awareness lies her criticism of Hartmann, who was discussed earlier. While Hartmann maintained that the male labour union is the driving force behind job segregation by gender, Cockburn looked at men as individuals and thought it necessary to analyse precisely how they behave, in and around the workplace or the union, in order to protect their supremacy over women by segregating women's jobs from their own (Cockburn, 1988).

Cockburn starts her case study with a historical overview of the printing industry, the formation and functions of men's unions and the process of technological innovation. Then, she notes the process of deskilling and reconstruction of skilled labour during the technological innovation following the 1970s and describes the changes that 'skill' and 'masculinity' underwent by examining the competition between skilled and unskilled workers and between men and women. Cockburn made it clear that it was the exclusion of women by the skilled workforce that brought about the concentration of women in unskilled and semi-skilled work areas. Even though the number of women employees has increased rapidly due to technological innovation, skilled workers' unions prevent women from participating in skilled work by saying that 'women are not supposed to do it' or that 'women should not do it'. Power relations that try to interpret and define 'skill' are at work here as individual men, and the organisations formed mainly by them, try to maintain men's dominance. 'Consent' on the part of women to such male hegemony is also part of this power relation. Through her analyses of historical and current situations, Cockburn performs a rigorous examination of both material and ideological processes and provides an excellent model for case studies for later researchers.[20]

An analysis of segregation by gender amongst medical professionals
Anne Witz criticised Hartmann's explanation – that women were excluded and segregated by men (labour unions and employers) – saying it was too narrow as an analytical framework, and that it did not agree with the historical facts. She suggested that a detailed examination of the complex 'patriarchal exclusion' process seen in history be carried out. Based on this rationale, Witz examined the historical process of change that occurred amongst professionals

in the medical field (for example, doctors, nurses, midwives and radiographers), areas with a concentration of women's professional jobs (Witz, 1992). In response to moves by women seeking to take up an occupation that has been a male preserve, men may start off using 'exclusion' strategies to protect their vested interests. This means excluding women from the formal acquisition of the necessary qualifications (for example women would not be admitted to a medical school). Another strategy is the 'demarcation' strategy, which draws demarcation lines between adjacent occupations. This strategy includes women but erects barriers based on the differences in skill levels, knowledge and qualifications needed to join any particular occupation. The relationship between a male doctor and a midwife is an example of this, with the latter being placed under the control of the former. Justifications for demarcation are sought in the prevalent gender norms at the time. These 'inclusion strategies', which maintain 'segregation' by means of demarcation lines, are the main factors in building a hierarchy based on gender differences in the occupational order. Women, on the other hand, have to develop complex strategies to counteract these moves. Women try their hardest to get qualifications and be 'included' but when they meet various forms of resistance and exclusion they also draw demarcation lines and engage in excluding activities (dual closure). The result, as with nurses and midwives for example, who each drew demarcation lines around their territories to protect their interests and positions, was a weakening of their qualifications and their increased subordination to doctors.

Witz's analysis notes the fact that the group being controlled recreates and imitates exclusion activities. Her analysis also describes the process of conflict between the genders, on an occupation-by-occupation basis, by giving a detailed analysis including the involvement of educational institutions, occupational associations and the state. Through this analysis, Witz has succeeded in grasping the dynamic processes which create occupational segregation by gender.

A comparative analysis of different strata of women employees
Rosemary Crompton and Kay Sanderson undertook comparative studies, based on case studies, of a number of groups of occupations (1990). In these studies their coverage of a wide range of occupations, from the higher types of occupations that require education and qualifications to those that form the lowest stratum of the labour market, indicates their ambitious intention to describe the stratification of

women employees into classes and strata. The occupations they studied include: pharmacists, traditionally a professional job for women; accountants, a profession with a recent influx of highly educated women; and management trainees and cashier-clerks in the building society industry. The lowest jobs were those held by women in the school meals service – public sector jobs whose numbers are rapidly diminishing due to social policy factors – and also jobs in the hotel and catering industry, where both genders are to be found because this is a segment of the labour market that does not require qualifications. The topics analysed for each occupation include the degree of women's participation, education and training, the effect of technological innovation, job segregation, career development and the degree of resistance against men's discriminatory exclusion activities.

As a whole, the lower the type of occupation, this comparative study shows a tendency away from the gendering associated with male participation. Among the higher types of occupations – cashier-clerks in the building society and pharmacists, for example – a pattern emerges of women still accepting the appearance of vertical segregation. On the other hand, among accountants and management trainees in the building society – who work side by side with men in the office and for whom, albeit only in principle, an equal opportunity path between the genders exists – women's anger and resistance seem to be quite intense when they are faced with actual discriminatory practices and a lack of career prospects. Crompton and Sanderson, who emphasise women's active selection of an occupation, conclude their research by indicating they see hope in this latter stratum, especially the generation in which men and women have received the same education. They also emphasise the importance of the 'qualifications lever' (Crompton & Sanderson, 1990, 156). While this aspect of their research has been criticised as 'too optimistic' (Devine, 1992), there is much to learn from their comparative analyses.

Crompton and Sanderson maintain in their study that previous theories that have tried to account for occupational segregation by recourse to gender, for example the theory of patriarchal exclusion, have not been refined enough. Although different jobs may share some similarities, a universal theory is impossible. They argue that it is essential to conduct and compare case studies in order to explain the complex realities of occupational segregation.

I have introduced here only a few examples of case studies. New, thorough research works are being published one after another. In recent years, workplace analyses have been undertaken, which pay particular attention to sexuality, power and organisational culture (Adkins, 1995; Halford, Savage & Witz, 1997; Bradley, 1999; and Fitzsimons 2002).

The tasks before women's labour studies in Japan

The significance of the negative summation given to the domestic labour debate, which acted as a trigger in opening up the way towards this new horizon and also towards the labour process debate, went unnoticed in Japan.[21] We are still prolonging the domestic labour debate. In concluding this chapter, I would like to suggest ways of overcoming two of the problems inherent in past studies in Japan.

Liberation from 'the special theory'

The first task is to overcome our insistence on the 'specificity' of women's labour. Undoubtedly, women's participation in the labour market is closely related to their life events such as marriage and childbirth and it is not surprising that importance was placed on these aspects when studying women's labour. However, when women alone are singled out and the focus placed exclusively on the relationship between their family responsibilities, employment and professional careers – on the grounds of their 'specificity' – there is a danger that it will become more difficult to see the whole structure of job segregation by gender, of which men too are a part. Furthermore, we must pay particular attention to the possibility of falling into the trap of considering the structure of job segregation by gender to be a given premise and leaving it altogether unquestioned. The reason for guarding against this is that when researchers fall into this trap they start off with the idea of women as 'special' subjects in their minds. This leads researchers to see women as carrying the double burden of entering the labour market while performing their domestic and child rearing roles. We can ill afford to have this idea that women lead a special existence re-confirmed as a characteristic of female labour through analyses of women's careers and other aspects of their labour. This is where the method of 'extrapolating' women's careers from domestic roles tends to suffer from its shortcomings. The 'universality' of men's labour and their career patterns has until now been guaranteed by the 'specificity' of women's labour. Research into women's labour that is wedded to the notion of a specificity has itself actually supported the universality of men's labour and men's labour studies. Methods that have as their starting point the gender-based division of labour in the family and that use this to 'extrapolate' women's careers and positions within the labour market, whatever their intentions, too readily accept the premise of the existence of a dichotomy of gender spheres.

Studies from a gender perspective should not consider actual segregation by gender as self-evident but rather should clarify why such segregation occurs and how the mechanisms which lead to it being accepted as 'natural' operate. There are many research works lacking an awareness of this, which have ended up merely describing labour phenomena that is related to women. Research in women's labour studies, conducted from a gender perspective, must draw a line between itself and the types of works just mentioned: its aims should be to move away from 'special theories' and to perfect and consistently apply a gender-based analytical perspective.

The enrichment of labour process analyses with a gender perspective

The second task is to find ways of overcoming the paucity of empirical analyses accurately describing reality. As mentioned earlier, because discussions of women's labour in the past did not contain sufficient theoretical momentum to drive research into women's paid work, there were extremely poor prospects for research moving into full-scale empirical analyses.

There are, however, a small number of macro-data analyses which provide valuable clues. Empirically, these have described the position of women in the labour market and changes to this position in post-war Japan by analysing statistical macro-data (Takenaka, 1989a and Shibayama, 1993). Mari Ōsawa has highlighted the marked differences between Japan and the West in regard to the 'feminisation of employment in the labour force' by analysing macro-data on the degree of segregation, based on gender and age, in the occupational structure. In her study, the trend in Japan is identified as dissimilar to the case in western countries, where this feminisation of employment was a result of the shift to white collar jobs and the growing importance of service industries in the economy. In contrast, in Japan blue-collar workers led the feminisation of employment, especially after 1985, when we saw both the entry of middle-aged and older women into manufacturing industries as part-timers and also an increase of middle-aged and older part-timers in tertiary industries (1993b). A task in need of attention, which suggests itself here, is an analysis of what is really happening in order to elucidate how the shift to part-timers has altered and reorganised job segregation by gender.[22]

Another analysis of the macro-data by Machiko Ōsawa has also identified some important facts. She does not support the theory of statistical discrimination that attributes the cause of wage difference between men and women in large companies to statistical discrimination in which women are not given equal opportunities for education and training because of their short period of service in the company. She has clearly demonstrated that the problem lies rather in the personnel management system of companies that places women in subsidiary jobs or in the rigid remuneration system (1993).[23] These findings raise issues that need to be examined more fully by case studies reaching down to every level of industries, companies and workplaces. The issues include: what is the theory upon which the allocation of jobs by gender occurs in women's places of paid work; what sort of restructuring was prompted by technological innovation; and how were new theories formulated at the time of this restructuring?

Kazuko Fukasawa depicts the features of the feminisation of the labour force in Japan through an international comparative analysis. In other advanced countries, feminisation of the labour force has developed through the changes made as a result of economic advancement. This is seen typically in the shift to a service economy, coupled with the state's social policies such as affirmative action policies and, more particularly, the ways in which the state takes responsibility for welfare services. On the other hand, Japan is characterised by the extremely limited involvement of the state (Fukasawa, 2000a). Fukasawa has made a more in-depth analysis, based on international comparisons, of the effect of social policy on women's labour. In this study Fukasawa has highlighted the fact that 'Japan has chosen a path for realising equality between genders which guarantees maximum freedom for companies, who hold direct authority in employment management, thus relying on the initiative of these companies rather than on the regulatory powers of the state'. She stresses the consequent need to disclose 'the practical actions of each of the participants – that is, companies and both male and female employees– concerned with the structure of labour' in Japan in order to explore the possibilities for realising gender equality in the place of work (Fukasawa, 2000b, 79–80).

Macro-data analyses, based on a gender perspective, suggest that the real state of labour relations in Japan cannot be understood, without a grasp of both individual company practices – such as the personnel management system, wage system, education and training, and job allocations – on the one hand and, on the other, the way male and female employees behave.[24]

More macro-data analyses are needed to enrich the body of case studies of the labour process from a gender perspective. Case studies are required because the actual organisation of capitalism in Japan, and the various conditions that sustain this organisation both in Japan and abroad, are changing, with the result that the structure of job segregation by gender is also showing subtle signs of change. Another reason is that company society, with its variations, cannot be bundled together as a whole. It is necessary to conduct careful investigations as to what combination of conditions changes the way in which individual industries, companies and workplaces respond. These types of case studies will enable us to recognise the direction of future changes and the various factors that underlie re-structuring. 'Men's labour studies' have accumulated a body of case studies, which although overwhelmingly concentrated on analyses of manufacturing industry, reach right down to the level of various companies and workplaces. Taking a lesson from this, it is imperative that we begin to see more case studies enriching women's labour studies.

Future Tasks

This chapter has shown that more effort must be devoted to case studies highlighting the various factors that determine women's paid work. For this purpose, what is most urgently required is the development of a methodology which enables the full-scale introduction of a gender perspective into analyses of the labour process. Since the mid-1990s, some case studies of workplaces based on a gender perspective and focussing on women's labour have been produced, albeit sporadically.[25] More research is needed alongside efforts to increase the completion rates for case studies. Building up case studies in this way will enable us to extract a realistic picture of the mechanism of gender-based work organisation, something that cannot be perceived through macro-data alone.

In order to achieve this, it is necessary firstly to build up a method for conducting case studies which is appropriate to the labour market and to the structures of the work organisation in Japan. We must perform thorough analyses of gender relations while identifying the many, wide-ranging factors that determine labour relations. If we are to mobilise fully the strengths of case studies, then we need an analysis of the various factors at work in the segregation by gender of occupations and jobs. This analysis, whilst paying particular attention to an analysis of macro-data, should regard these factors as processes of dynamic change and should also include an analysis of the possibilities for this change. We need to assume the broad involvement of various groups and factors – not only individual employees, but also work teams, labour unions, the management strategies of managing bodies, technological innovation and changes in government policy – and also to analyse the ways in which they are inter-connected. What is required is an accumulation of this type of research in order to demonstrate the superiority of analyses of the labour process which incorporate a gender perspective.[26]

2 Methodology and Subject

In this chapter I would like to discuss the methodology used in conducting the case studies, which appear in Part II (Chapter 3 onwards), and the subjects of these case studies. The historical survey of women's labour studies in the previous chapter established the need for these case studies to be carried out in a manner differing from the 'special theory' approach and with a solid gender perspective.

In Part II, I will look at the case of work in the retail industry, taking department stores and general merchandise supermarkets as the specific subjects, with the aim of putting the above approach into practice. Firstly, however, I will set out clearly the problem consciousness and methodological perspective of these case studies. Secondly, I would like to show the positioning of, and trends in, the retail industry. Lastly, I will show the relationship of this book to existing research on retail work.

The problem consciousness and methodology of the case studies

In this volume I have attempted to conduct case studies, which, as far as possible, put into practice the methodology proposed by Veronica Beechey. Consequently, I adopt a methodological position which thoroughly embraces 'the interpretation of gender within the very labour process itself' (Beechey, 1987=1993, 179), taking the labour process to be the place where gender is shaped and reshaped.

Job segregation by gender

The position of and themes in research into job segregation
The central theme in these case studies is job segregation by gender. As stated in Chapter 1, research into job segregation by gender, either picking up the issues raised by Heidi Hartman or criticising her, have become central themes in women's labour studies.[1] This theme emerged as a concrete analytical viewpoint in Britain in the 1970s

(Hakim, 1979), with a considerable amount of documented research having been accumulated following the 1980s, in particular.

In order to build up a concrete picture of the segregation of occupations and jobs by gender, let us attempt to understand the two levels of segregation – horizontal and vertical. Firstly, horizontal segregation refers to conditions in which there is a biased distribution of occupations and jobs, on the basis of gender. This can be seen from the example that nurses, health workers, midwives and nutritionists tend to be women and doctors tend to be men. This horizontal level attempts to seize upon the 'women's work'–'men's work' divide. Within this type of demarcation it is, in most cases, generally men who have high status occupations and jobs, as is clear from the example of doctors and nurses. However, this is not the whole story. There are also cases in which status relations do not play a role, as can be seen from the example that working in the schools' meals service is 'women's work' whilst waste disposal is 'men's work'. Then there is vertical segregation. This refers to a situation in which, even in identical occupations, men are assigned high social status jobs, which require specialist knowledge, technical qualifications and management ability, whilst women are assigned to typically low status jobs not requiring any decision-making responsibility, specialist knowledge or technical skills. If we look, for example, at the case of teachers we see a concentration of women in elementary education and of men from middle school education onwards, with men overwhelmingly the ones in management roles (Crompton & Sanderson, 1990, 32–35). High remuneration levels and the authority to exercise considerable influence are also, not surprisingly, conferred on high status jobs.

This segregation of occupations and jobs by gender became the central issue of concern in women's labour studies in an attempt to clarify why it was that although there had been a feminisation of employment, this still had not necessarily led to any improvement in women's standing in the labour market. The fact that women's average wages remained low, despite the increasing participation of women in the labour market, resulted from their continued concentration in lowly-valued and lowly-paid 'women's work'. Also, as large numbers of women entered skilled occupations, which had formerly been the monopoly of men, these came to be labelled 'women's work' and the levels of pay fell. It was not merely pay but also the social estimation and status of these occupations that declined. This led to the constant segregation of work into 'men's work' and 'women's work' but the main outstanding questions are to do with the identification of the various causes at work in this process and the elucidation of the underlying mechanisms.

Consequently, research into job segregation by gender is not simply a matter of focusing on a description of the state of jobs as segregated into male and female. How is the designation and labelling of specific jobs as female accomplished? Who, and by what logic, re-designates and redefines jobs, which have been carried out by men, as now being 'for women'. Are they appraising and deciding on the presence or absence of skills? How do large numbers of people agree with, approve of and accept this re-designation and redefinition? When we think about these kinds of problems we inevitably imagine the power relations and politics in the workplace. We need to isolate and examine the relations between the various actors participating in these power politics, starting with the company strategy, manpower strategy and the personnel management system. This effort is deeply bound up with the task of attempting to shed light on the whole of labour relations, working on the premise that the workplace is not simply made up of labour-management relations, but that gender relations are also woven into it. Individual subjects affected by job segregation by gender, whilst either conforming to or repelling it, cannot avoid the influence of this segregation on their own work identities. We need to elucidate the mechanisms at work in the formation and maintenance of the gender identity of these actors. The assertion by Alison M. Scott, who set up comparative research into job segregation by gender, that research in this genre is, 'important in order to attack the assumptions of gender neutrality which still permeate much social science thinking about work and labour markets' (Scott, 1994, 238) is by no means an exaggeration.

Strong forces of habit and the possibilities for change
In the past, job segregation by gender has been explained and interpreted in terms of either the physical differences between men and women or, alternatively, through analogies with the gender-based division of labour in the family. These are justifications of the divisions that exist based on the degree of physical strength and manual dexterity. It is also frequently the case that those jobs which are seen as being an extension of domestic work (for example, home help) are designated as being 'suitable for women' and jobs in which there are manifestations of the ability to care for others, which stems from women's domestic roles (for example, nursing), are seen as jobs suited to women's 'aptitude'. This type of popular 'belief'' plays a powerful role in job segregation

by gender and, when it comes to the employment of men and women, there are numerous cases of occupations with pre-existing, built in stereotypes. The biased employment of men and women, based on the translation of this belief into action, and also discrimination in terms of treatment is normal practice. The influential power of gender stereotypes, which are built into jobs in this way, is considerable. Labour unions and male and female workers, all working on this premise, end up strengthening their own gender identity in the process of carrying out their daily work duties. This, in turn, becomes a major factor prescribing the status of women in society (Collinson & Knights, 1986). Walby (1988, 28) made the point that we ought to go straight to the heart of an analysis of the various factors operating inside the labour process and not to be taken in by this kind of popular 'belief' early on, but it still remains an important problem today.

When looking at these types of powerful differentiation practices, we need to pay attention to the issue of the reproduction of gender stereotypes. We also need to turn our attention to those areas where technological innovation and changes in the labour market make it difficult to avoid changes to the pattern of job segregation by gender. The transformation of 'men's work' into 'women's work', or indeed the other way around, via technological innovation or changes in the labour market can be confirmed historically. There is also quite a large range of strategies regarding the utilisation of the labour force within individual enterprises, even when they belong to the same industry in the same period. We need keep these sorts of variations and changes firmly in mind. Consequently, rather than hasty generalisations, we need to seek, on the basis of thorough individual case studies, those aspects which instigate the reproduction of gender stereotypes and the possibilities for change.

Methodological points for consideration

In order to tackle this problem, in Part II of this book I consider the gender relations in the workplace which prescribe job segregation and the politics underpinning these, by going right down to the micro-level of the workplace. When doing this it is necessary to grasp how the two genders, and also the processes for change, in labour relations in an actual workplace are simultaneously forcibly intertwined and segregated in a variety of ways. I think that the following three points need to be considered in relation to this.

Firstly, job segregation by gender cannot simply be taken to be a structural matter; one needs to bear in mind the subjective acts which are part of the process. One aim in doing this is to connect the structure and institution with the individual subjects of job segregation in the workplace. Given that individual subjects act independently, another aim is to stress the process through which they tend to internalise the norms embedded in the structure around them once they have accepted these. When individual subjects feel that norms do not fit well, they tend to convert the existing structures in the workplace. We cannot talk about the mechanisms behind job segregation by gender while omitting the subjective participation of these individual workers. For this reason job segregation by gender is not just a plan for distributing jobs imposed from above; actors in the workplace actively draw the lines for the segregation that are put into practice on the basis of their own interests and concerns, thus locating these as 'segregation from below'. We also need to take these arrangements into consideration. Herein lies the strength of using case studies which go right down to the workplace. This approach also enables a dynamic description of the mechanisms behind job segregation. The efficacy of sociological methodologies, which stress reality, can be seen in this.

The second point to be considered is that in our analysis of job segregation by gender we must not neglect efforts to grasp labour relations in the workplace holistically. This is important because discussing the various factors concerned with job segregation as comprehensively as possible – including educational, generational and also gender discrepancies – and describing the aspects of and mechanisms behind job segregation by gender, as multi-dimensionally as possible and on the basis of reality, is indispensable to empirical analysis.

Thirdly, since the labour process is firmly located within management, we must investigate the links between the management structure and the labour process. Gender relations, which lie embedded inside the labour process, are not fixed and of a uniform type but rather contain many variations: we can think of them as metamorphosing along with changes in management strategy. In this sense, it is necessary to locate the relations between the labour process and management strategy.

Response and negotiating relations within the work organisation

The work organisation
I would now like to establish 'the work organisation' as the subject of deliberation in order to consider job segregation by gender. Up to this point, I have used the term 'labour process' in this book. However, labour is embedded within the work organisation, and without an understanding of the concrete context of an organisation we cannot understand the labour

process. In particular, when we approach the mechanisms behind job segregation by gender, from the sort of problem consciousness referred to above, we need to understand the workplace to be an organisational body made up of hierarchical structures and to locate the various actors as members of the organisation holding a given rank within it. It would be effective to understand the process of job segregation by gender in terms of the mutually reinforcing actions of all the members, shouldering their various ranks and roles within the organisation.[2]

As touched on previously, when occupations, which have been monopolised by men, become female occupations the interpretation of 'skills' also changes considerably, but it is the politics unfolding at this time around the definition and redefinition of skills in the work organisation that we need to consider. In order to make this politics clear we need to descend down to the level of the work organisation and try to decipher closely the power relations operating within it. When we do this it would be unrealistic to ignore the likelihood of the existence of norms and culture brought into the work organisation from outside, for mediation purposes, by individual subjects. However we need to understand how these norms and cultures come to be authorised and valued as being intrinsic to the work organisation and in this sense the core analytical concern must be, as far as possible, labour relations between the members of the organisation.

Response-negotiation relations within the organisation

In attempting to do this in this book I will also attempt to treat the work organisation from all angles, considering both its formal and informal aspects.[3] The reasons for this are as set out below. Formal procedures (procedures based on documented work rules) act as the premise on which the work organisation constructs and maintains order. The work organisation, in order to maintain this order, builds a scheme of authority and responsibility by allocating formal status and roles amongst its members. However, the order built up by the work organisation is not necessarily monolithic. Not surprisingly, since it is a work organisation it makes seeking profits for the firm its principal concern and the hierarchy of work positions that carry management's authority, which make this a reality, acts as the pivot. The formal rules, which determine matters from the distribution of work to promotion and remuneration for members of the organisation, are the important constituent elements of the organisation.

However, we cannot overlook that aspect in the practical workings of these formal rules in which compromises are made, taking into account the nature of the relations and the belief systems of the members of the organisation. The aims decided upon by senior management in the organisation, rather than being imposed unilaterally from above, are the subjects of overtures and attempts at propagation and persuasion aimed at individuals in various positions throughout the organisation. Individuals also respond to these efforts, using the authority that they are able to exercise in accordance with their respective positions, and occasionally they may refute, criticise or even ignore them. By the time aims, which have been determined in this top-down fashion, arrive at the bottom these various relations of response and negotiation intervene and we need to turn our attention to the process which ultimately furnishes the consent and approval of the bottom of the organisation. Labour unions also intervene in these response-negotiation relations. Of course, these response-negotiation relations by members of the organisation are not carried out by ignoring formal procedures, they are fundamentally carried out by following formal procedures. However, occasionally there are also cases of counter-acting the formal rules, in which members of the organisation seek to realise their interests and values through resistance and defiance.

As one would expect, there is an array of variations in these response-negotiation relations, according to the make up of each organisation, and there are certainly some organisations utterly lacking the scope for making responses from below. However, based on experience of the work organisations included in the survey to date, I see most organisations as possessing this scope. In this book I pay attention to the processes of manoeuvring and negotiation by individuals and groups, each with their own positions in the work organisation, as they receive decisions from above. This perspective is effective in gaining a dynamic understanding of the state of the organisation and management by taking the diversity of the members in the organisation sufficiently into account. Furthermore, this perspective makes it possible to locate correctly the meaning of the minute responses and resistance of individuals within the organisation.

Organisational culture
If we are to keep the above types of response-negotiation relations operating inside the organisation in our sights, we need to locate the organisational culture. The "belief" system within the organisation, as mentioned earlier, continues to explain and interpret a particular gender stereotype. Members of the organisation are not free of this. Their beliefs, attitudes and even value systems are influenced by

the organisational culture, through the belief system at work in the organisation. As a result of repeatedly experiencing the sense of 'men's work' – where men are in the majority – being the vibrant part of the organisation while 'women's work' is not seen in this way, members of the organisation come to view as 'natural' the perception that it is men who are the source of vitality in the organisation. The correct and appropriate manner in which each gender should conduct itself inside the organisation is not necessarily specified in the formal rules of the work organisation; rather, we must see members of the organisation as gaining their understanding of this through the culture, which is woven into the organisation.

Consequently, we can express what we call organisational culture another way – as the meanings, thoughts, values and beliefs, which are held in common in an organisation. However, these are not simply things devised unilaterally from above in order to unite the members of the organisation. We need to see the aims of management, which come down from above, as manifesting themselves by passing through processes of negotiation between the members of the organisation in their various positions.[4] By virtue of being part of the organisation, each individual is decisively influenced by the organisational culture, and this leads to the individual's own labour experience being prescribed by this. At the same time, however, when various individuals are unable to adapt to the organisational culture, they defy it and occasionally confront and resist it. There is scope for individuals, on the basis of the position they hold in the organisation and the differences in their concerns and interests, to struggle against the organisational culture. The organisational culture, which has been built up historically, plays the role of imbuing the organisation with its unique hue of solidity but there is the possibility that even the organisational culture once constructed could be reconstructed in order for individuals with heterogeneous value systems to negotiate with the mainstream organisational culture, without becoming steeped in the existing culture.

The subject and position of the case studies

The problem consciousness surrounding the choice of subject for the survey

'Making positive use of women' and 'realising women's latent potential'
In Part II, I will conduct case studies of the work organisation in large-scale retail firms, from the methodological perspective outlined above.

Let me set out, from the viewpoint of women's work, the position of these retail firms and the critical thought processes that went into their selection as the subjects of the case studies. As is widely known, women's entrance into the labour market is expanding irreversibly and, furthermore, they are increasing the extent of their long-term continuous service. The background to this is to be found in changes to the economic structure and to labour market conditions – such as the growing service and white-collar nature of the economy and also the increase in part-time employment – all of which stimulate opportunities for women to work. At the same time, women, for their part, have attained higher levels of education, delayed marriage and had smaller families than in the past. Tertiary industries in the 1990s, in particular, were conspicuous in attracting women employees, employing approximately over 70 per cent of women employees. Within this tertiary sector, the service, wholesale and retail industries exercised a particularly strong attraction for women employees.

In the midst of this process of women pouring into the labour market and coming to be regarded as indispensable by that market, companies which had adopted the strategies of making positive use of women and realising women's latent potential began to appear. This development was linked, in a timely way, to the emergence of ability-based personnel management (*nōryoku shugi kanri*), which underpins Japan's present-day labour relations. Ability-based personnel management was devised from the second half of the 1960s (Japanese Federation of Employers' Associations, 1969). There needed to be a commitment to assessing and treating everyone on an individual basis in order to modify previous collective management – based on gender, educational qualifications and the number of years of continuous service – and also in order to base decisions regarding salary increases, promotions and postings on one's ability to carry out a job. The status ranking system[5] *(shokunō shikaku seido)*, which places increased weight on personnel assessments of one's ability to carry out a job, was central to this change in management approach (Takahashi, 1992). The status ranking system, in order to assess ability in carrying out work, takes as its core a system in which classifications of status grades and ratings within a grade are interlocked. Because promotion on the basis of rating is to some extent possible without any promotion in managerial position, this ensures flexibility in the posting of employees. At the same time, individual assessment leads to increased competition between employees. However, we must bear firmly in mind the fact that it was only men who were ever considered for the above.

Management groups first began to pay attention to the exploitation of women's abilities, from the end of the 1960s onwards, with successive periods of attempts at ability-based personnel management (Kantō Employers' Association, Japan Federation of Employers' Associations, 1968). In the midst of a labour shortage, management broke free from its old assessment of women employees, who by now made up 40 per cent of the labour force, as merely 'workplace flowers' and aimed to do their best to manage women 'as professionals'. This change occurred because a continuation of the positioning of women as subsidiary employees, as had been the case in the past under the seniority wage system – despite the increased trend towards long-term continuous service by women – would invite a wasteful increase in wage costs. However, moves towards a personnel management system based on gender and modelled on the old 'view of women's labour' as 'short-term employees available until marriage', began to come to the fore from the mid-1970s (Takeuchi, 1992, 110–112). These types of strategies – of making positive use of women and shifting towards realising women's latent potential – did not contradict the direction taken by ability-based personnel management, which had originally only taken men into consideration. This is because individual assessments of ability are able to identify 'capable' women while restricting women who are not quite as capable to a low status grade. In this way, the separate management of men and women became flexible and the pursuit of individual personnel management, which would enable making positive use of women and realising women's latent potential under the one status ranking system for men and women occurred from the middle of the 1970s.

The position of women under the collective management of men and women

Whilst some industries took up this style of collective management of men and women, there were also other types of industries which persisted with separate management for men and women and which stuck, as in the past, to using women in subsidiary work. Large companies, with over 5,000 employees, are representative examples of this adherence to separate management: while remaining conscious of the need to take into account the Equal Employment Opportunity Law between Men and Women (enacted 1986), they selected a personnel management system based on career paths. These companies are found in finance and insurance industries and trading companies, such as banks, life insurance and securities companies (Senda, 2001). This system of separate courses in personnel management forges new and different paths between key and peripheral jobs, by adding the option or otherwise of transfers and also the presence or absence of possibilities for promotion and improvements in status. Because the possibility of transfers, including even moving house, is established in advance there cannot be any bias on the basis of gender in the individual choice of course when joining the company and, in practical terms, this is gender-distinct employment management. It is clear that companies which have adopted and adhered to this do not view men and women as equal employees. As is widely known, personnel management systems with separate career paths faced a situation in which career path divisions which were not objective and rational were regarded as illegal, following the enactment of the Revised Equal Employment Opportunity Law between Men and Women in 1999 (Asakura, 1999). It is a fact that debates surrounding women's labour studies, following the enactment of the 1986 Equal Employment Opportunity Law between Men and Women, have been liable to concentrate on personnel management based on career paths. However, in order to make clear the problems besetting women's work it is necessary to abandon gender-distinct management and instead concentrate on the types of industries which have been enthusiastic about 'making positive use of women'.

On this point, this book concentrates on cases of collective styles of management of men and women. The reason for this is that a work environment which treats men and women on the basis of an identical status ranking system, compared with personnel management based on separate career paths, holds considerably more possibilities for moving towards gender equality. However, as was mentioned also in Chapter I, the routine Japanese practice of locating male regular employees as the core workforce and restricting female regular employees to an inferior status, is widespread in the Japanese business world. Personnel management based on the status ranking system has the tendency to bind women tightly to the base in a 'pyramid-type work place structure', made up of a variety of levels of status grades and rating determined by personnel assessments (Kumazawa, 1986). Consequently, the incidence of women at the manager level was, on the whole, low and in the case of senior management, in particular, it was usual to find practically no women at all. Even though the status ranking system, with its framework for treating men and women identically, contains the possibility of moving towards gender equality, it does not function that way in reality. What are the factors limiting women to low status? Also, how do men and women respectively in the same work organisation accept this reality and how do they consent to it? Taking a broad, hard look at various matters such as job allocation, education and training, motivation, reshuffles and the ideal form of assessment, one could conclude that the exploration of the various factors causing segregation between the genders is simultaneously linked to the quest for the possibility of overcoming the rigid tying of women to the bottom of the pyramid.

With this type of problem consciousness as the starting point, large-scale retail industry can be seen as a suitable research subject. The status ranking system was introduced at a relatively early stage in this industry. That is not all, as will be seen later, large-scale retail firms are highly dependent on female labour and include a variety of employees in their work organisation – in terms of age, educational background and types of employment. This variety of labour relations makes large-scale retail firms ideal subjects for research surveys.

A historical outline of Japan's large-scale retail firms

Large-scale department stores as the motive power of retailers

In Part II, I will look at the case of the large-scale department stores and general merchandise supermarkets, which played a considerable role in the Japanese retail world, following the Second World War. Firstly, let us establish the historical position of Japan's large-scale retailers.

It was department stores that first secured predominance in Japan's sales and distribution network after the Second World War. Department stores developed around a central traditional type descended from dry goods stores, which were the longest established shops dating from before the Second World War – but which had experienced intermittent difficulties during wartime business. In 1955 pre-war levels of consumption had recovered and department stores grew rapidly, led by growing urban populations and the westernisation of lifestyles. The westernisation of clothing habits, in particular, accelerated the trend to ready-made clothing and presented department stores with an opportunity for rapid growth. In an attempt to attract the purchasing power of the residents along their railway lines the major capital behind private railway companies opened up a succession of department stores at the terminus of these railway lines at this time.

At the time of this change from Japanese clothing to western clothing, department stores lacked the human resources and funds to be able to respond adequately (Takaoka, 1997). Suppliers of goods (wholesalers and manufacturers) attempted to gain stability in their business relations with department stores by offering advantages to department stores, which were growing rapidly as the motive power amongst retailers. They introduced a unique purchasing system, the 'sales-based stock purchasing system' (*uriage shiire hōshiki*). Under this arrangement suppliers of goods are responsible for the purchase of merchandise, the determination of prices and even sales. That is to say, this was an arrangement in which, because ownership of the goods displayed on the sales floor remained with the suppliers of the goods, this same group also shouldered the risk of merchandise in stock going out of date and being left with stockpiles of remainders, as a result of changes in fashions. The suppliers of goods, who are responsible for bearing this sort of risk, transfer a collateral portion of the risk and also the personnel expenses of dispatching salespeople with specialist product knowledge, to the purchase price paid by the department store and end up receiving a good margin. This arrangement was attractive to department stores because it enabled them to avoid risk and keep a wide variety and small quantity of goods in stock and also to the suppliers of goods who shouldered responsibility for this system, because of the customer information brought to them from the sales floor by the salespeople whom they themselves had dispatched. (Kikkawa and Takaoka, 1997a, 124–128).

In this way, department stores relied on the 'sales-based stock purchasing system' and the system of dispatching salespeople to establish their position in the sales and distribution network by sharing the profit with the wholesalers and manufacturers. They became predominant in the competitive relations between small retailers on the basis of demonstrating their strength in keeping a good variety of clothing stock. Ordinary retail stores experiencing the threat posed by the rapid expansion of department stores, initiated the anti-department store movement and this eventually led to a Department Stores Law (1956) (Okada, 1991, 33). In order to protect small retailers, increases in the number of stores and any expansion in the floor area of department stores was subject to a licence system and their business hours and holidays were severely restricted.

As I discuss below, the supermarkets established later would usurp the department store industry's leading position in the retail world. This resulted from the fact that the introduction of unique business transactions for the buying of stock, resulted in department stores, which no longer made pricing decisions themselves and lacked any control over the composition of goods on the sales floor or the format of sales floors, suffering weakened merchandising functions (Tomizawa, 1993, 270–271) In the long term, these very features lowered the department stores' proportion of sales profits (Takaoka, 1997, 28). This became one of the conditions prescribing the ideal form for later department stores, and in turn, department store work.

The rise to prominence of general merchandise supermarkets
General merchandise supermarkets appeared in all regions of Japan in the second half of the 1950s and from the latter half of the 1960s, and grew rapidly with the development of chain stores. In Europe and North America, the term supermarket indicates a business with food goods as its core concern but in the case of Japan, it was the so-called general merchandise supermarkets, selling not only food items but also clothing, everyday and household electrical goods, which grew rapidly. This was because these early-period 'supermarkets' started off as small retailers buying relatively easy to handle goods, such as food, clothing, medicines and household electrical goods, with cash and selling them cheaply through a self-service system.[6] In this sense the 'general merchandise supermarkets' are a unique Japanese expression – they indicate 'supermarkets' which broadly stock a wide variety of essential goods (Koyama, 1993, 21) and, as far as strict advocates are concerned, these are more appropriately called 'big stores' (Azuchi, 1987, 25). Following the inauguration of self-service small retailers, which began with the opening of Kinokuniya in 1953, there was a spate of these types of businesses opening and, according to Katamasa Tateno, the period from 1953 until 1961 can be called the 'supermarket growth period' (Tateno, 1994). From that point on supermarkets grew rapidly and in 1972 Daiei Supermarket overtook Mitsukoshi Department Store in the area of total sales. The leading position amongst retailers shifted from the traditional department stores to the rising new supermarket chains. In this same year, five other supermarkets, apart from Daiei, held strong positions amongst the top ten retail firms: Seiyū Stores were fifth, JUSCO sixth, Nichii ninth and Yunii tenth. The above gives a sense of just how rapid the pace of growth was. The general merchandise supermarkets, with their plans for the development of multiple stores, became a threat to the position of department stores.

However, from the second half of the 1970s the growth of general merchandise supermarkets slowed, during the decline in consumption following the oil shocks, and from the 1980s convenience stores started to display rapid growth. This is because branch stores began to face difficulties under the restrictions imposed by the Large-Scale Retail Stores Law, which came into force in 1974. The food supermarkets, that is the original type of supermarket found in Europe and North America, had required time to establish management techniques for the three perishable foods amongst their stock – fruit and vegetables, fresh fish and fresh meat – but in the 1980s these supermarkets achieved full-scale prominence and rapid growth.

The differences between department stores and general merchandise supermarkets

The differences between department stores and general merchandise supermarkets, and also those between the original food supermarkets and general merchandise supermarkets, have come to be debated on the basis of the above historical circumstances. Toshiyuki Yahagi, who places convenience stores at the very vanguard of retail business reforms, argues that supermarkets (meaning general merchandise supermarkets for the purposes of this book), basically inherited the special characteristics of the sales forms employed by department stores, begun by the Bon Marché store in mid-nineteenth century Paris: that is, attractive displays, the freedom to peruse goods in store, cash sales, fixed prices, quality assurance and the sales principle of the freedom to return goods. Yahagi maintains that by also adding the new element of the self-service sales system, supermarkets brought about a reform of the retail business format. He holds that self-service sales are not merely a cost cutting policy but something which guarantees freedom and open shopping practices for the customer, with this openness inducing impulse buying and thereby acting as a factor capable of supporting the high customer unit cost. In this sense, the sales formats adopted by department stores ushered in the 'democratisation of consumption' in retail business and the sales formats of supermarkets, by promoting this democratisation even further, brought about the 'mass nature of consumption' (Yahagi, 1994, 53–55). However, seen from the viewpoint of Yahagi, who sees the innovations in distribution in terms of three elements – retail business, the supply of goods and organisation (particularly relations between organisations) – general merchandise supermarkets are strictly speaking no more than business reforms. This is because they achieved their growth by making ingenuous use – through large volume purchases – of the distribution channel structures and business practices devised by the large-scale makers of consumer commodities (Yahagi, 1994, 28).

Satoshi Azuchi, who emphasises the original food-centred supermarkets, characterises the social function of general merchandise supermarkets as being identical to that of department stores (Azuchi, 1995, 50–51). The special characteristics of the original food-centred supermarkets are consistently those of food goods chain stores aspiring to standardisation, simplification, specialisation and concentration. This is because their reformist nature is to be sought, above all else, in the fact that they succeeded in bringing about an enormous expansion of retail industry. That is to say, the food supermarkets introduced one stop shopping through their large-scale stores to which customers could make one trip and find their shopping needs assembled in one place.

These reforms by large stores are to be found precisely in the achievement of low prices, using the facilities and techniques of chain operations, which can respond to the structure of Japanese food consumption with its regard for the level of freshness in pricing policy (Azuchi, 1995, 52–53). Until now it has largely been argued that the introduction of the self service system was generally connected with cost reductions, achieved via the removal, to whatever extent possible, of the energies directed towards customers. However, Azuchi focuses on the decisive differences in scale between the self-service and the original small-scale food stores and argues that the aim behind the introduction of a self-service system lies in 'efficiently disposing of a large number of items (for example several thousand items) to a vast number of customers (for example several thousands)' (1995, 58). Consequently, he says, the essential elements that distinguish the sales formats of supermarkets are not to be found in the introduction of the self-service system in order to 'sell at bargain prices', but in the refinement of one stop shopping through the realisation of low gross profit ratios and high turnover and shops where one can shop for everything needed for meals eaten at home.

Seen from Azuchi's viewpoint, 'general merchandise supermarkets', which experienced a rapid rise in Japan, were similar to quasi-department stores.[7] 'General merchandise supermarkets' certainly targeted cities comprehensively and their construction of stores adjusted to a city scale – with features such as a comprehensive range of goods, including almost anything one could want, and its floor plan allotting the uppermost level to a food court and play area – closely resemble a department store. The previously mentioned Department Stores Law (1956) was responsible for this development. This same law restricted the opening of new branch stores in the existing department store industry and brought about a conservative trend in the branch strategy of departments stores. Despite the fact that the development of urbanisation opened up possibilities for increased business opportunities for department stores, they were unable to mount an adequate response. Rather, because general merchandise supermarkets were not subject to the restrictions of this law, there was a rapid succession of businesses as they turned their original stores in the busy streets of large cities into branches and adopted the floor plans and assortment of stock that made them pseudo-department stores (Azuchi, 1995, 72–75). In this way, the new 'supermarkets' took on the appearance of department stores, without encountering the restrictions faced by the latter. The influence of department stores notwithstanding, in their broad adoption of the self-service policy and their idea of creating chain stores through standardisation and concentration they were also influenced, from the outset, by the food supermarkets (Azuchi, 1995, 73).

Department stores, as we saw earlier, lacked the power to decide prices and also control over the format of sales floors and the composition of goods on these floors. In contrast with this, general merchandise supermarkets faced a confrontation with the manufacturers of consumer goods. The manufacturers of consumer goods, in order to achieve price stabilisation, systematised sales companies and used them as a trump card in their countermeasures against distribution channels but eventual confrontation over this was inevitable. As is typically demonstrated in the relations of Daiei Supermarket – whose founder was known as a 'fighting trader' (*tatakau shōnin*) – with Matsushita Electrical Industries and Kao Soap, supermarkets saw the need to challenge the price setting rights of manufacturers. However, following a fixed period of 'battles' both sides built mutual dependence relations (Yahagi, 1993, 128–139). When seen from this angle, as Yahagi contends, general merchandise supermarkets did not change existing distribution channels and transaction practices, they were able to grow by making use of them (Yahagi, 1994, 28). For example, general merchandise supermarkets, with their high rate of turnover on the sales floor, are attractive outlets for processed food manufacturers, who offer incentives such as progressive rebates on sales, giving rise to the establishment of cooperative relations between manufacturers and supermarkets (Kikkawa and Takaoka, 1997a, 136–143). This was different from the case in department stores but even in this respect general merchandise supermarkets have a strong pseudo-department store aspect, thus setting them apart from what Azuchi calls the 'original supermarkets'.

Branch restrictions and technological innovations

The transition from the previously mentioned 1974 Department Stores Law to the to the Large-Scale Retail Stores Law encompassed department stores and general merchandise supermarkets, intensifying the competition between them. Under the Department Stores Law, upper limits had been placed on closing hours and the number of holidays and these stores were not free to expand their hours of business. Under the Large-Scale Retail Stores Law, restrictions on closing hours and the number of holidays were revised and a notification system was introduced, allowing for these to be increased through advance reporting. Because this law sought to alleviate the restrictions on business hours, this led to an inevitable intensification of competition in sales formats and naturally also between firms.

In addition, in 1979 the floor space occupied by stores, which were the subject of branch regulations, was reduced to 500m^2 and then in February 1982 administrative guidance from the Ministry of International Trade and Industry made it necessary for branch stores to have a local letter of mutual agreement. The result of this, in practice, was checks on the new branches of large stores, followed by a marked decline in the number of these branches. Alongside this, in the 1980s these branch stores sought to come to grips with changes in the supply of goods and relations between organisations, whilst also being affected by the chain store operations of food supermarkets and convenience stores. The introduction of new technology, which would make up the store's information systems – an area in which convenience stores in particular had taken the initiative – spread also to general merchandise supermarkets. This new technology included computerised ordering machines and systems such as EOS (electronic ordering system). A correct understanding of individual sales trends, based on POS (point of sales/control of information at the time of sale), also contributed to improved accuracy in the ordering of goods on the basis of sales forecasts. These systems were introduced by 7-11 stores from the end of the 1970s on (Yahagi, 1994, 22), but became widespread in department stores and then general merchandise supermarkets from the middle of the 1980s (Dateki, 1990). Food management techniques pioneered by food supermarkets, for example the pre-packaging system, were also established in the 1980s (Azuchi, 1995, 67–78) but these took about ten years to spread to the food departments of general merchandise supermarkets[8] (Kikkawa and Takaoka, 1997b, 290–298).

In this way, the technical innovations pioneered by convenience stores and food supermarkets, also spread to department stores and general merchandise supermarkets and became a platform for looking to the 1990s. General merchandise supermarkets, in particular, also set about accumulating know-how regarding chain operations based on technical innovations. Even so, large general merchandise supermarkets strengthened their tendency to become more like department stores. An outstanding example of this can be found in the composition of their stock. In the midst of declining sales, as they targeted the introduction of a group of goods that would increase the total rate of profit, they filled the sales floor with items such as household electrical goods, cameras, watches, cosmetics, furniture and goods for interior use, and also searched for higher quality clothing. This was the reason for the tendency of large general merchandise supermarkets to lose their own sales format identity (Orihashi, 1996, 118–120).

Further, the 1990s saw the stimulation of more intense competitive conditions. As a result of the relaxation of the regulations of the Large-Scale Retail Stores Law in 1994, branches below 1,000m^2 in size were free of restrictions. In cases where the number of holidays exceeded 24 days per year there was no reporting requirement and it became possible to extend closing hours from seven until eight pm. Under these changes there was competition to increase the number of days of business and to extend the hours of business, as competition to open up branches intensified. Further, in 1998 the Large-Scale Retail Stores Law was repealed and the newly enacted Large-Scale Retail Stores Industrial Location Act (*Daikibo kouri tenpo ritchihō*) led to an investigation into store branches, emphasising environmental countermeasures to problems such as traffic and rubbish.

Large-scale retail trends

Next, let us identify trends for large department stores and large general merchandise supermarkets, using Tables 2.1, 2.2 and 2.2, compiled from the *Census of Commerce* (Ministry of the Economy, Trade and Industry), which has national wholesale and retail places of business as its subjects.[9]

The first thing that we need to note, above all else, is that food supermarkets have been growing rapidly since the 1980s. Taking 1982 as 1, in 1999 they have brought off a 4.3 fold increase in the number of stores and a 4.1 fold increase in annual sales. The sales share held by general merchandise supermarkets was limited to a mere 4.4 per cent in 1982 but throughout the 1990s they persistently increased this, ultimately reaching 11.6 per cent in 1999. Numerous local chain stores fall into this business category and the fact that they continue to display their strength can be verified through the establishment of chain operation techniques suited to the structure of Japanese food consumption, with its stress on the freshness of food products (in particular, the establishment of management techniques for fruit and vegetables, fresh fish and fresh meat).

In contrast to this, between the years 1982 and 1999, large department stores extended their annual sales volume no more than 1.3 fold and large general merchandise supermarkets only 1.6 fold. As is seen in Table 2.1, large department stores have been reducing their store numbers over the period from 1982 to the present. In the case of annual sales volumes (Table 2.2), large department stores experienced an upward trend in annual sales volume from the 1980s until the

Table 2.1: Changes in the number of stores by sales format

Sales format		1982	1985	1988	1991	1994	1997	1999
Department stores	Store Numbers	461	438	433	478	463	476	394
	Component Ratio %	0.0	0.0	0.0	0.0	0.0	0.0	0.0
Large department stores	Store Numbers	416	403	407	395	398	404	365
	Component Ratio %	0.0	0.0	0.0	0.0	0.0	0.0	0.0
General merchandise supermarkets	Store Numbers	1,507	1,634	1,851	1,683	1,804	1,888	1,670
	Component Ratio %	0.1	0.1	0.1	0.1	0.1	0.1	0.1
Large general merchandise supermarkets	Store Numbers	1,293	1,198	1,302	1,152	1,360	1,546	1,461
	Component Ratio %	0.1	0.1	0.1	0.1	0.1	0.1	0.1
Food supermarkets	Store Numbers	4,358	4,707	4,877	14,761	16,096	17,623	18,707
	Component Ratio %	0.3	0.3	0.3	0.9	1.1	1.2	1.3
Total other supermarkets	Store Numbers	59,914	60,809	55,354	78,093	93,949	135,307	193,191
	Component Ratio %	3.5	3.7	3.4	4.9	6.3	9.5	7.3
Convenience stores	Store Numbers	23,235	29,236	34,550	23,837	28,226	36,631	39,628
	Component Ratio %	1.3	1.8	2.1	1.5	1.9	2.6	2.8
Total other retailers	Store Numbers	1,631,990	1,531,820	1,522,687	1,486,731	1,359,410	1,227,771	1,243,294
	Component Ratio %	94.8	94.1	94.0	92.6	90.6	86.5	88.4
Total retailers	Store Numbers	1,721,465	1,628,644	1,619,752	1,605,583	1,499,948	1,419,696	1,406,884
	Component Ratio %	100.0	100.0	100.0	100.0	100.0	100.0	100.0

Source: Yearly editions of *Shōgyōtōkeihyō* (*Census of Commerce*)

Table 2.2: Changes in annual sales volume and sales share by sales format (million yen)

Sales format		1982	1985	1988	1991	1994	1997	1999
Department Stores	Sales volume	7,314,060	7,779,717	9,062,759	11,349,861	10,640,330	10,670,241	9,705,460
	Share %	7.8	7.6	7.9	8.0	7.4	7.2	6.7
Large department stores	Sales volume	7,207,984	7,696,326	8,993,474	10,985,997	10,364,486	10,380,356	9,517,559
	Share %	7.7	7.6	7.8	7.7	7.2	7.0	6.6
General merchandise supermarkets	Sales volume	5,223,325	5,970,902	6,748,886	8,495,702	9,335,933	9,956,689	8,849,658
	Share %	5.6	5.9	5.9	6.0	6.5	6.7	6.2
Large general merchandise supermarkets	Sales volume	5,175,873	5,537,054	6,247,445	7,033,787	8,069,330	8,986,997	8,264,234
	Share %	5.5	5.4	5.4	4.9	5.6	6.1	5.7
Food supermarkets	Sales volume	4,120,066	4,788,381	5,177,527	11,296,961	13,197,669	14,768,134	16,747,995
	Share %	4.4	4.7	4.5	7.9	9.2	10.0	11.6
Total other supermarkets	Sales volume	6,996,813	8,395,809	8,980,851	10,012,318	12,280,562	15,657,522	15,421,967
	Share %	7.4	8.3	7.8	7.0	8.6	10.6	10.7
Convenience stores	Sales volume	2,177,609	3,382,902	5,012,549	3,125,702	4,011,482	5,223,404	6,134,896
	Share %	2.3	3.3	4.4	2.2	2.8	3.5	4.3
Total other retailers	Sales volume	68,139,318	71,401,103	79,857,356	98,010,590	93,859,089	91,467,125	86,972,576
	Share %	72.5	70.2	69.5	68.9	65.5	61.9	60.5
Total retailers	Sales volume	93,971,191	101,718,814	114,839,928	142,291,134	143,325,065	147,743,115	143,832,552
	Share %	100.0	100.0	100.0	100.0	100.0	100.0	100.0

Source: Yearly editions of *Shōgyōtōkeihyō* (*Census of Commerce*)

beginning of the 1990s but, we see a worsening of actual sales results from 1997 and their sales share in the whole retail area fell from 7.7 per cent in 1982 to 6.6 per cent in 1999. Large general merchandise supermarkets have increased their store numbers fairly consistently and have also managed to maintain an upward trend in annual sales volumes. The sales share held by large general merchandise supermarkets has stabilised from 5.5 per cent in 1982 to the 1997 peak of 6.1 per cent. With regard to employee numbers (including regular employees who are regular part-time and casual employees employed for over 18 days) (Table 2.3), large department stores have grown to around approximately 190,000 but entered basic conditions of decline from the mid-1990s on. In the case of large general merchandise supermarkets, numbers have continued to increase fairly consistently, extending in 1999 to an approximately 1.7 fold increase over 1982 figures. However, these are figures that in no way approach the 4.6 fold increase experienced by food supermarkets.

As seen above, one perceives an ebbing trend in large department stores, in sharp distinction to the food supermarkets. The latter continued their relentless offensives even throughout the 1990s, said to have been a period of sluggish consumption. Large general

Table 2.3: Changes in employee numbers by sales format (regular employees)

Sales format		1982	1985	1988	1991	1994	1997	1999
Department Stores	Employee Numbers	201,396	188,991	193,116	206,548	205,493	186,493	168,343
	Component %	3.2	3.0	2.8	3.0	2.8	2.5	2.1
Large department stores	Employee Numbers	197,794	185,968	190,870	198,400	199,282	179,493	165,289
	Component %	3.1	2.9	2.8	2.8	2.7	2.4	2.1
General merchandise supermarkets	Employee Numbers	177,916	193,922	204,394	232,103	272,426	302,503	320,422
	Component %	2.8	3.1	3.0	3.3	3.7	4.1	4.0
Large general merchandise supermarkets	Employee Numbers	175,858	177,368	187,013	185,731	232,669	268,699	296,905
	Component %	2.8	2.8	2.7	2.7	3.2	3.7	3.7
Food supermarkets	Employee Numbers	161,564	183,589	200,597	399,945	497,556	568,919	742,991
	Component %	2.5	2.9	2.9	5.7	6.7	7.7	9.3
Total other supermarkets	Employee Numbers	359,620	403,179	407,448	422,525	534,927	734,388	774,697
	Component %	5.6	6.4	5.9	6.0	7.2	10.0	9.6
Convenience stores	Employee Numbers	129,996	208,036	305,829	189,611	302,233	406,490	536,927
	Component %	2.0	3.3	4.5	2.7	4.1	5.5	6.7
Total other retailers	Employee Numbers	5,338,934	5,150,897	5,539,951	5,549,494	5,571,542	5,151,919	5,485,178
	Component %	83.8	81.4	80.9	79.3	75.5	70.1	68.3
Total retailers	Employee Numbers	6,369,426	6,328,614	6,851,335	7,000,226	7,384,177	7,350,712	8,028,558
	Component %	100.0	100.0	100.0	100.0	100.0	100.0	100.0

Source: Yearly editions of *Shōgyōtōkeihyō* (*Census of Commerce*)

merchandise supermarkets also continued to experience a slowdown in growth.

Looking at Table 2.4 and the male/female ratio[10] amongst regular employees (including regular employees who are regular part-time and casual employees employed for over 18 days), in all retail businesses from 1991–1997 the proportion of females shows no more than a mere increase from 52.2 per cent to 56.6 per cent. Compared with this, it is widely known that large department stores and large general merchandise supermarkets are far more dependent on women. The ratio of females in large department stores reached the 60 per cent mark in 1991 but between 1991 and 1997 this showed a 0.5 per cent increase. In large general merchandise supermarkets, on the other hand, where this figure had already reached 70 per cent in 1991, it continued to grow finally reaching 78.6 per cent in 1997. This extremely high dependence on women is a well-known feature of large merchandise supermarkets.

Table 2.4: *Changes in the proportion of regular female employees by sales format*

Sales format		1991	1994	1997
Department Stores	Regular employees	206,548	205,493	186,493
	Female regular employees	128,553	127,176	117,701
	Proportion of females (%)	62.2	61.9	63.1
Large department stores	Regular employees	198,400	199,282	179,493
	Female regular employees	124,312	123,918	113,369
	Proportion of females (%)	62.7	62.2	63.2
General merchandise supermarkets	Regular employees	232,103	272,426	302,503
	Female regular employees	167,127	202,849	236,830
	Proportion of females (%)	72.0	74.5	78.3
Large general merchandise supermarkets	Regular employees	185,731	232,669	268,699
	Female regular employees	133,958	173,895	211,065
	Proportion of females (%)	72.1	74.7	78.6
Food supermarkets	Regular employees	399,945	497,556	568,919
	Female regular employees	278,320	362,128	417,506
	Proportion of females (%)	69.6	72.8	73.4
Total other supermarkets	Regular employees	422,525	534,927	734,388
	Female regular employees	264,249	350,587	483,480
	Proportion of females (%)	62.5	65.5	65.8
Convenience stores	Regular employees	189,611	302,233	406,490
	Female regular employees	98,307	165,010	225,549
	Proportion of females (%)	51.8	54.6	55.5
Total other retailers	Regular employees	5,549,494	5,571,542	5,151,919
	Female regular employees	2,719,088	2,904,460	2,679,733
	Proportion of females (%)	49.0	52.1	52.0
Total retailers	Regular employees	7,000,226	7,384,177	7,350,712
	Female regular employees	3,655,644	4,112,210	4,160,799
	Proportion of females (%)	52.5	55.7	56.6

Source: Yearly editions of *Shōgyōtōkeihyō* (*Census of Commerce*). Employees who had been employed for over eighteen days were treated as regular employees.

Looking at 1999 (Table 2.5) makes it possible to understand the distinction between the regular work force, who are on the company's regular payroll, and those who are part-time or casual. From a look at this we can see that part-timers and casual workers made up 44.7 per cent of the workforce in the whole of the retail industry, as compared with 34.7 per cent in large department stores and if we exclude 'other retailers', the dependence on part-timers is extremely low amongst all other business formats. In contrast to this, the figures for large general merchandise supermarkets were 74.2 per cent but if we line this up alongside food supermarkets (73.9 per cent), then these figures lag behind convenience stores (81.8 per cent), the most heavily dependent on part-timers and casual workers. Since we can only glean the figures for 1999 from the *Census of Commerce*, let us ascertain the proportion

Table 2.5: A breakdown of regular employees by sales format (1999)

Sales format		Full employees	Part-timers and casuals	Total
Department Stores	Number of employees	110,160	58,183	168,343
	%	65.4	34.6	100.0
Large department stores	Number of employees	107,995	57,294	165,289
	%	65.3	34.7	100.0
General merchandise supermarkets	Number of employees	82,180	238,242	320,422
	%	25.6	74.4	100.0
Large general merchandise supermarkets	Number of employees	76,603	220,302	296,905
	%	25.8	74.2	100.0
Food supermarkets	Number of employees	193,867	549,124	742,991
	%	26.1	73.9	100.0
Total other supermarkets	Number of employees	336,927	437,770	774,697
	%	43.4	56.5	100.0
Convenience stores	Number of employees	97,788	439,139	536,927
	%	18.2	81.8	100.0
Total other retailers	Number of employees	3,618,574	1,866,604	5,485,178
	%	66.0	34.0	100.0
Total Retailers	Number of employees	4,439,496	3,589,062	8,028,558
	%	55.3	44.7	100.0

of female employees and part-timers (converted to an eight-hour day) in the six largest department stores and five largest supermarkets, from the *Yearbook of Distribution Companies* (Nihon Keizai Shinbun) (Figures 2.1 and 2.2). In the case of the six largest department stores, they have always had a low proportion of part-timers but they have been gradually increasing this since the 1980s. Following the fluctuations of the bubble economy and the adjustment period that followed immediately after, the proportion of part-timers has increased again, following 1995. In contrast to this the proportion of regular female employees has been following a slow downward trend and it is clear that, in recent years, it has declined to a level that is slightly greater than that for part-timers. Even in department stores, where there is a strong internal impetus behind the trend towards part-timers as a result of the dependence on dispatched salespeople (*haken hanbaiin*) (dispatched by manufactures and wholesalers), we can see that the part-time trend is gradually growing with the steady advance in the changeover of regular female employees to part-time work. Also in the case of the five largest supermarkets, in 1975 there were approximately equal numbers of regular and part-time employees, but after this time

Figure 2.1: Changing employee profile in the six largest department stores

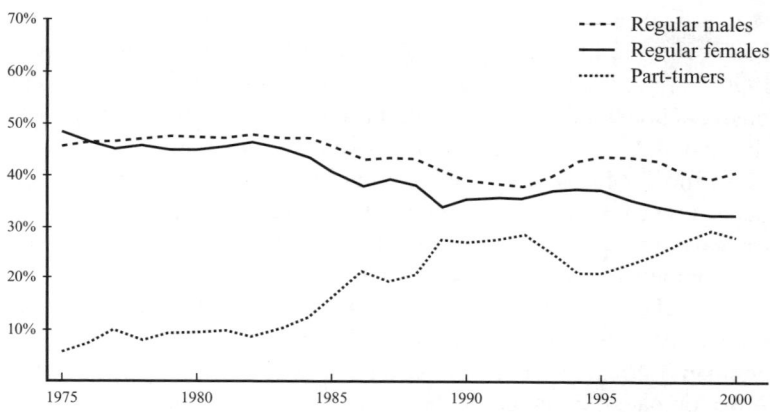

Source: *Ryūtsū kaisha nenkan* (Yearbook of distribution companies) (Nihon keizai shinbunsha, publisher) for each year.

Figure 2.2: Changing employee profile in the five largest supermarkets

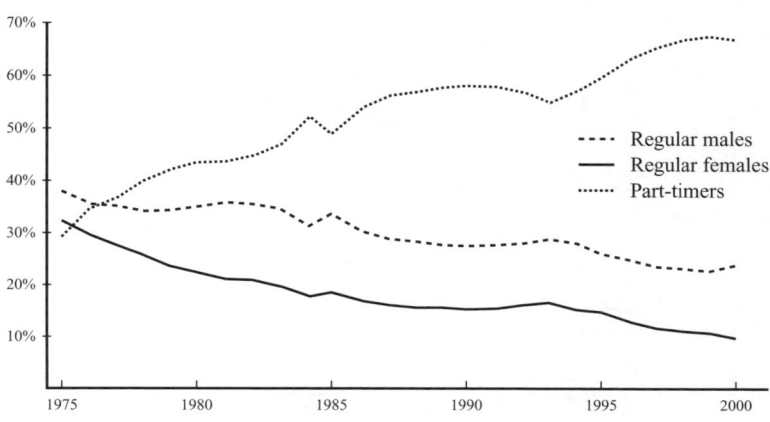

Source: *Ryūtsū kaisha nenkan* (Yearbook of distribution companies) (Nihon keizai shinbunsha, publisher) for each year.

they increased their part-time numbers fairly consistently and the changeover of regular female employees to part-time status shows an even more striking rate of increase than was the case in department stores. The supermarkets' increasing tendency towards part-timers has been even more noticeable particularly since the middle of the 1990s. This development can be seen as a response to the extended business hours and business days, brought about by the relaxation of restrictions in the 1994 Large-Scale Retail Stores Law.[11]

As indicated by the above trends, we can see that both large department stores and large general merchandise supermarkets are increasingly replacing regular female employees with part-timers: this development can be said to be particularly striking in the case of large supermarkets. However, we ought not to lose sight of the point that regular female employees are not retiring immediately after joining the company, rather, they are prolonging their years of continuous service. If we compare the changes in the average age of men and women in the six largest department stores and five largest supermarkets taken from *Yearbook of Distribution Companies* (Figure 2.3), we can see that the average age for both men and women is getting considerably older in

Figure 2.3: Changes in the average age of regular employees

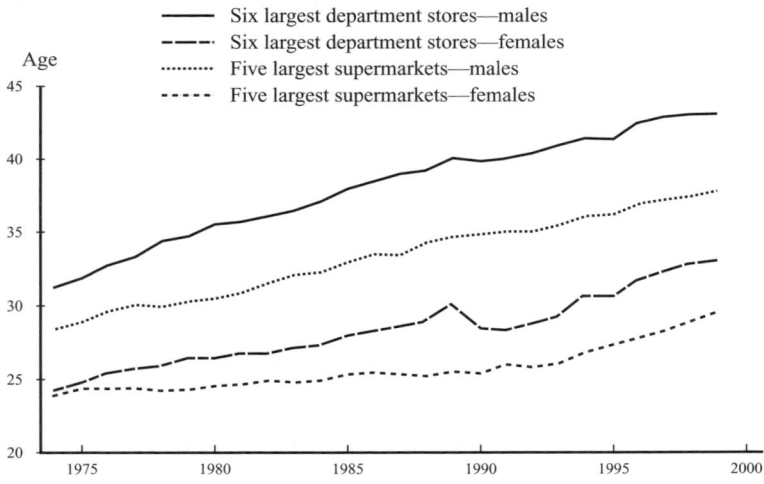

Source: *Ryūtsū kaisha nenkan* (Nihon keizai shinbunsha, publisher). Compiled from the average age for each company

department stores. In the case of supermarkets also, the prolongation of women's years of continuous service, even whilst lagging behind men, is noteworthy. If we turn our attention to points of this nature, then we can say that careful analysis of the role that a handful of male and female regular employees, with long years of continuous service, are playing in the midst of this increasing trend towards part-time work, is an important problem for research into work in retail industries.

Research trends regarding work in retail industries

Available research into job segregation by gender, in the area of retail work, is practically negligible in Japan but when we look at the English language field a certain amount of work is being done. A representative work dealing with job segregation by gender in retail businesses is Alison M. Scott's research (1994). Scott notes that retail business not only occupies an important position in the still-expanding service sector, but that its dependence on female employees is extremely high and also that it is following the kind of move to large-scale operations, automation and organisational innovation which had previously occurred in manufacturing industry with the introduction of high level technology. On the basis of an analysis of detailed interview surveys of thirteen stores, Scott clarified that the feminisation of sales work is not merely an economic factor, motivated by the use of cheap labour, but that it is interlinked with expectations of a demonstration of the abilities of salespeople themselves, who are in a position linking goods and customers, and also the expectations of customers. That is to say, Scott makes clear that we cannot simply explain away job segregation by gender in terms of economic reductionism – it can also be changed by employees' strategies. Scott also shows that we ought to approach job segregation by gender from a broader perspective: that is, not simply as an economic factor but as the interaction of social and cultural factors. Originally, interest in Scott's research into job segregation by gender was along the lines of 'Why should there be such marked segregation between men and women within the same type of work and if women are such a majority at the lower levels, why do so few reach higher levels of management?' (1994, 236). Since then research focussing on the question of female managers in retail business has begun to accumulate (Brockbank & Traves, 1996) (Tomlinson et al., 1997) (Broadbridge, 1998, 1999a and 1999b). In addition, there has been research taking note of the point that it is women who bear the brunt of the non-standardisation and flexible nature of employment, as represented by part-timers in retail industry (Perrons & Hursfield, 1998 and du Gay, 1996). All of the above works share the characteristics of empirical research of a hypothetical investigation type, using data built up from a series of detailed interview surveys.

Amongst the excellent works compiled using survey materials, there are two particular pieces of research on department stores and supermarkets, the subjects of this book, deserving special mention. Alice Lam has carried out a case study of a Japanese department store in the 1980s (Lam, 1992). The critical line of inquiry in Lam's work was an attempt to clarify the types of changes brought to bear on Japan's labour practices as a consequence of any of the following three developments: the advent of the 1985 Equal Employment Opportunity Law between Men and Women, internal company motives and foreign pressure resulting from internationalisation. Lam points out that Japan 'is often regarded as representing an extreme case of sexual inequality and is often criticised as building its economic vitality upon the exploitation of women workers' (1992, 7). Lam took the recently established, large department store, Company E, as her case study and targeted questions regarding changes to the personnel system, changes to the company image and the female subjects who were affected by these. This case study made substantial use of questionnaires, interviews – conducted both in 1984 before the Equal Employment Opportunity Law between Men and Women and again in 1988 – and also participant observations on the sales floor. Alice Lam concludes that the method of 'making positive use of women', which appeared in Company E following the Equal Employment Opportunity Law between Men and Women, amounted to the formation of a sphere of 'women's characteristics', through the fostering of university graduates and the establishment of specialist jobs and women's teams. Although this opened up the way for a group of 'capable motivated women', it did not threaten the pathways fostering management jobs exclusively for men. There was also a simultaneous deepening of the tendency for the vast majority of women to become ever more entrenched in sales jobs at the base of the pyramid. Lam summarises the situation saying that the question 'Why is it that Japanese management is able to preserve the male-dominated employment system?' (1992, 235) persists as an unresolved theme. One key to answering this question can be thought of as lying in the fact that top management's strong intention to promote the position of women in the company was not felt 'down the line' and also in 'the persistence of a deep-rooted male prejudice against the idea of promoting equal opportunity for women' (1992, 172). What is needed now is a searching analysis, which extends to the mechanisms reproducing male dominance inside this type of organisation, alongside an investigation of whether policies at the top have been adequate? This point is one of the themes of the present work.

The other work deserving special mention is that of John P. Walsh, who selects a large, multi-regional supermarket chain superstore in the United States as the subject of his research survey. Walsh scrutinises, historically, the determinants of technological and organisational innovation; and considers the power relations which determine the directions of change, including management strategy, market environment, labour union, customers and the responses of all levels of employees. The fundamental critical concern of Walsh's work is to criticise the deskilling thesis (Harry Braverman), which is one of the influential theories to date regarding technological change. In the course of his critique, Walsh is particularly conscious of attempting to describe the dynamic and complex processes brought about by innovation.

I will attempt to highlight the points made by Walsh, on the basis of analyses of interviews with people working in one of the biggest supermarkets (' a superstore') in the United States and publications in a leading trade journal for the industry, which are related to the same period that I cover in this book. The first point is that whilst the computer automation of ordering processes progressed, the number of people engaged in this work was reduced dramatically but it did not have the effect of devastating the essential nature of the work tasks. This was because the ordering process, one of the high status jobs because it was one of the most difficult jobs in the store, was simplified and knowledge about product trends became widespread as something belonging to the people at the bottom of the store (1993, 90–105). Also, superstores, which make possible one stop shopping, responding to the many and varied needs of customers, render the decentralisation of operations inevitable. As store managers cannot possibly have knowledge that extends to details of the sales floor, they entrust this to those on the spot and it is instead their communication abilities with employees and customers that end up being important for store managers. For example, the people possessing a thorough knowledge of which salads in the salad bar will sell best to customers in a particular region are not the store mangers but the rank-and-file employees at the very shop front. The role of the store managers lies in managing in a way which draws out the motivation and a feeling of job satisfaction in the people working at the bottom of this type of organisation (1993, 112–114). In a sense, employees at the bottom end up monopolising knowledge about their individual sales floor, as a result of increasing decentralisation as the store grows larger. Consequently, they are provided with increased scope for autonomy and the complexity of their jobs (for example, the complexity in decisions about which mixed salad to make at different times and about various combinations of ingredients) becomes the thing that brings them job satisfaction (1993, 117–140).

This type of analysis leads Walsh to assert that it is market conditions and the resistance of employees from every level which decide the ultimate form of organisational innovation and also to reject the oversimplistic thesis of 'deskilling'. The ability to pose empirically based questions about the motivations and decisions of work organisations is one of the extremely significant contributions of empirical analyses. Walsh succeeds in gaining a deep understanding of work through the thoroughness of his methodological perspective, which sees every individual and group as subjects responding to organisational change by mobilising the resources that they possess.

However, the theme that Walsh was unable to resolve is the problem of 'the gender component'. His analytical perspective did not include a gender viewpoint at the outset, but what he did reveal, on the basis of his detailed survey and analysis of 'the intersection between the labor process and organizational structure' (1993, 37) is the problem of jobs carried out by women being 'defined' inside the organisation as nothing more than 'seemingly' low skilled, despite the high levels of skill actually inherent in these jobs. The knowledge and skilled nature of the service jobs carried out by female employees at the point where the store comes face to face with the customers (at checkout counters, the delicatessen and seafood shops) is of a high level, not easily passed on to newcomers and incapable of being set out in manuals. All of this notwithstanding, women's jobs attract low wages and a low market price (1993, 139–147). Walsh ultimately arrived at an understanding of the importance of the problem created by women being confined to specific areas of customer service, such as at checkout counters, and of being labelled as 'low skilled 'without proper acknowledgement of the reality of their work'. Walsh concluded that the elucidation of this problem was a subject for further discussion. He points out the issue of 'cultural perceptions in determining the "skill" of a job' – that is, the importance of the gender component (1993, 146). Recognition of the importance of research into job segregation by gender arose from Walsh's painstaking empirical research. This book is heavily influenced by his understanding of jobs and also by his understanding of the subjects inside a work organisation.[12]

It could well be said that Japan has no research that is equal to that outlined above. Certainly from the 1980s on research which takes as its subject work in retail industries has also been appearing in Japan and there are some works amongst these which focus on female labour. However, these locate large-scale retail industry, with its extensive experience of female employment, as a 'perfect field' for women's problems in gaining promotion. Alternatively, they select a small number of women, who work in management positions or who have attained high rank, and through interviews looking at career development, suggest tips on the possibilities for women to gain promotion (Nakamura, 1998) (Yashiro, 1984 and 1992). Even research which has gone down to the workplace level and explored the possibilities for skills acquisition is limited by its narrow problem consciousness of attempting to conceive a policy for 'making positive use of women' by thinking about how to find 'capable women'. This research lacks a broad perspective interested in investigating the structural problems in work organisations, including the issue of men. What is needed is the expansion of research concerns to include empirical analyses of work organisation analysis from a gender perspective[13] (Wakisaka, 1986a; 1986b).

Part II

3 Job Segregation Mechanisms: Excessive Work Duty Gendering

The task of this chapter is to elucidate the mechanisms at work in job segregation by gender. In order to do this I will consider the case of Department Store A. As I mentioned in Part I, the department store sector is acknowledged as a progressive industrial sector, one which tackled the issue of 'making positive use of women' at quite an early stage. It was the department store's high degree of reliance on female labour, from its beginnings, and its abundant experience in managing female employment that made this possible. Consequently, as we will see in more detail later, department stores introduced a status ranking system (*shokunō shikaku seidō*) and abandoned separate personnel management for male and female employment comparatively earlier than others in the industry. Department stores are also worthy of attention in the field of women's labour research because of their pioneering role in showing the fruits of 'making positive use of women', particularly in the promotion of women in managerial positions and also the employment of fourth year female university graduates. Company A was part of the department store world, which was distinguished by progressiveness in these matters, and constructed an up-to-date personnel management system, which led the entire distribution industry from the first. This chapter directs its attention to Company A and analyses the mechanisms at work in forming the structure of job segregation by gender within this company. To pre-empt the conclusion slightly: this analysis will reveal a tendency for women to be concentrated in low ranking managerial positions, even in this type of progressive company. What are the mechanisms at work, at the concrete level of the workplace, which give rise to this state of affairs? This is the question that I would like to ponder in the rest of this chapter.

Department Store A: the personnel management system and the trend towards 'making positive use of women'

An overview of company A

Firstly, let us gain a clear picture of the nature and status of Company A. The data for the following discussion is based on interviews with the personnel departments of various department stores, including Company A, and interview surveys of male and female employees in Company A. This survey was carried out between July 1992 and March 1994.[1] Women make up about 70 per cent of the approximately 6 000-strong labour force in Company A, which is part of the group of the six largest department stores. The average age of this labour force is 30.3 for women and 39.1 for men. The average length of continuous service is 16 years and 11 months for men and 9 years and 7 months for women. If we look at the respective figures for 1970 – 10 years and 4 months and 4 years and 0 months – then we need to note that the increase in the continuous length of service for women in particular is striking. As a result of a shift from the second half of the 1970s towards the employment of university graduates, the figures for male educational background were: university graduates 64 per cent, junior college graduates 2 per cent and high school graduates 34 per cent. The employment of female university graduates commenced in 1969 but this was limited to a very small number each fiscal year. Although the full-scale employment of university graduates got going from 1982, even ten years later, in 1992, they made up no more than eight per cent of female employees. Junior college graduates represented 38 per cent, senior college graduates 54 per cent and women who had not graduated from university were a distinct majority. Even within the department store industry, Company A stands out with its high proportion of women and the striking trend towards increases in their years of continuous service.

Trends in personnel policy

Let us take a look at the personnel and women's policies in Company A. Table 3.1, in order to grasp the evolutionary processes undergone by the various internal personnel management systems, deals exclusively with the formation process surrounding the status ranking system and the women's policy. According to this table, attempts to fashion a status ranking system began from the quite early period of the beginning of the 1960s, with repeated cases of trial and error, such as the exclusion of the seniority element and an effort to shift the emphasis onto status grade. At the time of the survey, the time of the 1992 revisions, these attempts had taken on a systematic framework, as seen in Figure 3.1. According to the company history, in 1970, the basic form of the status ranking system was finalised, the separate personnel management systems for men and women were abolished and an examination system for promotion was established, which did not take note of gender or educational difference. Via this system, the move up from the clerical to the leadership tier, seen in Figure 3.1, became possible regardless of gender or education. In the year in which this examination system was introduced (1970) a large number of capable veteran women sat this examination and 29 female chief clerks were created. In 1989 the status ranking system and categories of occupational groups were introduced and a virtual prototype of the present system, with its three tiers and seven status grades, took shape. In 1992 management and specialist groups were integrated as 'career track employees' and specialist work was abolished as the company shifted to a way of thinking which viewed sales specialists as management trainees too. We also notice a jump in grade level, after a year, from rank-and-file grade levels two to the career track group. This system selects only those university and junior college graduates who raise their hands in order to express an intention to seek promotion at an early stage. Individual assessments are carried out twice a year, on the basis of evaluation charts for each status grade and status pay, which forms the basis of wages, is decided. If we look, for example, at grade two we see that it is divided into seven ranks and that the wage difference between top and bottom is 14 400 yen (per month).

This round of revisions to the status ranking system was fundamentally motivated by a desire to address the problem of insufficient positions due to the ageing of male employees and also to nurture their administrative and management abilities. In particular, the establishment of the jump in status grades, from the level two grade up, was aimed at identifying at an early stage any capable men of talent. According to what I heard in other department stores, apart from Company A, this state of affairs is almost universal throughout the department store industry. Preparations for a status ranking system, that is, were hastened mainly with a view to nurturing capable men of talent and not in order to bring women into the picture. Department Store B carried out practically the same system reforms as Company A but, according to what I was told by its personnel department, this

Table 3.1: The development of Company A's personnel management systems

* = Related to the status ranking system
○ = Related to the female employee support system
● = Related to the promotion and expansion of occupational areas for women

1956	○	Maternity leave (8 weeks before and after the birth)
1961	*	Proposal to union for an investigation into switching over to 'work'-centred wages
	○	Childcare leave (1hour per day with pay)
1962	*	Completion of a status ranking pay system (regular pay + allowance for supervisory post + family allowance)
1964	●	'Substitutes system' – appointment of women as Assistant Sales Managers
1965	○	Re-employment of women workers system
	●	Creation of position in charge of sales service in each section (as assistant to floor manager)
1966	●	Appointment of women as Sales Managers and to departments dealing with sales to outside customers
1969	●	Appointment of women as Buyers and Assistant Buyers
1970	*	New personnel systems and new wage structure
	●	Examination for appointment to managerial positions (creation of 29 female chief clerks)
1971	○	System of childcare leave (more than six months in three years)
1973	○	System of temporary reduction of working hours for pregnant women and those with infants
	○	System of retirement age of 60 for women (move to same system for men and women)
1979	*	System of specialist occupations for all employees and new wage structure
1982	●	Large-scale employment of fourth year female university graduates
1985	●	Projects for administrative planning by female regular employees
1986	●	Overseas purchasing teams composed of female clerks
1989	*	Introduction of status ranking system and occupational groups
1992	*	New personnel system
	●	New establishment of sales masters

Source: Internal company documents and interview surveys.

was dependent on men's aspirations regarding management work. 'We did not particularly have women in our sights. We have a fairly substantial women's policy so this is certainly not a case of gender difference but rather a matter of individual success or failure,' they argued. In the case of Department Store C, it responded to the ageing of its male workforce by pouring its efforts into establishing multi-step managerial positions and opening up a path, not to management

Figure 3.1: Company A's status ranking system

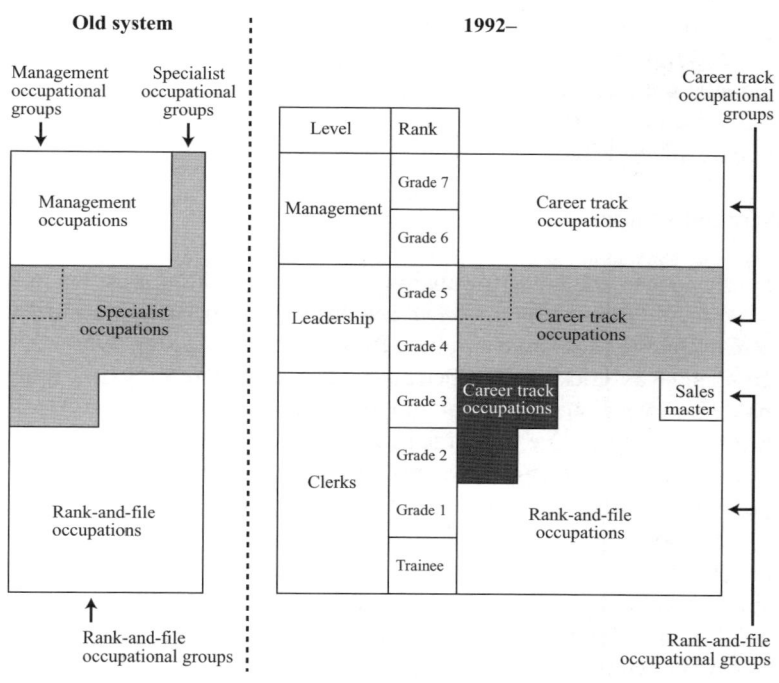

positions but, towards an evaluation of expertise in sales skills. According to its personnel department, men (particularly high school graduates) described the result of this as producing, 'rather, a shocking effect as the seniority system and paternalism disappear and the conduct of promotion reviews and decisions about increases in status occur without reference to gender or education'. This is because men with limited management abilities are screened out of consideration as salespeople with expertise and discriminated against. In Company A also, in the same sort of way as in Company C, the rank of 'Sales Master', which is restricted to the low status grades, level three, was established following 1992.

The above type of arrangement of a personnel system can be described as having been constructed with the enduring pivotal concern of nurturing the management abilities of male employees; there was only a weak sense of the need to act in order to start making 'positive use of women'. As I mentioned in Part I, Chapter 2, the status ranking system, by virtue of making it possible for men and women to have their status grade considered equally, in a general sense, gives women also the possibility of promotion and increased status. However, it probably goes without saying that, understandably, this alone is not enough to promote making 'positive use of women', in the sense of nurturing women who have built up extensive work and management skills.

Women's policy

In what sense, then, has Company A promoted making 'positive use of women'? Returning to Table 3.1, let us look at the special features of Company A's women's policy. In the early half of the 1960s the company was quick to introduce guarantees of child rearing time (one paid hour per day) and a re-employment policy, aimed at employees who had resigned due to marriage or pregnancy, and then in 1971 a system of child rearing leave (more than six months in a three year period). In other companies in this same sector re-employment systems were, generally, not introduced until after 1975. Company A's progressive nature is illustrated by its early setting out of measures to support women who face work difficulties as a result of childbirth and child rearing and policies opening up the way for the re-employment of women who have left work because of marriage or childbirth.[2]

Companies began thinking about using women in low-level management positions from the 1960s. A system whereby women filled in for managers was established in 1964 and the position of assistant attached to a floor manager was introduced the following year. This was a position in which female regular employees acted as substitutes for male managers in responsible positions, when the latter were absent from the workplace, and responsibility was transferred to these women, as they played the role of advisers to male managers. This was, however, only ever an advisory role and we should not lose sight of the fact that it was not necessarily imagined that this sort of position would provide a foothold for regular female employees to advance beyond it.

New paths were opened up for the appointment of assistant sales managers in 1964 and then sales managers in 1966. The company was also searching for ways to expand occupational areas and embarked on the posting of women to departments dealing with sales to outside customers from 1966, increasing numbers at a stroke in 1976 from zero to eighteen. Thereafter numbers stayed at around 30, rising to 37 in

1988. It has been an extremely slow process but the company has been increasing the number of women assigned to the department dealing with sales to outside customers. From 1969 the company opened up the way for their appointment as buyers and assistant buyers. However, as we will see later, whilst the appointment of assistant buyers progressed smoothly, in its own way, advances into the buyer level by women proceeded at an extremely slow pace. Since 1970 appointments have been limited to a few people but the numbers from 1985 show that there were a mere nine people at this level.[3] Company A began its efforts in the area of maximising women's contribution to the company from the 1960s, making it an 'industry leader' but substantial steps in the expansion of occupational areas did not occur at all quickly. In the 1980s the company assembled teams for designing for special issues and for overseas purchasing and pursued new initiatives, such as the formation of women only teams, to promote the expansion of occupational areas for women and also the utilisation of the product knowledge held by women.

As outlined above, alongside its opening up of opportunities for intermittent work and re-employment for women, Company A, has been one of the first to venture into the area of appointing women to key advisory roles. From the start of the 1980s it has sought to make 'positive use of women' on the basis of the new idea of assembling women's teams. However, at the time of the survey, conditions in the company were a long way from any idea of selecting women for more senior positions while speeding up the pace of fostering the training of women for these positions, in a manner befitting the reality that they make up 70 per cent of the workforce. This is immediately obvious from the status and managerial positions of women at the time of the survey.

Women's status and managerial positions

As already mentioned, the tendency towards women's increasing length of continuous service has been striking and this has certainly been reflected in their appointment to high-level status grades. As can be seen in Table 3.2, there were 100 women at level four (chief clerk class) in 1985, with this number reaching 123 (19.9 per cent of the entire fourth level) in 1993. However, the women who have made it above level five are limited to an extremely small number: a mere 4.6 per cent at level five (section head class) and 2.2 per cent at level six (department head class). It is common knowledge that there is a

Table 3.2: Changes in the number of employees by status grade level

Year	Males						Females					Total males and females
	Status rank grade					Total males	Status rank grade				Total females	
	7	6	5	4	3–1		6	5	4	3–1		
1970	15	94	165	450	480	1,204	-	-	29	2,658	2,687	3,891
1975	29	119	224	575	546	1,493	-	-	61	3,730	3,791	5,284
1980	43	133	327	580	457	1,540	-	4	98	2,909	3,011	4,551
1985	47	162	478	521	528	1,736	-	16	104	3,454	4,059	5,795
1990	61	216	613	433	505	1,828	4	25	125	3,209	3,363	5,191
1991	62	236	625	468	457	1,848	5	29	122	3,360	3,516	5,364
1992	62	258	633	487	448	1,888	6	31	124	3,412	3,753	5,461
1993	62	269	645	496	486	1,958	6	31	123	3,531	3,691	5,649

Source: Internal company documents. Number of employees as of June each year.

clear divide between level four and levels five and above. However, we should not forget that an even greater divide exists between level four and levels three and below. Whereas 24.8 per cent of all males are to be found in levels one to three, as many as 95.7 per cent of women are found in these levels. Whilst men are seen climbing up the career ladder within an excessively short period from their entry as new employees, the figures show that a considerable number of women stay at a low status grade, level three and below, despite their increasing years of continuous service.

Let us look at the annual trends by managerial positions in Table 3.3. According to these figures, we can verify that, as a whole, the appointment of women is progressing, despite the fact that there is a mere scattering of women in the occupational levels. It is at the buyer level, as mentioned before, that this increase has been at its lowest and although there was a modest increase following 1985, women were limited to 8.9 per cent of all buyers in 1994. In the case of sales managers also the figure is only 11.5 per cent. These sales managers and buyers are both selected from level four but their numbers do not even reach the approximately 20 per cent figure, which is the proportion of women at level four. We can say that, in terms of the appointment of women, both sales manager and buyer are managerial positions with walls around them, which are hard to penetrate.

In contrast to this, the appointment of women is proceeding apace in those managerial levels with the title 'assistant' selected from level three. Women make up 47.7 per cent of assistant buyers, climbing to numbers virtually comparable with men. In the case of assistant sales

Table 3.3: Number of women in managerial positions in the workplace

	Assistant Sales Manager	Sales Manager	Buyer	Assistant Buyer
Females				
1970	7	119	4	15
1975	11	73	1	9
1980	9	102	2	15
1985	26	149	9	30
1991	20	204	6	58
1992	24	205	7	80
1993	28	214	8	90
1994	22	216	9	93
Males				
1994	169	40	92	102

Source: Internal company documents.
Note: The number of employees for the initial year of the system are as given below.

    Sales Manager: 2   (1966)
    Assistant Sales Manager: 41   (1964)
    Buyer: 2   (1969)
    Assistant Buyer: 14   (1969)

managers, the numbers of women climbed to around 100 from 1970 and then to 200 in 1991. In 1994 the numbers reached 216, running well ahead of the 40 men in that category. The vast majority of assistant sales managers and assistant buyers are women high school and junior college graduates who have worked their way up from the shop floor as salespeople. Women with over ten years of continuous service make up 26.5 per cent of all women in the company (1990) but the majority of this group are restricted to the assistant sales manager and assistant buyer levels. We see also that appointments from managerial positions with titles, such as 'assistant', attached to them to sales manager and buyer positions are limited to an extremely tiny number of women.

As we can see from the above, in Company A, with its pioneering approach and 'industry firsts' such as a women's policy, women are, to a limited extent, progressing on to level four as the years of continuous service increase for women. A steady stream of assistant sales managers is also appearing. There have also been a certain number of appointments to assistant buyer positions. However, it is clear that the pace of progress on to higher levels is slow and, just as in the past, although women are being appointed they are stopping in the assistants' roles of assistant sales manager and assistant buyer. Also, there is a strong trend towards the overwhelming majority of women, who are high school and junior college graduates, staying at the level of regular employees in the rank-and-file grades, with no title. This state of affairs attests to the fact that Company A's progressive women's policy is concerned with giving women the opportunity to accumulate a certain degree of experience and access to advisory roles in the workplace – where they gain this experience – but that it is definitely no more than this. Even in Company A, which abandoned the separate management of men and women at an early period and which showcased its progressive women's policy, there is a tendency for women to be stuck in managerial positions, which are at the very bottom of the status grades or which are merely advisory. Indeed, we could say that the increase in length of women's years of continuous service neatly exposes this state of affairs. This type of women's policy and the mechanisms behind job segregation by gender in the workplace in Company A are not mutually contradictory, in fact, they prop each other up.

Job segregation by gender amongst regular employees

Survey subjects: general conditions in the workplace

Let us now go right down to the level of the workplace, which forms the very base of the work organisation, in an attempt to understand the structure of job segregation by gender. The focus of this investigation will be Shop C, an average shop for Store B and part of Company A, which is located in the heart of Tokyo. What I mean by 'average' is a shop with working hours, determined by the goods handled, hours which are neither too long nor too short and also one in which the product knowledge required for serving customers is neither too complex nor too simple. The goods sold in this workplace, in the women's clothing department, are heavy women's clothing items such as coats and suits and the estimated customer time is in the order of 30 minutes to one hour per person.

The job allocations of the 27 staff – 6 male and 21 female – in this shop are set out in Figure 3.2. Apart from these there are some who are not regular employees: 3 part-timers and 50 dispatched salespeople (*haken hanbaiin*), called 'goods suppliers' employees' (*torihikisaki shain*). In Company A, at the beginning of the 1990s, apart from the case of newly opened suburban stores, there was little reliance on part-timers and these employees were assigned to peripheral, assistant-type jobs.

Figure 3.2: Distribution chart of personnel in survey shop

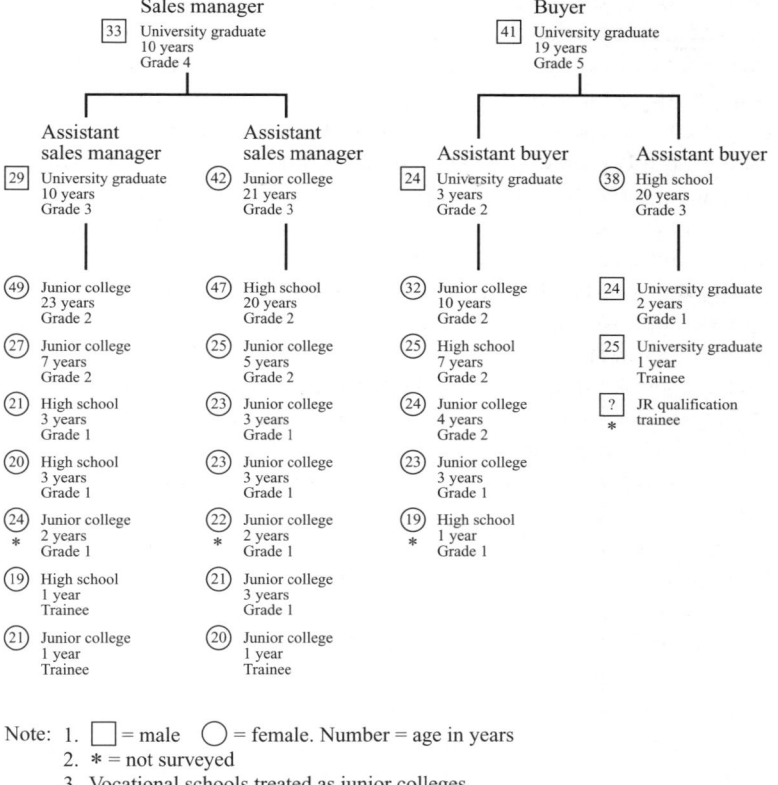

Note: 1. ☐ = male ◯ = female. Number = age in years
2. * = not surveyed
3. Vocational schools treated as junior colleges.
4. Other figures indicate length of service in years.

Source: Interview surveys.

In contrast to this, dispatched salespeople, both in terms of numbers and nature of work, were active as the main force in sales. I will deal with dispatched salespeople in more detail later but for now let us first attempt to understand the situation regarding job segregation, with a focus on regular employees. In the following discussion I will be using data based on surveys of 24 employees from this shop, excluding part-timers. I conducted these intensive interviews with close to 90 per cent of the members of one workplace in order to gain a detailed understanding of the organisational structure of the workplace and thereby highlight, in a multi-dimensional way, the job distribution mechanisms and labour relations.[4]

Educational background and gender

Worth noting from the outset is the problem of the overlap between gender and educational differences. When we look at the composition of the educational backgrounds of regular employees in this workplace, we see that all the men are university graduates and that the women are made up of eight high school graduates and thirteen graduates from either junior or other colleges. Because female university graduates are not posted to this workplace, male/female differences and educational differences clearly overlap. As a result of this, employees find themselves in an environment in which it is easy to regard the differences in treatment, which actually exist between male and female employees, as being the 'natural' result of gender rather than educational differences.

Let us look first at educational differences with regard to the speed of increases in status grade and of promotion. Status increases and promotions, in the case of high school graduates, were of the order of level three after twelve years of service, with a promotion to level four after a further six to seven years. Graduates from junior and other colleges reached level three after ten years of service, and level four after a further six to seven years. University graduates, by contrast, reached level three after an average of three and a half years of service, progressing on to level four (chief clerk class) after about four and a half years, thus securing their passports to the positions of sales manager and buyer (around 30 years of age). Then, with thirteen years of service, they reach level five (section head class) and after 20 years of service level six (department head class). What we ought to note here is that educational differences are a decisively large factor in the time needed to rise up to level three. University graduates, in addition to having the time spent graduating from university taken into account, are assured a strikingly rapid rise in status grade. Further, the time deemed necessary to advance to level four is a mere eight years for university graduates, as compared to eighteen to nineteen years for high school graduates and sixteen to seventeen years for junior college graduates. University graduates actually rise in status grade at about twice the speed of high school or junior college graduates.

Since the employment of men has been narrowly limited to university graduates for a considerable amount of time, it is naturally women who are the focus of our interest here when comparing and contrasting high school and junior college graduates. As mentioned previously, the vast majority of high school and junior college graduates actually remain below level three. Only an extremely tiny number from amongst these women advance to level four but, even on these occasions, as the above figures show, it takes them twice as long as university graduates. Assistant sales managers and assistant buyers, selected from amongst level four employees, are positions which, as far as university graduates are concerned, represent a step up to a higher job level but as far as female high school and junior college graduates are concerned it is no exaggeration to say that they are the limit of the highest level which they can be expected to reach. As seen in Figure 3.2, young, regular, female employees in Shop C are stuck at level two even after seven to ten years of continuous service. Of the four women with over 20 years of continuous service two are stuck at level two and the other two have been selected as assistant sales manager (aged 42) and assistant buyer (aged 38).

The Personnel Department's routine practices regarding the timing of these increases in status, just as in the case of the women's policy looked at previously, lead to the company's female human resources consistently being seen as nothing more than rank-and-file grade employees. Alternatively, women can, at best, be expected only to fulfil an assistant's role after long years of service. In Company A the basic approach is to devote the nurturing of management ability and high-level job skills solely to a small group of men. Following the narrowing down of male employment to university graduates, from the second half of the 1970s, educational differences were seen as overlapping with gender differences. I will discuss this in more detail later but before the large-scale employment of fourth year female university graduates in 1982, the fact that men walked over women in their rise in status and promotions was viewed as perfectly normal by women themselves. The appearance of a limited number of female university graduates saw the beginning of a new stage with the potential to smash this status quo. However, female university graduates, who still make up no more than eight per cent of all females, are not necessarily in a position to have a decisive impact on the workplace.

The distribution of work duties

Just how are work duties distributed and roles allotted in the workplace? The segregation of labour by gender, which says that 'women should sell and men manage', is clearly evident even within the types of work common to sales occupations. Even after long years of service there are extremely large differences in job allocation between men, who expect to be trained as the future managers, and women, who do not. Women are given sales jobs and subsidiary sales jobs while men are given all other work duties and managerial duties. Below, I will take a more detailed look at the conditions surrounding the division of labour between male and female regular employees but first let us look at Figure 3.2, which deals with the age, education, years of continuous service and skill levels of the interviewees.

Female regular employees, as seen in the case of one veteran female employee (aged 47) with as many as 20 years of continuous service, are – as regular employees in the rank-and-file grades – responsible only for sales. Contrasted to this, younger female regular employees in the rank-and-file grades, from their mid-twenties to thirties, deal with all sales floors, training and complaints. Assistant sales managers and assistant buyers are assigned to the management and supervision of these women. The young women, 'even while being trained by the older women', perform the jobs that are secondary to sales (such as, check out, supplies, packing, checking the accuracy of sales slips and cleaning). Whilst there are some differences amongst women – as in this sort of assigning of roles according to years of continuous service – women, in general, are responsible for jobs directly related to sales.

In the case of young, male regular employees in the rank-and-file grades on the other hand, basically one out of three men with short employment histories will stand on the shop floor during busy periods while the other two replenish the shelves with goods from the storerooms, take care of the paperwork for deliveries and for unsold goods that are to be returned to the supplier, check the accuracy of sales slips for marked down goods and arrange the bargain corner for unsold merchandise. They also follow the work of the assistant buyers. Although men are also, in part, associated with sales, they are mainly responsible for work duties which differ completely from those of women. One 24 year-old man with two years of service said, 'since there is a lot of irregular work to do, I have to work efficiently'. He stressed the points of difference with women's jobs saying that female high school and junior college graduates can get by with limited product knowledge but 'we have to know about all the products and everything to do with the shop floors'. Another 25 year-old man with one year's service said, 'I clump up and down the stairs to the fifth floor storeroom many times each day to replenish items which are running low. This is not simply because I am still in my training period, all men do the same thing. The men work as a team, arranging and restocking products as well as finalising sales accounts, after shop closing hours.

We even work overtime in order to be able to get data ready quickly, not only at work but also at home.' This differs from women's jobs in that men are responsible for physically heavy carrying tasks; a greater volume of knowledge; and jobs to be done after shop closing hours. A further striking detail is that in this workplace organisation, occupied by a majority of women, the small numbers of men work as a team.

The nurturing of men

These young men's senior, a sales manager (male, ten years' service, aged 33) relates that, 'while men carry out these daily work duties, they are being nurtured, along the way, as management trainees. They perform all of the lowest level work duties during their one-year training period and after this year they need to be able to understand how absolutely everything works. Since they will be in a senior status grade to women who are older than them, they must possess a sense of themselves as leaders.' From the very first stages of joining the company, there is a fundamentally different method for nurturing men than that adopted for women, who make up the majority of the workplace. One result of this, according to what I heard in the Personnel Department, is the creation of an atmosphere in which, even the female regular employees all around them end up feeling, 'it is because he is a man' and 'I am no match for a man'. Consequently, female regular employees' generally give high appraisals of the ways in which male regular employees work. For example, one woman (aged 24) with four years' service said that even though 'there are individual differences...men shoulder responsibility for the shop floor. If they make mistakes they are shouted at and they work longer hours than women.' Another woman (aged 21) with three years' service sees men's way of working as a case of, 'no matter how hard they work men are faced with a seemingly endless amount of work and they work excessively, arriving before the shop opens and staying after it closes: it is to be expected that there will be a difference in the ways that men and women are treated.' As we will see in more detail later, men's strict training and the high regard in which they are held is decisively different from the case with women's work duties.

Not surprisingly, there were also displays of defiance: 'even though it is women who do all the serving of customers and the selling that directly makes sales profits, their male superiors say things like, "Why can't you sell?" When I hear them scolding, I always think, "You are not the one doing the selling everyday!"' complained one woman (one year's service, aged 21). This defiance is based on women's sense of indignation that men, who tend to specialise in management work, intervene in their spheres of work duties. It is not certain which is the stronger: this type of response or the one which says 'it is because he is man' and 'I am no match for a man'. One thing that emerges from the interview surveys is the unique format of the nurturing of male regular employees. This is not the type of approach to nurturing talent in which there is a hidden curriculum and in which before anyone quite realises it the workplace is imbued with gender specific roles. Rather, a quite obviously special programme is assigned to men from the very first stages of joining the company and we can see that a sense of camaraderie, like a men's club, supports this. Although a feeling of camaraderie can sometimes lead to a sense of competition between individuals, from the moment that men first join the company they are placed in an organisational culture, which is different for each gender, and in which the sense that 'naturally I am different from women' is clearly acknowledged by both individual men and others. There is basically no working in teams for women. The type of team formation by women seen in Figure 3.2 was devised when the current sales manager took up his position and it is no more than a feeble attempt to stimulate some consciousness on the part of senior women of their educative role towards younger women. In contrast to this, men, a numerically small force in the workplace, from the very outset of joining the company, are thrown into men-only teams and shoulder all the responsibility for the workplace as though they were the elite troops of a reserve army.

The difficulties faced by female regular employees

Women face their own peculiar difficulties under this type of structure for the distribution of work duties. Although they are compelled to push themselves and work hard, this is a different situation from men's jobs, in which one can feel a sense of fulfilment at assuming responsibility for the workplace. A sense of boredom and futility haunt women. One 49 year-old woman, a veteran regular employee in a rank-and-file grade of 23 years' service, tells, 'it makes me happy when customers like something that I have selected myself but this sort of thing does not happen often. There are also times when I feel a sense of futility at my intermediary role of simply selling something made by someone else. There is no sense of fulfilment, no sense of satisfaction. This is because I am so used to sales. I end up thinking that it does not matter who does the selling.' She adds, 'even without any decision-making power, just being given the opportunity to select the colour and shape of goods, along with the assistant buyer, gives me a sense of 'participation'. I think that the pleasure of selling a product that I myself have made, along with others, is very important.' However, the opportunities for being able to experience this sense of 'participation' are actually few. These types of opportunities are not incorporated into the everyday work duties of female regular employees. If they were able to have some insight into all of the processes regarding sales and the movement of goods, then there is the possibility that they would be freed from a sense of 'boredom' and 'futility' but they seldom come across this kind of opportunity.

One woman in a rank-and-file grade (aged 27) with seven years' service and who has been given the role of chief substitute (*daikō*) says, 'even in the area of ordering stock, I cannot act without, above all else, first consulting my "superior" (assistant sales manager)'. Once, when she asked about something that she was well capable of doing on the basis of her own judgement alone, after a pause for thought, she got a reply, 'to the effect that, on rainy days, I should double the paper bags for customers'. Another woman (aged 25) with five years' service, recounted, 'I find no interest in selling goods that my superiors have stocked. It is interesting when I see the whole flow of things. For example, when I help the assistant buyer with pricing I understand the cost price and grasp the flow of the whole process. But lately I have become a little bored.' A woman (aged 47) with 20 years' service, talked about the leeway open to her as a veteran, 'when I am in charge of sales, there are no assigned tasks so if I think that I would like to loaf around on the job, I can.' However, as we shall see in more detail later, this leeway that they have is born from the fact that it is actually dispatched salespeople who are the main strength of sales.

We can see that the work duties assigned to female regular employees in the rank-and-file grades are boring. This is a point which differs considerably from the case of male regular employees in the rank-and-file grades. The scarcity of room for exercising discretion and the weakness of the decision making power inherent in women's jobs compound this. Further, the inability to develop a clear view of the work process, as a whole, and therefore a sense of 'participation' in the work organisation are problems specifically borne by female regular employees.

As seen above, there are clear differences in the assignment of work duties between men and women, with men possessing ten years service being strictly trained for the future. In contrast to this, it is as if there are no expectations of women after ten years. Women are assigned to work duties which tend typically to lead to boredom and they are not required to have a sense of 'participation' and be challenged.

Gender differences in working hours

As might be expected, these types of differences in the allocation of work duties between genders are linked with clear differences in working hours. Working hours for men, who are trained in a manner different from women from the moment they join the company, are extremely long and overtime hours, in particular, soar to massive levels. Female regular employees in the rank-and-file grades, who are high school and junior college graduates, basically keep to a shift system of working hours, which is divided into an early shift (9.45–18.40) and a late shift (10.35–19.10). Their overtime is only in the order of approximately two to three hours per month, at stocktaking time. Men, on the other hand, are already at work when the early shift arrives and stay there at least until the late shift leaves. They regularly do overtime in order to arrange stock after shop closing hours, to calculate sales and to enable the rapid collection of data. On occasion they also take work home. Even one man with one year's service (aged 25) does two to three hours of overtime daily. This corresponds to the monthly overtime hours for female regular employees. This man also has no regard for the distinction between early and late shifts, arriving for work at nine in the morning and leaving at nine at night. In addition, he takes home approximately two hours of overtime per fortnight. Another man (aged 24) with two years' service recounts that on top of one to three hours of overtime per day, he has approximately one hour of take home overtime every day, this amount rising at times to two to three hours of work every day.

An assistant buyer (aged 24) with three years of service says that aside from the overtime that he puts in at work, he has had take home overtime everyday since joining the company. He says, 'this happens because I have many miscellaneous duties and also a lot of work that has been entrusted to me. Men are given more and more work from the time of their cadetships. I do not keep to the hours of the shift system. Even on rest days I have various things to do, connected with understanding my work, so that I do not have a proper rest. This is relatively difficult work so I strive telling myself, "I have to do it!" What I would like more than anything else right now is time.' A sales manager with ten years' service does one and a half hours of overtime everyday. He arrives for work a little before the beginning of the early shift and leaves at the end of the late shift, making his overtime approximately a fixed one and a half hours per day. There is also 'sometimes' take home overtime. A male buyer with nineteen years' service arrives for work at nine twenty in the morning and leaves at eight or nine at night, thus putting in approximately three hours of overtime everyday.

As shown above, men's pattern of working ignores the shift system of working hours and, either out of a sense of responsibility for their managerial positions or in response to their level of mastery, they must do copious amounts of overtime. The testimony, quoted earlier, of a woman with three years' service that, 'no matter how hard they work, men are faced with a seemingly endless amount of work. They work excessively, arriving before the shop opens and staying after it closes' reflects accurately the reality for male regular employees.

Women, on the other hand, are able to stick to the working hours of the shift system and face an extremely small amount of overtime every month. However, once one attains the managerial position of assistant conditions change significantly. A female assistant sales manager (aged 42) with 21 years' service does 20 hours of overtime per month, overtime hours that are far removed from those of female regular employees in the rank-and-file grades. Her hours of attendance at work have also changed: she must wait until both early and late shift employees leave work. However, being able to keep to the working hours – at least those of the late shift – is different from the men, who already in their first year with the company, work without regard to the working hours of either the early or late shifts. Generally, her overtime hours are also fewer than those of men. Another female assistant buyer (aged 38) with 20 years' service does two to three hours of overtime everyday. She arrives for work with the early shift and leaves with the late shift. She says that she does her take home overtime on the evenings of her rest days. Since this ruins her rest days she has had to give up going skiing, which she used to enjoy. This case is similar to that in which men find themselves. As women are promoted to the grade of assistant, they end up being drawn into the same endless working hours faced by men.

The desire for promotion

As is clear from the preceding section, from the very instant of joining the company men do approximately the same amount of overtime as their male seniors, while observing and learning from the working patterns of these senior males. Women, in exchange for their boredom-inducing jobs, gain abundant free time. Their leisure activities, such as skiing, scuba diving and foreign travel, are extremely lively and colourful. However, once selected as assistant sales manager or assistant buyer, and regardless of the fact that their overtime hours are considerably shorter than those of men, women are drawn into a seemingly endless work pattern, similar to that of men; even having to do take home overtime on their rest days. The young high school and junior college graduates, amongst the female regular employees in the rank-and-file grades, see before their eyes the hard working pattern of male employees, including the newcomers, and also that of their female seniors who have become assistant sales manager and assistant buyer. It is not surprising that these females think 'I cannot work like that' and say 'I want to quit when I get married'. This is because what these young women are seeing is completely different from the working pattern to which they have become accustomed.

The ways in which expectations and training methods work and also the ways in which work duties are allocated in the workplace all have an impact on the gender differences inherent in work consciousness and the can do spirit with regard to work. As a look at the desire for promotion up the managerial positions shows, in contrast to the fact that all male employees responded that they wished to be in positions higher than where they were now or that they clearly had jobs in higher positions in their sights; female employees, even those with long years of continuous service, in complete contrast, displayed a desire to stay in low positions. Only a mere two out of thirteen high school and junior college graduates, one in her teens and the other in her twenties, responded, 'I would like to become an assistant buyer or assistant sales manager'. Most of the women had no wish to be promoted saying, assistant sales managers and assistant buyers 'become busy' and 'it looks so hard', 'I want to marry and leave work by the time I am 30'.

Even women who are selected to become assistant sales managers and assistant buyers do not aspire to further promotion. This is because they have been left disoriented by having been drawn abruptly into the working hours and responsible positions familiar to men, without any acknowledgement of the fact that they have been tied to sales and have come through an organisational culture so clearly different from that surrounding men from the moment they entered the company. One 38 year-old assistant buyer (20 years' service) has been shaken by precisely this experience. She is living a life in which she leaves for work at seven (or seven thirty) and returns home after midnight. It is not just work that brings her home so late, but also the fact that after completing her overtime she goes out to dinner and karaoke bars with her colleagues in order to relieve stress. She is thinking of starting over from the beginning by either going back to being a 'sales employee in a rank-and-file grade with no responsibility or moving to a new post, in order to free herself from this type of lifestyle. However, she says that despite being busy everyday she feels, 'as one season ends, I want to give another season a try. I want to stop but I cannot'. Her superior has recommended that she try for the qualifying exam for Grade four, but she is hesitating, 'because the working hours will become even more dreadful'. This is because lacking, from the outset, any desire for promotion, she has admitted to herself that she is in a different position from men. Another female assistant sales manager (aged 42) with 21 years' service says, 'I have no wish to become a sales manager because I prefer to meet customers rather than to manage people'. Another woman with ten years' service (aged 32) says that her selection as an assistant sales manager is planned to take place in half a year but, 'I really do not want to become one. My superior says that I am running away from an opportunity but I am not cut out for it. Part of me wants to quit work, and I also want to get married.' She ends up wanting to run away from a move to a situation, which is decisively different from her working pattern of the past ten years, and at this time what comes to mind is the word 'marriage'.

As we have seen, women, even those with long years of service, characteristically have a low desire for promotion. This is the complete opposite of men who, from a young age, have an eye on the next level up or are aiming for a clearly higher position at work. Even in 1994, as we have already seen in Table 3.3, the fact that women themselves are not wishing for promotion to higher managerial positions, as they continue to experience longer working hours, can be seen as one of the reasons for the extremely small numbers of women reaching the high managerial positions such as sales manager and buyer. Behind this is the fact that from the moment that they join the company women are tied exclusively to sales related jobs and also the fact that they have come through an organisational culture which is different from that experienced by men. Females in the rank-and-file grades, who for a variety of reasons have established good work reputations and long years of service, also do not react at all positively to being 'selected' for higher managerial positions. Even so, after they have been selected, as assistant sales managers and assistant buyers they are thrown into a system of long working hours, of which they have no previous experience; but at the same time, they are swayed as they savour the sense of accomplishment, which they also have never experienced before. Notions regarding when to stop working and when to get married are provided by the norms encountered before joining the company. Undeniably all influence the state of the can do spirit with regard to work and the work consciousness of female regular employees.

However, it was not just women in their teens and twenties but also those in their thirties who again and again, in the course of these interviews, halfway through talking about their work uttered the words, 'I also want to get married'. We can find the background to this in the fact that these women, since joining Company A, have lived in the midst of a completely different organisational culture from that of men; one in which increases in status and promotions belong to another world, which has nothing to do with them. These women vaguely consider marriage as a way of avoiding either 'boredom' or being drawn into work patterns like those of men. In this sense, job segregation by gender and gender relations reproduced by job segregation itself can be seen as playing a major part in spurring on women's marriage aspirations.

Inconsistencies resulting from job segregation by gender

The problem of the status-less 'grade level three'

As we have seen in the preceding discussion, both the daily allocation of work duties in the workplace and the organisational culture found in the workplace are strictly segregated along gender lines. Even though a workplace organisation so thoroughly permeated by job segregation by gender is capable of stimulating a moderate regeneration of women, it is inconsistent with making 'positive use of women' effectively in the workplace. Inconsistencies continue to surface particularly given the trend towards longer years of continuous service by female high school and junior college graduates, who are in the majority. As the links between the trend towards an increase in the years of continuous service by women and the growing trend towards women in large cities not marrying have become clear, those in charge of personnel matters are also increasingly becoming aware of this fact. As many as 25 per cent of high school and junior college women graduates in

Company A are continuing to work beyond the age of 30. This invites a situation in which the company must fundamentally consider policies for 'maximising the contribution of these women to the company'. In fact, even Company A's Personnel Department has acknowledged 'the lack of desire for self-advancement and a tendency towards intentional negligence' amongst female regular employees, in the 30 to over 40 age range. They have termed this the 'problem of the status-less grade level three'. The Personnel Department is increasingly turning its attention to a female stagnation trend in which women, even after having reached grade level three, reject the idea of becoming an assistant sales manager or assistant buyer or simply grind to a stand still becoming unsuitable for promotion thus evading the need to reject promotion. The question of how to motivate and nurture these women has become one which cannot be ignored in future personnel strategies.

However, we can probably say that even if women show 'a tendency towards intentional negligence' regarding work, this is an inevitable consequence of the way in which work duties are divided and the position in which female regular employees are placed. According to company documents, see Figure 3.3, the annual income of junior college and high school graduates continues to show a widening gap compared with that of university graduates, from the time of joining the company, reaching approximately half that of university graduates after 20 years of service. It is extremely difficult to expect any 'desire for advancement' amongst these women given the meagre levels of work stimulation, responsibility and authority and also the fact that they have reached the uppermost limit of pay. As far as these women are concerned, the assistant sales manager and assistant buyer, who have no alternative but to descend into the same difficult working conditions as men, do not stand out as attractive role models. Even Company A, with its rich history and wealth of experience in 'making positive use of women' in the workplace, has come to be permeated by what can rightly be called a conservative posture towards women, who are seen as unreliable for stable long-term employment.

This conservative posture arises from the fact that although the company has a certain degree of awareness of the benefits of 'making positive use of women', ultimately they have always operated a safe policy on the basis of experience. This is a policy in which the company has fundamentally come to rely on a workplace management system with men, from whom they can anticipate long term employment, as the pivotal players. Improved treatment and a reorganisation of the allocation of work duties in the workplace, taking into account the

Figure 3.3: Average annual income model by educational background (Company A)

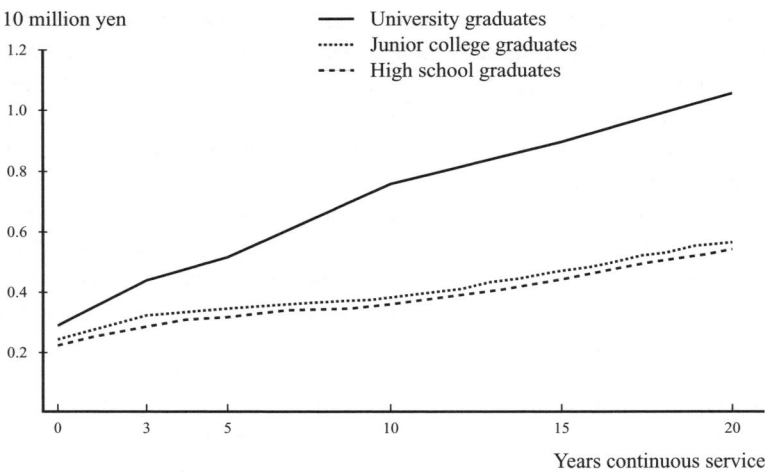

Source: Internal company documents

presence of women with increasing years of continuous service, would be an indispensable step towards solving this problem.

The situation of female university graduates who are in a grey zone

Another area, which we can describe as being in the eye of the storm, is that of the trends displayed by female university graduates who have been employed as regular employees since 1982. The very presence of female university graduates upsets the state of equilibrium preserved by the work organisation, in which gender and educational differences overlap with one another.

Since no female university graduates were posted to the shop, which served as the subject of this interview survey, I conducted a special interview survey with eleven female university graduates on the same floor in the women's clothing section.[5] Jumping ahead a little, the clear conclusion of this survey was that female university graduates find themselves in, as it were, a 'grey zone'.

That is to say, by virtue of being university graduates they overtake female high school and junior college graduates and are promoted to higher positions than these other women, just like male university graduates. There is, however, at the same time an entrenched notion in the workplace that because they are women, 'they must be able to sell'. Consequently, whilst carrying out the same sales and related work duties as the female high school and junior college graduates, they are also required to acquire product management knowledge and management skills, like male university graduates. This means that, although they are university graduates, they are still drawn into 'women's work' and end up occupying a middle ground somewhere between male university graduates and female high school and junior college graduates.

According to the Personnel Department, at the time of the survey, the numbers of female university graduates had declined to a third of their original numbers by age 30. These numbers were at a considerably higher level than the retention rate for female high school and junior college graduates (approximately 25 per cent). The dilemma faced by female university graduates is that as a consequence of being promoted above female high school and junior college graduates, like male university graduates, they are required to develop the same skills as male university graduates; but this notwithstanding, they are also expected to pour their energies into sales. In addition, their appearance awakens a strong awareness of the educational differences between them and female high school and junior college graduates. This comes about as a result of these young women being promoted over female high school and junior college graduates who are their seniors. It is in this context, whilst fielding stern looks from other females, and as their superiors see fit, that these female university graduates are assigned work duties centred on sales and others similar to those carried out by men. The grey middle ground in which they find themselves is surprisingly wide. This makes the pattern of their rise in status all the more one of constant trial and error and, unlike male university graduates, there is no stable programme and course to aid their upward movement.

The working hours for female university graduates also differ from those of male university graduates. As mentioned earlier, it is basic practice for men to disregard the hours of the shift system, turning up for work with the early shift and leaving with the late shift. In the case of female university graduates, they generally observe the same shift hours as female high school and junior college graduates, sharing only the same overtime as men. There are a number of female university graduates who work exactly the same hours as their male colleagues but there is a paternalistic atmosphere in the workplace which says, 'Women go home early!' and most women comply with this. Once women reach assistant sales manager or assistant buyer levels, they have to endure the same working hours as their male counterparts.

The originality of female university graduates

When we look at the way in which female university graduates appraise their male colleagues and their consciousness of gender differences in this 'grey zone', a very interesting fact emerges. As one woman in her first year of service says, 'I think it is terrible to work that much, like men, without even an overtime allowance. There are even some men who ruin their health, as they comply with their superiors' orders. There is nothing that can be done about it as men rapidly become assistant buyers.' There is an awareness of the fact that even though they are all university graduates, there is a gender difference in the speeds at which they are promoted. This occurs because female university graduates, with their extra responsibility for 'women's work', are prepared for management roles more slowly than men. As a result, they rate the way in which men work – with their tendency to slide into overwork – from a different perspective. A female university graduate (aged 25) with two years' service says, 'one man does the work of two to three women on his own and because he is surrounded by so many others who are driven in their attitude to work, there is a tendency not to go home leaving things half finished. I used to be troubled by the difference between this type of male consciousness and my own. Up until now it has been men who made up the practices and rules in this company. The women who are able to work along the lines of men's way of working may be fine but I think that it is important to think about women's physical condition and pace of work in considering their work in future'. Because these women are placed in a middle ground between being treated as university graduates and being treated as women, they inevitably have different experiences from those of either male university graduates or female high school and junior college graduates. In this situation, we can see them cultivating unique value judgements as they accumulate continuous years of service.

A female university graduate (aged 30) with seven years' service says, '(in my own case) I am seen more as a woman than as a university graduate in the workplace. The nurturing of men and women is completely different. I think that for this reason there are many dissatisfied women (university graduates), but unless they can grit their teeth and wait tenaciously (for a chance), then they cannot survive.' On the basis of two failed attempts at the examination for chief clerk, she adds that she thinks that, 'failure in the examination has its causes in other factors (being a woman) rather than in ability'. She says that this became the basis of her thinking 'that merely being above others is not work'. Another female university graduate (aged 31) with nine years' service and who is a buyer says, 'the educational differences are greater than the gender differences. When you join as a graduate, there is a pay difference (with high school and junior college graduates) and you have to work in a way which makes this difference clear. I can well understand that female high school and junior college graduates do not want any work responsibility and also their feelings of not wanting to do any more work than they are paid to do. Since I am in a management position, I, necessarily, have to assume a different posture regarding work. In the past I used to think that I certainly did not want to rise up but once I failed the chief clerks' examination, possibly because of some self-awakening, I grew bolder. It is strange to consider why it is that men can simply think, "I will rise up the managerial positions" right from the start. In the case of women, however, there are many who would like to stay in the same post for a long time.'

The third way for female university graduates

We can gather from this utterance the individuality of experience of female university graduates, as distinct from that of men who, from the moment they join the company, work as a team, learn from their seniors and concentrate their efforts on climbing up the positions in the company. Female university graduates, whilst acquiring 'tenacity', are attempting to develop a work objective, which differs from either 'standing above others' or 'climbing up the ladder of managerial positions'. They have also developed a critical view of the way in which men work. Even a female university graduate (24) with one year's service, states that, 'men have a much stronger sense of rivalry towards female university graduates, who joined the company at the same time as them, than I had thought. They say to women, "Do not outdo your male peers!"' Another female university graduate (aged 32), a sales manager with nine years' service, says, 'men are on the side of the company. When I look at the fact that they see it as the thing to do to stay behind until ten or eleven o'clock, I think that there must be some secret training given to men. I think that female university graduates, along with other women must build themselves an alternative way. Even my women seniors have said this to me.' This woman is searching about for a way of working, 'that will not lead me to become the same sort of sales manager as a man'. Returning to the case of the female university graduate (a buyer, aged 31) with nine years' service, she says that, 'there are many women above the chief clerk level who like to do things their own way' whereas 'men are always conscious of the company and even communicate vertically'. We can see that there is a tremendous difference between the genders regarding their respective sense of values and perspective inside the organisational culture.

There are also big differences between men and women in the setting of targets for the future. Three out of five female university graduates, who are in the rank-and-file grade, hope to rise above the assistant buyer level but none of the six who are already above the assistant sales manager and assistant buyer level have any particular wish to advance above their current position. This reflects the minority position of female university graduates. They clearly possess a work will and work orientation different from men's and they are, moreover, attempting to find a more flexible way of working. As individual female university graduates, the fact that they have, to some extent, had the experience of working their way up through sales makes them decisively different from male university graduates – as does the fact that their training has taken place amongst the female high school and junior college graduates. They hope to become sales managers who have been moulded by these former experiences – they are particularly interested in searching for an image of the sales manager which is different from that held by men. Alternatively, they are interested in becoming buyers with some level of discretionary powers and who can work in their own way. The orientation of female university graduates is clearly different from that of male university graduates; they look with indifference upon the aim to be promoted, which is considered a matter of course by male university graduates. To this extent, they do not see male university graduates as either role models or rivals. The problems caused by job segregation by gender and its inherent contradictions are clearly visible in the dual issues of the excessive working hours of male university regular employees and the 'boredom' experienced by the vast majority of women. However, the presence of female university graduates serves to highlight this state of affairs and they must inevitably search about for their own way. The unexpectedly high resignation rate amongst female university graduates, referred to earlier, may indeed be related to the fact that it is not at all easy to find this 'third way'.

The fact that female university graduates find themselves in a grey zone and having to go through this much trial and error, is a result of a lack of clear policies regarding the use and treatment of these graduates in Company A. This is notwithstanding the fact that ten years have passed since Company A first began hiring female university graduates as regular employees. It is not that the company has rapidly increased the number of female university graduates being employed. Rather, the fact that it has left the matter of nurturing the career development of these women to male superiors on each shop floor – that is, ultimately, to on the job discretion – is basically the result of efforts to safeguard workplace practices, which were developed with male university, female high school and junior college graduates in mind. To the extent that this is the case, it will be difficult for the unique views of female university graduates to be incorporated into the organisation.

Gender relations in the workplace and the sales and distribution network

The status of dispatched salespeople

The excessively sharp gender-based segregation, which we have been looking at, runs the risk of creating inefficient conditions for the whole workplace. Mr C., former Senior Manager of Company A, declares, 'the department store industry is unique regarding the extent of the impact that the abilities of sales staff have on sales'. If this is the case, then the 'tendency to intentional negligence' by female high school and junior college graduates, who are in positions where they need to display their sales abilities, is a serious problem. I have touched on this already but the Personnel Department, whilst aware of this problem, has no sense of it being a fundamental and pressing problem; that is, of the urgent need for the revision of job segregation by gender (currently practised) amongst regular employees. This is because it is not regular employees but someone else who carries out the core functions underpinning sales ability, which is the department store's lifeline now. It is precisely the dispatched salespeople who are assuming this role.[6] This has been brought about by the unique position occupied by department stores in the post war sales and distribution network and to that extent, it is no exaggeration to say that the gender relations, which we have been considering between regular employees in the workplace, are sustained from below by this sales and distribution network.

Department stores, by their very nature, characteristically sell a large variety of goods whilst stocking only small quantities of these goods. The purchasing capacity, product planning abilities and sales capacity of department stores are their lifelines. However, as I explained at length earlier, because the department store industry has come to hold a predominant position in the post war sales and distribution network, it is able to deal with superior suppliers of goods and this strength has made them behave as if they owned this network. That is to say, as mentioned previously, this is a unique purchasing system in which one purchases only the portion of stock which one has been able to sell. The department store relies on wholesalers and makers for their skills in stocking goods, determining the price of goods and even sales; there are no purchasing formalities for the department store at the stage where these groups line up the assortment of goods which they have put together for it to sell. It is only once the customers have finished the business of buying the goods that the stock purchasing formalities begin. This is called the 'sales-based stock purchasing system' (*uriage shiire hōshiki*) (alternatively, the 'consignment business system' (*itaku torihiki seidō*). On the basis of this system, department stores can avoid the various risks which accompany the buying and selling of a wide variety and small quantity of goods and they also gain access to dispatched salespeople who possess product knowledge and selling abilities (Okada, 1991, 112–116). The merits of this system for the suppliers of goods who meet the labour costs of these dispatched salespeople reside in the opportunity to obtain detailed information about consumer trends at the very point of retail sales and also in being able to sustain stable business relations in an extremely competitive environment. However, according to the contract with the company dispatching the salespeople and meeting their personnel costs, the gross profit rate for the department store is kept at a low level (25 per cent) and one which differs considerably from the United States and European levels (approximately 40 per cent)(Okada, 1991, 120).

According to the recollections of Mr C., the former Senior Manager of Company A quoted earlier, dispatched salespeople were used, from around the mid-1950s, in areas such as cosmetics, jewellery, time pieces, artworks and the foodstuffs of long-established shops – product areas in which regular employees lacked product knowledge and sales skills. In the 1960s the makers of women's clothing also set their sights on this system and started sending along their own salespeople. Then, particularly from 1985 on, the number of dispatched salespeople increased steadily in response to the rise in the brand name orientation of consumers.[7] What was the actual workplace standing of these dispatched salespeople, who had thus become an indispensable labour force to department stores and how are they related to job segregation by gender?[8]

The actual situation of dispatched salespeople in Shop C

In order to grasp the actual situation of dispatched salespeople in Shop C, the central subject of the survey in this chapter, I conducted an interview survey with salespeople who are usually sent to Shop C (October 1993–March 1994). I selected eight companies, from amongst the twelve currently dispatching salespeople to Shop C, and interviewed one person from each of these, giving a total of eight people. The comments below come from the results of this survey and also from what I heard in the Personnel Department of an influential women's clothing manufacturer, which also sends salespeople to Shop C. The subjects of this survey, as can be seen from Table 3.4, are made up of four women aged between 50 and 52 and another four aged between 42 and 44. My information regarding the attributes of dispatched salespeople in Shop C, obtained from the subjects of the survey covering the eight dispatching companies, is that they are all women, with 32.4 per cent in their twenties, 5.4 per cent in their thirties, 43.3 per cent in their forties and 18.9 per cent in their fifties.

We should note that the employment relations and conditions of dispatched salespeople are completely different from those in the dispatching company itself. As we see in Table 3.4, there are a variety of employment relations in the dispatching company, including regular employees, junior employees and contract employees. Pay is divided into daily and monthly pay and there are also wide disparities in the conditions of treatment according to the dispatching company in areas such as the number of days of paid leave and the provision or lack of bonuses. With regard to employment history, there are many dispatched salespeople with long careers in sales work behind them. Furthermore, the number of dispatched salespeople who have already been employed in Shop C for over ten years is not small, with the longest period stretching to fifteen to sixteen years. There are two work chains of command for dispatched salespeople. The first of these is the chain of command within Company A. The sales manager mainly gives out instructions at the morning meetings but dispatched salespeople actually have more frequent contact with the assistant sales manager. They say that, 'When [sales manager and buyer] patrol [the shop floors], it is unwise to look idle' and that this increases stress. One woman with experience of having been sent to another department store recalls, 'because I did not get along (temperamentally) with the assistant sales manager [there] and because it would have been awkward to trouble my company I just resigned (got herself dispatched to another company)'. We can sympathise with these women that their relations with their superiors, in the companies to which they are sent, are important. However, what we need to stress, above and beyond this, is the chain of command from the dispatching company. Assessments, which have a direct bearing on pay and bonuses, are carried out on the basis of consultations between those in charge of business from the dispatching company, who visit shop C daily, and the superiors in direct control in the dispatching company. The situation regarding the achievement of daily sales targets, which are set individually, play an important part in this. This explains the severe competition to sell the products of one's own company. However, because this severe sales competition, based on their respective companies, invites customer distrust and runs the risk of damaging the shop ambience, Company A has taken the lead in 'clearing away the fences between the dispatching companies'. However, it is still the amount of sales of one's own company products which has a direct bearing on the assessment of dispatched salespeople.

The management of targets in each of the dispatching companies is, as one would expect, rather rigorous. Each company determines individual yearly, monthly and daily sales targets, based on the previous year's results. We get a sense of the severity of target management from the following comments. 'There is a lot of pressure. If we do not fight in a cut throat way with other companies, then we cannot achieve our targets.' 'Every day, every hour, we sell while calculating how many items there are still to sell.' 'I constantly have the target figures in my head. We have to spur each other on, calling out, "How many to go today?" to other members of the team (made up of salespeople sent by the same dispatching company). The pressure is enough to give me a stomach ache from the morning.' There were also people who expressed critical views about companies operating a cash bonus system, in which individual shares were added each month on the basis of the rate of accomplishment of sales targets. 'They (salespeople) make sales quickly and those who cannot sell are

Table 3.4: Attributes of dispatched salespeople

Age	Employee status	Salary Form	Length of service in survey shop (years)
42	Contract employee from Mannequin Club (chief)	Daily and monthly pay	10
43	Associate employee	Daily and monthly pay	8
43	Associate employee (chief)	Monthly pay	3
44	Employee (chief)	Daily and monthly pay	6
52	Employee (chief)	Daily and monthly pay	13
51	Contract employee	Daily and monthly pay	15–16
52	Contract employee (leader)	Monthly pay	13
50	Contract employee (star manager)	Monthly pay	15

Source: Interview surveys.

soon made to quit.' Given this, fellow dispatched salespeople are in a situation in which they, 'do not have conversations with each other about pay' and they certainly do not discuss differences in their terms and conditions with people from other companies, or indeed with people from their own company.

The 'sales professional' perspective

Dispatched salespeople generally have a strong sense of being professionals. Amongst female regular employees, however, even those with long years' of service, comments indicating that they 'had hardly any discretionary freedom' and that they 'were bored' were, as mentioned previously, conspicuous. In contrast to this dispatched salespeople say, 'we cannot sell if we do not have the scope for discretionary freedom'. In short, dispatched salespeople, who are in the front line on the job site, must make decisions and act independently. Comments such as, 'with good products, the will to sell is there spontaneously' and 'if the products are good, we can sell them easily. We gain satisfaction from the fact that they have been sold', give an insight into their professional nature. The statement which best illustrates the sense of professionalism of dispatched salespeople is, 'as long as I have good products to sell, I will sell out of them '.

I never heard any of these statements, full of a sense of sales professionalism, from female regular employees. One can imagine the scathing looks of the dispatched salespeople looking at female regular employees. Dispatched salespeople with experience in other department stores unanimously rate the female regular employees in Company A as being better at sales than those in other companies. Even so, they expressed the following types of views. 'They are taught how to sell by us, while they earn much better pay than us. Sometimes we think, work harder, in order to be worth your pay.' 'They are in a daze. They work differently from us.' 'They have no selling ability at all. Their movements are slow. If you build up your career and have a sense of responsibility, then selling ability follows but perhaps this is not possible until you are over 30.'

Conversely, how do female regular employees view dispatched salespeople? Basically, they rate the selling ability of dispatched salespeople highly. 'They are good at making recommendations.' 'They have a will to sell.' 'They have a greater hunger for making sales than company employees. They are not sentimental.' 'There are many outstanding sales veterans. They really know how to sell.' However, the female regular employees simultaneously point out the problems, which are the reverse side of this type of high sales ability. 'When there are people who forcibly recommend (items), then they become the source of customer complaints.' 'Unlike company employees, they tend to proceed on the basis of "selling" rather than valuing the customer.' 'They are extremely knowledgeable about the products but they fight over getting customers. There are even times when we have to say, "That's enough!"' 'They are conspicuously people selling only their own manufacturer's products. Company employees must follow their lead (on this point)' I also heard the following sorts of opinions. 'They are scattered (individually) and cannot have any sense of being one group. They appear to be inflexible as they attempt to sell their particular manufacturer's products.' 'Company employees are the only ones who are capable of recommending from amongst the whole range of available products.' Female regular employees also point out that dispatched salespeople are not proficient in related jobs. 'They have sales abilities but they are inexperienced in handling receipts and grievance procedures.' 'There are people who just cannot deal with sales slips no matter how many times you explain it to them.' 'They are not trained in the way that company employees are.' From the position and logic of dispatched salespeople, since their role is centred on sales and also since they are not appraised on anything other than sales, they do not want to encumber themselves with the duties of regular employees. Alternatively, we can see them as sales professionals avoiding related duties out of a sense of it being their duty to devote themselves to sales.

Various lines of segregation within the workplace

As we saw previously, male regular employees have little to do directly with sales and whilst occupying the same workplace, constitute a separate world. In contrast to these male employees, dispatched salespeople, who are playing an indispensable role as the heart of sales ability, and female regular employees, who are in touch with sales jobs, are bound together with strong links to the same workplace. However, with the decisive differences in their employment relations and their prescribed ways of managing sales targets, both parties are mutually segregated and mutually very critical. We cannot overlook the fact that there is a tendency for them to be mutually torn apart, including psychologically, by the divisions originating from their employment relations; the age differences amongst them; and the differences in life experiences which follow on from these. One female regular employee (aged 24) frankly expresses her view of dispatched salespeople. She points out that dispatched salespeople, 'are largely people working to support themselves, because they are divorced or because their husbands have failed in previous ventures. When I realised this, I was shocked. They are people from a different social group.' The female high school and junior college graduates, who eulogise the workplace status and conditions of being a regular employee, in what at first glance appears to be a showy department store, have no assigned tasks and are left instead to endure 'boredom'. Female university graduates are searching for a 'third way' but they hardly give any thought to the existence of dispatched salespeople. The dispatched salespeople, for their part, keep working in circumstances and with motives drawn from a variety of life experiences, and in this shop they demonstrate their abilities as sales professionals, while enduring severe working norms. Not once in the course of these interviews did either of these two parties utter any friendly words towards the other. Rather, it was as if, despite their comparatively long relations in the same workplace, both parties were living in separate worlds.

As we have seen in the preceding discussion, we must pay attention to the fact that lines of segregation have actually been drawn between several strata in the one workplace. These are not only gender and educational differences but also lines of segregation drawn on the basis of differences in life experiences, in turn arising from age differences. Objectively, these are structural divisions born of differences in employment relations, which are brought about by the unique sales and distribution network. However, for the parties concerned, individual attributes – generational differences and social class differences resulting from life experiences – are seen as decisive factors. Also, amongst the dispatched salespeople there are further complex lines of segregation, drawn in multi-layered ways.

The mechanisms behind the gendering of work

This chapter has looked at gender relations, principally job segregation by gender, in a single workplace, which represents the smallest unit of the work organisation within Department Store A. Surveys were conducted on the basis of intensive interview surveys with all levels of rank-and-file regular employees and dispatched salespeople. I would now like to consolidate the main points highlighted by the preceding discussion.

The excessive gendering of work duties

Let us look firstly at regular employees. If we take a detailed look at workplaces, which can be said to be of the 'dependent on women type' in the sense that they employ large numbers of female regular employees, then we see that 'male management' actually occupies a central position; that there is an accumulation of workplace practices devised by men; and that this tradition is still dominant. Even when women move from positions as regular employees to assistant sales manager or assistant buyer, they end up being drawn into these traditions. Although the women carrying out these assistant roles have reached considerable numbers, the fundamental structures of 'male management' have not changed. Under this regime female high school and junior college graduates find themselves pegged to positions in the rank-and-file grades and even when they are assigned to assistant roles, these become dead end positions for them. There has not necessarily been any thought given to them moving on to the next step. In this work I refer to these types of conditions – job segregation by gender in the workplace – as conditions of 'the excessive gendering of work duties' in the workplace. This implies that work duties are distributed on the basis of gender, in an extremely rigorous manner. This is because there are clear gender-based differences extending into all areas, including job postings, informal training and working hours and because there is extremely scant scope for male and female regular employees to share work duties with each other and to cooperate in their roles. They both experience a completely different organisational culture from the time they join the company.

The very first by-product of this is men's excessive conformity and excessive integration into work. Men join the company under a system of long working hours and appear to have a sense from the outset, of 'carrying the workplace on their shoulders'. Men see this type of working pattern as a male only thing and they separate themselves off from their female colleagues. At the end of the 1970s the employment of male high school graduates ended and only male university graduates were employed. This led to fierce competitiveness within the homogeneous group of regular employees who were male university graduates. With role models who were older males, the male regular employees set achieving 'a higher standing' and 'achieving high rank' as reasonable targets for themselves.

On the other hand, young female high school and junior college graduates, under a rigidly constructed job distribution system, experience 'boredom', 'resignation' and 'despair' and recollecting, 'I had from the start only seen this as a "stop gap" ' and 'I want to get married', they resign. There is no denying that they bring to the workplace the gender identities impressed on them before having become a part of this workplace (for example, a consciousness which sees work as something 'stop gap'). However, we should not overlook the considerable influence on this of the gender relations created by the type of excessive gendering of jobs discussed above. The excessive gendering of jobs reinforces the gender norms brought in from outside the workplace and helps to cement a gender-based lifestyle value system. Talented women with long years of service are picked out in this system and assigned assistant roles and, albeit reluctantly, they are abruptly drawn into men's excessive working patterns. These women swing between thinking 'I am quitting tomorrow' and finding the work interesting. The 'status-less' 30 to 40 year old women gain extensive free time by eschewing hard work, despite having hit the uppermost limit of pay. However any spirit of challenge regarding higher managerial positions and, understandably, a can do spirit with regard to work itself are in short supply amongst this group.

Gender relations which are difficult to alter

This 'uneven distribution' of work, giving disproportionate emphasis to gender, dampens female regular employees' will to work and gives rise to inefficient conditions. The fact that, this notwithstanding, Company A to date has not treated this as a serious matter which needs to be dealt with immediately, is the result of dispatched salespeople having the main role as the force behind sales. They have a strong sense of themselves as sales professionals and they display amazing levels of energy in cutthroat sales competition against other companies. However, dispatched salespeople, even if they have worked shoulder to shoulder in the same workplace for over ten years, exist as if they were nothing more than 'strangers' in the eyes of regular employees. Dispatched salespeople do not even develop chummy relations amongst themselves. When we take a broad view of the workplace, including dispatched salespeople, gender relations in the workplace organisation appear to be far more complex and multi-layered structures than would be suggested by a consideration of company employees only. As long as a management policy reliant on the unique sales and distribution network created by the dispatched salespeople system continues to be adopted in Company A, it is difficult to think that any significant change will occur in the conditions creating the excessive gendering of jobs.

Former Senior Manager, Mr C., reminisces that before the use of dispatched salespeople became widespread, the department store 'was healthy'. The person in charge of personnel with a women's clothing manufacturer, and one of the dispatching companies, says that since the move towards a sales-based stock purchasing system, 'department stores have declined'. This has happened because of the development of a situation in which, 'products are now always available without incurring any risk'. This has probably led to a situation in which as long as business runs smoothly, the company is not at all inconvenienced by the continuation of the present job segregation by gender, even if this means that individual companies do not need to vie with other companies in arranging original products and that the department store itself does not concentrate its efforts on fostering product planning and expertise in selecting products. If this is the case, then the implication is that there is extremely little motivation within the work organisation to change the structure of work duties, which has become excessively gendered.

The image of gender in personnel policy

What needs to be stressed in particular at this point is the problem of the image of gender embedded within personnel policy. As I have mentioned frequently, Company A has an established reputation as having been the first in the industry to develop a women's policy. This was certainly a policy which, alongside opening up the possibilities for the intermittent employment and re-employment of women, also attempted to create assistant roles in the place of work. However, there was not necessarily a conscious attempt to promote women, by structuring these assistant roles to act as a step to even higher managerial positions. At best, the company only attempted to select women for higher managerial positions, by fishing out a few, after having assured themselves of their performance in the assistant roles. It is understandable that this women's policy was seen as progressive at the end of the 1960s. The problem lies in the fact that, with the passage of time, women continue to build up long years of continuous service but still have not broken free from the image which sees women in assistant roles. Because there has been no reconsideration of men's long working hours, even the increasing numbers of women carrying out assistant roles, such as assistant sales manager and assistant buyer, still have not produced any option but for women but to be drawn into men's excessive working hours as a matter of course. These assistant roles have given them their first taste of the interesting side of work. At the same time, however, they are constantly oppressed by the long hours of work. This way of working fails to impress their young female juniors as attractive.

Meanwhile, female university graduates, wedged between male employees and female high school and junior college graduates, continue their various trial and error efforts. Even at the time of this survey, over ten years since the company embarked on the regular employment of female university graduates, no training policy had been established for them. Matters of training were left entirely to the discretion of their direct superiors. This implies that the company has not decided upon a personnel policy which asks itself how to 'make positive use' of female university graduates. In this environment, women, having understood that the will to 'make positive use' of female university graduates does not exist in Company A, are leaving the workplace early. The women who are still left in the workplace, over and above not being able to regard male university graduates as role models whom they wish to emulate, are attempting to formulate their own independent work image and, what may even be called, their own philosophy of work. Actually, women sales managers gradually continue to appear from their ranks. Theses female university graduates are, objectively, in a position to disentangle educational and gender differences and they have within themselves the potential to shed light on the problematic nature of the excessively gendered structure of the distribution of work duties.

The image of women, upon which personnel policy is based cannot be said to have kept pace with changes over time. Rather, despite the revelation of the contradictions brought about by the excessive gendering of jobs, in the form of the problem of the 'status-less level three', the personnel department's awareness is simply limited to 'the perplexing tendency towards intentional negligence'. This is a matter of conjecture but, we might ask whether the image of women contained in Company A's personnel policy has been powerfully influenced by the image of female employees established in the past. In the Company A history we find the remark that, 'it is the duty of the company to receive girls from good families as employees, to educate and train them and to arrange marriages for them'. The thinking behind this was that these people would become good housewives and good customers for Company A. The women's policy of the 1960s, in addition to being an extension of this way of thinking, also backed up women's desire to work, in a way which anticipated the changing times. However, the company did not give serious thought to the policies needed to put this into effect. Also, in the case of the regular employment of female university graduates, it did not act to clarify the status of these women or to set up training plans for them. The company's basic strategy, based tenaciously on the sales and distribution network surrounding the department store, which has sought to maintain the, 'women should sell and men mange' structure, remains unshakeable and its women's policy for responding to present times is nothing more than frills around the edges, as it were. As I stated at the beginning of this chapter, the revision of the status ranking system is, as usual, actually only concerned with policies for making the most of the capacities of male employees.

The primary factors behind changes in gender relations

As we have seen in the preceding discussion, the interest in bringing about reform of the accumulated workplace practices responsible for the excessive gendering of jobs, driven by spontaneous concern for the problem from within Company A, is weak. Given this, will these types of gender relations continue to be sustained into the future?

Trends in Company A's management strategy are noteworthy in this regard. Under the intensification of competitive relations known as the 'department store wars' and also competition between retailers, including supermarkets, there has been an ongoing revision of management strategy in Company A. These changes have been aimed at strengthening the company's 'robust operating powers' and also towards the cultivation of its regular employees' selling abilities, product planning ability and also their expertise in product selection. In practical terms, the company has started pursuing the possibility of developing its own brand products and establishing independent shops; forming women only overseas buying teams; and, furthermore, reducing the numbers of dispatched salespeople. The reduction of dispatched salespeople, in particular, is very significant because it increases gross profit rates and, in addition to increasing the regular employees' own purchasing skills, this reduction in the use of dispatched salespeople also has the very revolutionary effect of building up the sales abilities of regular employees. If the company were to proceed along these lines in earnest, the inevitable result would be the reorganisation of the current excessively gendered organisation of work duties. It should be possible to tie this type of trend in management strategy to the search by female university graduates for a 'third way'.

4 Response-negotiation Relations in the Work Organisation: the Segregation Line between 'Them and Us'

The task of this chapter is to examine – after first gaining an understanding of the labour relations woven into the work organisation – the conditions surrounding job segregation by gender. This examination will show that it is the manner in which work duties are allocated in the first place which gives rise to these conditions. In addition, in this chapter I look at the internal segregation found at an even deeper level of the work organisation – at its very bottom. I give particular emphasis to a consideration of the meaning of the fact that the workers at the very bottom of the organisation themselves draw a line segregating 'us' from 'them'. In order to do this I chose Company X, one of the large general merchandise supermarket chains, and carried out a case study of the labour in one of its stores. Company X, in common with other Japanese large retail companies, has an extremely small ratio of women to men at higher management levels, even though its general level of dependence on women's labour is high. However, the company is characterised by its speedy promotion, starting in 1996, of the policy of 'making positive use of women': a policy of appointing women to lower managerial positions in its stores; placing women in the food section where there had traditionally been few women; and also of 'creating female store managers'. The discussion of Company X will continue in Chapter Five, along with a consideration of the impact of the 'creation of female store managers' policy on the work organisation.[1]

Job segregation by gender in store work

An outline of Company X – a general merchandise supermarket chain store

Structural features of the labour force

Firstly, I will give an outline of the general merchandise supermarket chain, Company X, based on information taken from Company X's *Financial Report*, internal documents and data collected through interviews. Company X has been operating for about 30 years. It is one of the top companies in the industry with over two hundred stores in Japan. Its main business form is general merchandise supermarket retail. In the year 2000, there were more than ten thousand regular employees, with men and women in a ratio of about two to one. As seen in Figure 4.1, while the number of both men and women regular employees is increasing, the increase in part-time employees is much greater. This trend has been apparent since 1985, but accelerated noticeably after 1995. This seems to have been the result of labour cost pressures under stagnant consumer spending. The proportion of part-time employees (calculated on the basis of eight working hours per day) was over 65 per cent in 2000, which is about average for the industry. The rate of increase in the number of female regular employees is slowing down compared to that of male regular employees, with the number of female employees remaining virtually flat through the 1990s. Even so, in 2000, about 36 per cent of regular and nearly all of the part-time employees were women. This shows that the composition of the labour force is highly dependent on women.

The average age of regular employees was 35 for men and 27 for women in 1987 and 37 and 31 respectively in 2000. About 65 per cent of women and 33 per cent of men were under 30, indicating that the female workforce was comparatively younger than the male. The average for years of service (Figure 4.2) was relatively short in 1975, being 4 years and 10 months for men, and 2 years and 10 months for women. These figures grew steadily until 1995, when they were 12 years and 10 months for men and 7 years and 9 months for women. In 2000, the average years of service had declined to 10 years and 1 month and 7 years and 2 months respectively. The decline was due to the many mergers that occurred in the late 1990s when Company X took over stores in a particular region, where the company was expanding. What we need to grasp here is that women as well as men have been moving towards longer years of service since the 1970s. In

Figure 4.1: Changes in the number of employees

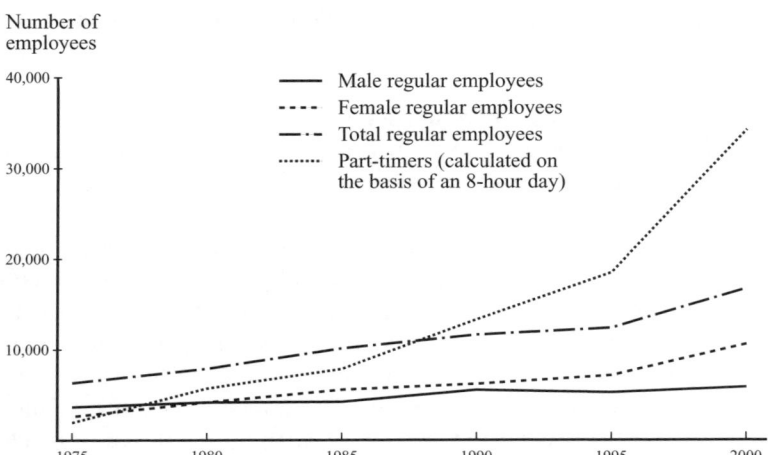

Source: *Yūkashōken hōkokusho* (Financial statement) for each year

terms of educational background, new recruits are now more likely to have a university degree. As many as 79 per cent of new recruits were university graduates in 1998 and over 40 per cent of these were women. Another 14 per cent had completed junior college or technical college and over 50 per cent of these were women. A mere 7 per cent were high school graduates, and 70 per cent of these were women. The shift towards higher educational qualifications in the younger age group has been striking.

An overview of the personnel system

The status ranking system in Company X is set out in Table 4.1. It is Company X's basic policy regarding the career development of regular employees that all staff members, including those in the Headquarters and the Business Operations Division, must start by experiencing work in a store. This is because the stores are positioned as 'the foundation of management'. The first hurdle to clear in status grade advancement is the move from Grade 5 to Grade 6. The criteria for assessment are the results of written tests, interviews and personnel assessments. Once the applicant passes these tests, he or she will have satisfied the requirements to become a section head in a store. New recruits who are high school graduates start at Grade 1 and move up

Figure 4.2: Changes in average length of continuous service

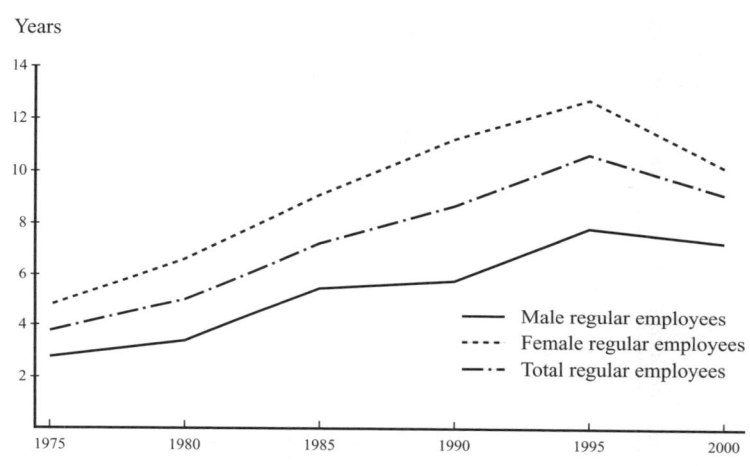

Source: *Yūkashōken hōkokusho* (Financial statement) for each year

to Grade 4 in their fourth year of service. University graduates start at Grade 4. After about two years at Grade 4, both high school leavers and university graduates move up to Grade 5. Most employees are expected to advance to Grade 5.

Advancement to Grade 6 or above is determined by a personnel assessment, a written test and an interview set at each stage. One employee, described as 'an energetic person' by the Personnel Department reached Grade 7 at the age of 28. Employees on the 'elite course' become store managers after fifteen years of service and will go on to become managers of the Business Operations Division.

Thus, Company X does not have a dual personnel system, but there are separate career paths depending on one's choice of area in which to work. The work areas leading to the 'nation-wide path' include overseas countries as well as the whole of Japan, whereas in the 'area-specific path', employees are limited to a specific area although relocation may require moving house. The 'store-specific path' means there is no relocation that requires moving house and, in fact, it often means continuous service at one store only. There is no upper limit in status grade for the nation-wide path, whereas the area-specific path is limited to Grade 9 and the store-specific path to Grade 5. According to the Personnel Department, selecting the nation-wide path does not confer any advantage over other paths at the time of preferment examinations

Table 4.1: Status ranking system and corresponding positions in Company X

Ability grade	Basis for evaluation	Position in stores	Position in Business Operations Department	Position in Headquarters
Grade 12	Recommendation			
Grade 11	Recommendation	Head of Area Operations Division	HQ	Department head
Grade 10	Recommendation	Head of Area Operations Division Store manager	Department head	Department head
Grade 9	Recommendation	Store manager Assistant store manager	Department head	Section head
Grade 8	Merit rating, written test, interview	Store manager, Assistant store manager Store manager	Section head	Section head, In-charge In-charge
Grade 7	Merit rating, written test, interview	Assistant store manager Section head	Section head	In-charge
Grade 6	Merit rating, written test, interview	Section head, Supervisor	Section head, In-charge	In-charge
Grade 5	Merit rating, written test, interview	Chief Clerk, Leader	In-charge	In-charge
Grade 4	OJT	Leader	In-charge	In-charge
Grade 3	OJT	In-charge		
Grade 2	OJT	In-charge		
Grade 1		In-charge		

Source: Compiled from data supplied by Company X
Note: OJT = On-the-job training

or personnel assessments.[2] Employees, aged between 29 and 44, can apply to change to another career path every five years. However, changes are accepted every year for moves to the nation-wide path from either the area-specific or store-specific paths as Headquarters intends to increase the numbers in the nation-wide path and also to attach greater importance to this path.

The work area selection system was introduced in 1993, when Company X was actively pushing ahead with a national expansion of stores. However, a significant number of regular employees were reluctant to relocate to a wider region. Also, it was a time when the employment situation was such that it was difficult to recruit new employees to positions with a prospect of nation-wide relocation. Then a system was put in place in which selecting areas of relocation would be left to individual employees in order to secure 'good human resources' even though there was a concern that this system might stifle flexibility in personnel transfers. Concern over the issue was limited only to male staff and the issues of female regular employees were not at all taken into consideration.[3] But as will be discussed later, it was the case that mainly female regular employees, particularly married women, took the store-specific path. Even before the introduction of this system, married women had often continued to work for one particular store because of family considerations. The formal system that was developed consequently resulted in the ratification of this practice. As a result, a stratum of employees was formed that was identified by the system as not being the subject of personnel transfers between stores. Incidentally, in 2001 51.8 per cent of the total regular employees chose the 'nation-wide path', 32.8 per cent 'the area-specific path' and 15.4 per cent 'the store-specific path'. The percentage of women in each path was 18.4 per cent, 38.7 per cent and 90.0 per cent, respectively. This, as will be discussed, is closely connected to the internal segregation of work organisation, which this chapter aims to examine.

The status ranking system, which in principle did not provide for demotion, was abolished for part-time employees in the late 1980s and the current personnel management system is based on specific duties. This means that wages are determined by a type of duty pay, which is calculated on the ranking of the duty for which the part-time employee is responsible, and evaluation pay, which is determined by personnel assessment. The chief clerk, who is the part-time employee's immediate superior, and the section head conduct this personnel assessment every six months, which is the term of the contract. The assessment system has five grades and comes to an end when an employee attains the highest grade and starts anew form the lowest grade in the next rank. Although the abolition of the status ranking system has resulted in longer periods of service no longer warranting better pay, a high proportion of part-time employees are working for long periods of time. This will be discussed later.

Job segregation by gender in store work

The tendency for women to be concentrated in lower managerial positions

The focus of this section will be the store workers, seen by Company X as the 'foundation of management'. Firstly, I will analyse the conditions in which job segregation by gender occurs by looking at the nation-wide data for the company. Then I will consider the work organisation of a large store located in a regional town, from the inside.

The ratio of male to female regular employees who engage in store work is 55 to 45. Compared to the ratio of men to women across the whole of Company X, which is about two to one, we can see the higher dependency on women employees in stores. The organisational structure of the store being discussed in this section is shown in Figure 4.3. In addition to the General Affairs Section, which is an administrative workplace giving behind-the-scenes administrative support in the area of sales, the main part of the store is divided into several sections according to the three categories of merchandise handled on the sales floor (apparel, food and other household goods).

Each section has a section head. These sections are further divided into smaller sales areas for their specific types of merchandise, with a chief clerk posted to each floor. Under the chief clerk, there are regular employees in the rank-and-file grade (hereafter rank-and-file regulars), who are divided into employees who are either 'leaders' or clerks. 'Leaders' are chosen from Grades 4 and 5 and clerks belong to Grades 1 to 3. The store manager is in control of the whole store and in larger stores may have an assistant manager.

Figure 4.4 shows the 1999 nation-wide distribution of managerial positions for men and women in business occupations. These are staff members in the stores and in the Specialised Business Operations Division including the Merchandise Department. From this figure, it is clear that there is an overwhelming concentration of women at the lower managerial positions. Women account for 52.4 per cent of clerk class employees, 66.8 per cent of leaders and 40 per cent of chief clerks.

Figure 4.3: Schematic representation of distribution of in-store positions

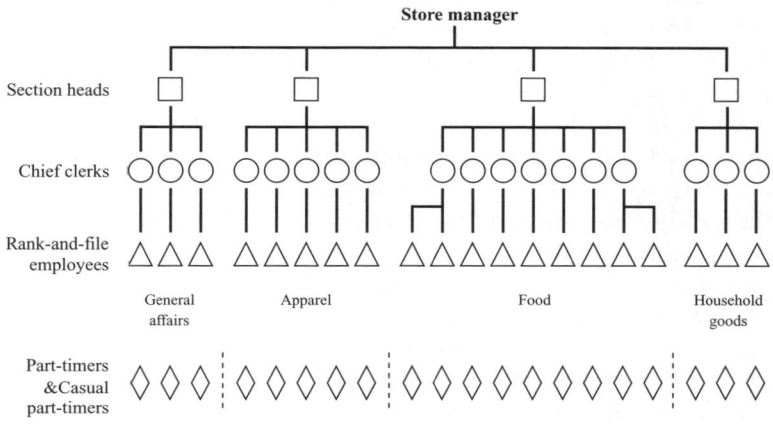

Figure 4.4: Numerical composition of positions by gender (regular employees in sales)

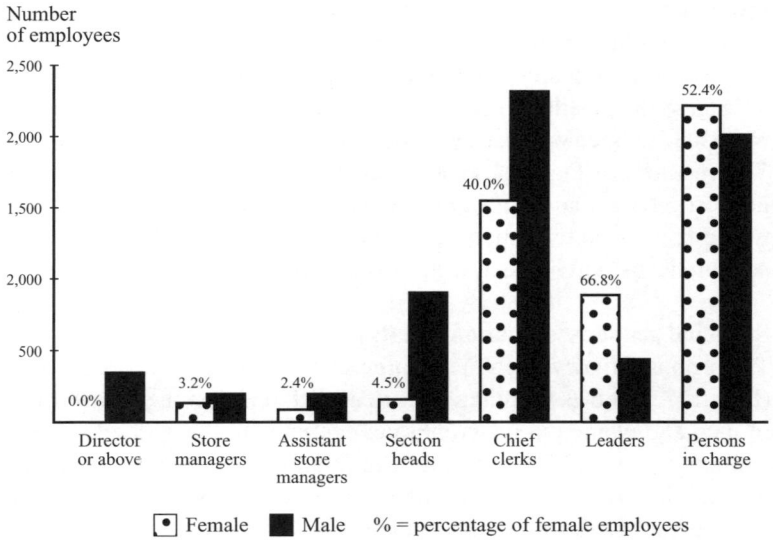

Source: Internal company documents

Women occupy more than half of the leader positions because of the tendency, as will be discussed later, of many long-serving women to remain in these positions. When it comes to section heads, however, only 4.5 per cent are women and as few as 3.2 per cent of store managers are women. There is a glass ceiling just below the position of section head that seems to be very difficult to break through. A further point needs to be noted in regard to what this data for 1999 shows us. As mentioned at the beginning of this chapter, Company X has been actively promoting the policy of 'making positive use of women' since the mid-1990s and women have been progressively appointed as chief clerks, section heads and ultimately as store managers. It is necessary, therefore, to keep in mind that these figures for 1999 were produced in the midst of this change. Prior to this change, the policy of 'making positive use of women' primarily took the form of selecting capable women for a position in the Area Business Operations Division or in the Merchandise Department within Headquarters. Some of these women, albeit very few, have been trained and appointed as section heads. In the stores, on the other hand, although there are a high proportion of long-serving regular female employees, most of them have remained rank-and-file regulars.

Both male and female university graduates have been given equal access to the path that leads to the position of chief clerk within the same period of time. Only recently has attention turned to female high school leavers in view of the policy of 'making positive use of women'. The company promoted the appointment of relatively young women to the position of chief clerk and also the promotion of highly motivated women who had been rank-and-file regulars for a long time.[4] This resulted, as Figure 4.4 shows, in an increase to 40 per cent in the proportion of female chief clerks, a phenomenon which ten years ago would have been extremely rare. One can expect that future female section heads will be born from this expanding stratum of women.

Sectional gender segregation and its causes
The proportion of women in the three sections of Company X's stores (Figure 4.5) shows that there is a clear difference in the distribution of men and women in different sales sections. In the apparel section, women represent 72.9 per cent of rank-and-file regulars and 50 per cent of chief clerks, while in the food section, no more than 7.3 per cent of chief clerks are female and only 30.8 per cent of rank-and-file regulars are women. In the household goods section, 31.6 per cent of chief clerks and 54.1 per cent of rank-and-file regulars are women.

Figure 4.5: Proportion of women in each department (National 1999)

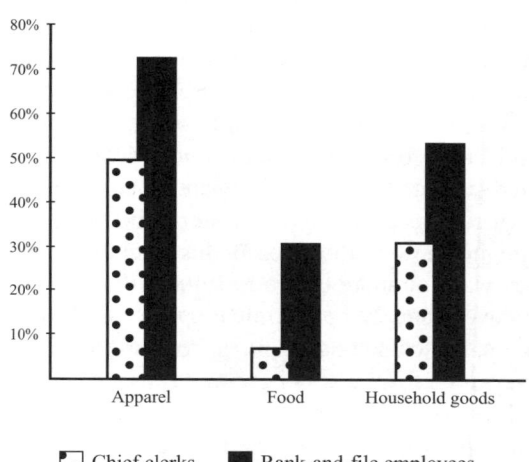

Source: Company X's internal documents

The proportion of women in this section falls between the other two sections. Thus, it looks as though the apparel section is 'a women's workplace' whereas the food section is 'a men's workplace.' What types of factors contribute to such a gender imbalance in the distribution of employees A personnel officer in the Personnel Department said that 'the food section involves a certain amount of dirty work and there is a perception that heavy physical work is required there. As a result, the company tried to avoid placing women in the food section and female employees themselves also had a strong aversion to it.' Let us take a closer look at this issue by examining a specific store.

The store examined here is Store A, a large-scale store with about 100 regular employees and located in a regional town. The discussions in this chapter are based on three types of survey data. Firstly, data was collected from interviews with individual employees who work in Store A. The store manager was asked to select the interviewees so that they were mainly women but so as to include all the strata of employees as evenly as possible. He was also asked to seek a balanced representation of the different sections. The interviews were conducted in November 1999. Interviews with three additional employees were carried out at Stores B, C and D in order to gain an understanding of female employee types not found in Store A, such as a female section head, or an unmarried female chief clerk, whose career is comparable to those of her male colleagues (conducted between December 1999 and January 2000). See Table 4.2 for details of the interviewees.[5] Secondly, data was collected from questionnaires sent to the employees of Store A in June 1998. Answers were collected from 45 regular employees and 66 part-time employees.[6] Thirdly, data was collected from questionnaires, identical to the one used in Store A and distributed in exactly the same manner, to employees in eight stores (including Store A). These stores, including Store A, were all within the purview of the Area B Business Operations Division. (This survey was conducted in June 1998 with responses from 198 regular employees and 299 part-time employees.)[7] In addition to the questionnaires, I also used data gained from in-company documents, observations, and informal small group discussions.

Store A does not have a female section head. According to Table 4.3 (1999), the proportion of female rank-and-file regulars[8] within the apparel section is as high as 92 per cent, a figure higher than the national average.

Store A is a female dominated workplace as, in addition to the above figures, all of the part-time employees are also women. Closer observation reveals that the few male regular employees on the sales floor are placed only in limited sales areas: men's-wear, footwear, and children's wear. There are no males in either of the sales areas of women's wear or lingerie. The type of merchandise determines the gender distribution of regular employees on sales floors. In the household goods section, there are an increasing number of female chief clerks, as a result of the active promotion of long-serving female rank-and-file regulars to the position of chief clerk. This sales area – which sells electrical appliances among other things – is similar in nature to the apparel section in that a large amount of face-to-face customer service is required. In the food section, by contrast, men make up the majority of regular employees. This is an area in which in the past there was a concentration of male postings, with female employees having been concentrated only at the check out and customer service counters. In other words, the major part of the sales area in the food section consists of regular male employees and part-time female employees.[9] The division of work duties by gender is just as evident within sections as it is between sections.

Let us use the interviews conducted with the different levels of employees in Store A to consider the factors which prompt job

Table 4.2: Overview of interviewees (Store A)

	Position	Sex	Age	Educational background	Marital status	Length of service (years)	Section
Store A	Store Manager	male	53	university	married	21	
	Section Head 1	male	44	university	married	14	apparel
	Section Head 2	male	39	university	married	18	food
	Chief Clerk 1	female	27	high school	married	9	food
	Chief Clerk 2	female	34	high school	married	15	food (cashier)
	Chief Clerk 3	female	36	vocational college	married	16	apparel
	Chief Clerk 4	female	42	high school	married	22	apparel
	Chief Clerk 5	male	37	university	married	11	food
	General Employee 1	female	25	high school	single	6	food
	General Employee 2	female	28	high school	married	9	apparel
	General Employee 3	female	47	high school	married	10	household goods (electrical appliances)
	General Employee 4	female	40	high school	single	19	food
	General Employee 5	male	39	high school	single	5	food
	Part-Time Employee 1	female	36	high school	married	6	household goods (books)
	Part-Time Employee 2	female	33	high school	single	9	food
	Part-Time Employee 3	female	41	high school	married	6	food
	Part-Time Employee 4	female	52	high school	married	20	household goods (cosmetics and pharmaceutical)
Store B	Section Head 3	female	38	university	married	15	apparel
Store C	Chief Clerk 6	female	26	university	single	3	food
Store D	Chief Clerk 7	female	24	vocational college	single	3	apparel

Note: 'General employee' = rank-and-file employee.

Table 4.3: Number of employees by section in Store A

	Apparel	Food	Household goods	Backroom	Total
Regular employees					
Section Head	1 (0)	1 (0)	1 (0)	3 (0)	6 (0)
Chief Clerks	8 (4)	9 (3)	9 (5)	4 (3)	30 (15)
General employees	25 (23)	18 (9)	20 (12)	4 (2)	67 (46)
Total regular employees	34 (27)	28 (12)	30 (17)	11 (5)	103 (61)
Part-time employees	47 (47)	106 (104)	44 (43)	23 (23)	220 (217)
Casual part-time workers	30 (25)	106 (60)	43 (27)	8 (0)	187 (112)
Total employees	111 (99)	240 (176)	117 (87)	42 (28)	510 (390)

Source: Compiled from data (in 1999) provided by Store A
( ) = number of female employees. 'General employees' = rank-and-file employees.

segregation by gender and employees' perceptions of this segregation. During his two years in the position, the store manager of Store A appointed two female regular employees to the food section. 'What makes it hard is that there is resistance to working in the food section on the part of female employees. They want to avoid the food section if they can, because they don't like heavy work such as carrying milk cases,' he says. Female Rank-and-File Regular 1, who was transferred from the household goods section to the food section, confirmed this, '[Two years ago,] I was transferred to the processed food sales area. I was very upset. Female regular employees have a certain image of it – "Not the food section!" we say. It is rumoured men need to work in the food section in order to get a promotion, but for women [the food section] has a bad image.' This is consistent with the observation made by the Personnel Department that there is 'a tendency for female employees themselves to try to avoid the food section.'

However, we should take note of the remark added by Female Rank-and-File Regular 1: 'After I actually started working in the food section, I realised that systematisation [including ordering] is well-advanced in all aspects of the food section and I learned a lot from it.' Female Rank-and-File Regular 4 also pointed out that the food section is 'livelier because the merchandise turnover is faster' than in other sections. To be sure, there is a perception that the food section is 'hard' and 'dirty' among female regular employees, but the view that male employees use that section as a gateway to promotion – because of its more advanced systems of operation – probably contributed to it being perceived as a workplace for men. As seen in Table 4.3, chief clerks in the food section are responsible for a much greater number of part-time, casual, and male subordinates, and accordingly are required to exercise stronger leadership. This seems to have contributed to the perception of the food section as a man's workplace. This means that the areas in which women can learn and build up their ability have been restricted. The remark by Female Rank-and-File Regular 1, quoted previously, suggests that women are preoccupied with this perception and distance themselves from 'advancement'.

As mentioned earlier, however, increasing numbers of female regular employees are being posted to the food section. Female Rank-and-File Regular 4 volunteered to move to the food section from the household goods section. She worked as a cashier in the food section for her first four years with the company. She then worked in the processed food area for nearly ten years before moving to the book area, which is part of the household goods section. She subsequently volunteered to move to the food section because she 'liked its lively atmosphere' and also because she thought 'the age group would suit her better, as there are older part-time employees, especially in the vegetable area.' The chief clerk at the checkout counter in the food section (Female Chief Clerk 2) observed that the food section is 'a man's workplace' as far as the regular employees are concerned, despite the need for a housewife's keen sense in everyday matters in this section. She added that 'the opinions of part-time employees are often sought in order to gain insight into the housewife's mode of thinking in everyday matters'. This point was also the reason why long-serving Female Rank-and-File Regular 4 chose to work in the food section: because it is a workplace in which she can make use of her knowledge and sense as a housewife that she has gained from her own life experience.

Job segregation by gender and organisational efficiency
Although women might try to avoid the heavy physical work involved in the food section, we must remember that other sections can require physical work as well. Female Chief Clerk 3 in the apparel section said, 'Sometimes, I am aware of the difference between men and women in doing heavy work. But we women have to do by ourselves what is assigned to our team. Boxes full of underwear are very heavy. Perhaps not as heavy as a box of seasoning in the food section, but any box full of merchandise is very heavy.' Female Rank-and-File Regular 2 in the apparel section said, 'talking about physical strength, the boxes are really heavy even in the apparel section. The lingerie area has many sales and we need a good deal of physical strength to stack up all

these cardboard boxes. Whichever section it is, you need to do some physical work. Even in the babies' section, there are heavy products like car-safety seats. If there are men around, we might ask them to help us, but basically we must manage on our own.' On the basis of these statements, the perception that the food section alone involves heavy lifting is a fiction.

The preceding discussion suggests that the reasons for the perception of the food section as a man's workplace are not due exclusively to the image held by the female regular employees that it is a 'hard' and 'dirty' workplace. We must remember that the prestige attached to the food section, as an essential stepping-stone for male regular employees to climb up the career ladder, creates an environment in which it is relatively easy for women to distance themselves from this section. Male Section Head 1 in the apparel section said, 'the ratio of male to female chief clerks in the apparel section is 1:1. This makes it more interesting because we can encourage each other in many respects. If there were more women in the food section and the same number of female chief clerks as male chief clerks, then I'm sure that it would help to broaden the view in the section.' Store A has proportionately more women than the national average and there are three female chief clerks in the food section. Two of the female chief clerks were in so-called 'women's workplaces' – that is, the checkout counter and the service counter – but the third is in the kitchenware area of the food section. As a result of the gender-biased job allocation that has been practised in the particular sections and areas, no female employee has become chief clerk in the fresh food sales areas. The fishery products, livestock products and agricultural products areas will remain a 'man's domain' for some time yet.

In 2001, however, a new female regular employee with a university degree was employed in the food section. Male Chief Clerk 5 said, 'physical strength is essential in the seafood area. Until recently, there were no females stationed here because we believed that women don't like it here, because it is cold and smells of fish. But the new employee who has joined us is a graduate of a university fisheries department and she is very enthusiastic.' Although concerned about her physical strength, 'she is so slow at cutting up frozen products', he nevertheless values her, 'I think she can overcome this problem in due course as long as she has enough drive. I expect she will become a chief clerk.' He also noted: 'there are an increasing number of women who want to work in the food section. This is because the turnover of merchandise is very fast and it's exciting to get an immediate result.

So, it's rewarding to work for this section.' The current state of job segregation by gender within and between sections, which is the result of an accumulation of the biased allocation of jobs over a long time, cannot be turned around in a short period of time. But the fact that many female regular employees, especially married women, choose the store-specific path means that organisational fluidity may be compromised unless transfers between sections are introduced. If this fluidity is low, the operation of an organisation depends on the abilities of its long-serving employees who, having learned to perform the daily routine, can ensure that the organisation maintains a stable level of performance. On the other hand, because this situation introduces no new perspectives to daily routine, there is a danger that such a workplace might lack a sense of challenge and consequently stagnate. In this sense, the barrier between 'men's workplaces' and 'women's workplaces' should be lowered in order to improve organisational efficiency. If the store managers' will to make positive use of women could be combined with the women employees' strong preference for joining the food section, or their eagerness to make full use of their life experience and knowledge on the job, then reform would not be impossible; although nurturing human resources does take time. Company X is on the verge of change, albeit gradual.

Mutual relationships between chief clerks, rank-and-file regulars and part-time employees

The characteristics of chief clerks and rank-and-file regulars

This section will examine how labour relations operate within the work organisation of Store A and how gender difference is intertwined with them.

The core tasks of store work are ordering, preparing merchandise, taking out the merchandise from the storeroom, stocking and restocking shelves and tidying up. This sequence of tasks is repeated over and over again as customers move around items on neatly stocked shelves and remove others as they make purchases. The lifeline of the business lies in prompt ordering to retain the appropriate amount and variety of merchandise on its shelves. Needless to say, the distribution system supports this work. In addition to these tasks, there are other tasks such as attending to customers in person, as required, and getting displays ready for sales or special events. A team consisting of a chief clerk, rank-and-file regulars and part-time employees carries out these core tasks. Each team occupies a sales area, which is a subdivision of a section. The chief clerk is responsible for the sales floor and gives directions to the rank-and-file regular and part-time employees. The chief clerk is responsible for achieving sales targets. As the sales section is subdivided into numerous small sales areas, often it is the chief clerk who has the most intimate knowledge of the merchandise in his or her sales area. Decisions are made at store manager meetings and the monthly and weekly sales policies come down via the store manager and the section heads; but, it is the chief clerk who is responsible for interpreting and delivering these directives more specifically at the level of the sales area.

Now let us examine the relations between the three parties that constitute the corps that performs shop work – the chief clerk, rank-and-file regulars, and part-time employees.

First, I will analyse the mobility paths selected by chief clerks and rank-and-file regulars to find the reasons why certain regular employees choose certain paths. As shown in Table 4.4, the number of rank-and-file regulars and chief clerks who have selected the store-specific path, in which employees are not moved to other stores but stay in Store A, is as high as 64.5 per cent. It is noteworthy that almost 90 per cent of these are women; many of them married women. As indicated in Table 4.5, many of the women who selected this path had served for a long time. Quite a few relatively young women, who have advanced to the level of chief clerk at a speed comparable with men, as well as some single women, have wedged themselves into the store-specific path. Only an extremely small number of male rank-and-file regulars – those, for example, obliged to care for an aged family member – have chosen this path. Common amongst female rank-and-file regulars is an aversion to moving between stores and a strong inclination to make Store A their only workplace for the sake of stability. If we consider that part-time employees – all of whom but one were women – are directly employed in the store, then the overwhelming majority of those carrying out store work are women. It is this feature that gives this store its unique aspect as a workplace. In contrast, those who have selected the area-specific path, not to mention the nation-wide path, are relatively young men and women who aspire to the position of chief clerk or section head. The female regular employees who have chosen the store-specific path rarely aspire to higher managerial positions, as will be discussed in detail later. However, in recent years, the appointment of women as chief clerks has been encouraged and those female rank-and-file regulars

Table 4.4: Distribution of mobility paths selected (Store A)

	Apparel		Food		Household goods		Backroom		Total
	R/F regulars	Chief Clerks	R/F regulars	Chief Clerks	R/F regulars	Chief Clerks	R/F regulars	Chief Clerks	
Nation-wide path	5 (3)	2 (0)	6 (0)	4 (0)	3 (0)	2 (0)	0 (0)	0 (0)	22 (3)
Area-specific path	1 (1)	1 (0)	2 (0)	2 (0)	4 (3)	2 (2)	0 (0)	0 (0)	12 (6)
Store-specific path	19 (18)	4 (4)	10 (10)	3 (3)	13 (12)	5 (3)	4 (2)	4 (3)	65 (55)
Total	25 (22)	7 (4)	18 (10)	9 (3)	20 (15)	9 (5)	4 (2)	4 (3)	96 (64)

Source: Compiled from data provided by Store A
( ) = number of female employees; 'R/F regulars' = rank-and-file regular employees.
* In addition, there is a female part-time employee who is a supervisor in the food section.

Table 4.5: Years of service of female employees on the store-specific path (Store A)

	Apparel		Food		Household goods		Backroom		Total
	R/F regulars	Chief Clerks	R/F regulars	Chief Clerks	R/F regulars	Chief Clerks	R/F regulars	Chief Clerks	
≤ 5 years	1	0	1	1	0	0	0	0	3
5 years < 10 years	8	0	4	0	6	0	0	0	18
10 years ≥	9	4	5	2	6	3	2	3	34
Total	18	4	10	3	12	3	2	3	55

Source: Compiled from data provided by Store A
'R/F regulars' = rank-and-file regular employees.

who have management abilities are being selected for promotion. The length of service of female chief clerks is mostly sixteen to seventeen years or longer – 83 per cent have worked longer than sixteen years. Their career advancement is slower than that of men.

Only 25 per cent of male chief clerks have worked as long as the majority of female chief clerks. For the bulk of the male chief clerks, the shortest period served is two years and the longest is fourteen years. Furthermore, many of them have selected the nation-wide path.

When we look at the qualifications of female regular employees on the scale of the status ranking system, the characteristics of female chief clerks and female rank-and-file regulars stand out more clearly. From Figure 4.6, we can identify the figure of the male rank-and-file regular advancing steadily from Grade 1 onwards. Male chief clerks, too, progress to Grade 5, continuing up the career ladder without a hitch. Female rank-and-file regulars, on the other hand, are concentrated at

Grade 4. When we look at the length of their service, we can see that nearly 20 per cent of women have served over fifteen years, a figure that would be exceptional for male rank-and-file regulars. A further 21 per cent of women have served between ten and fifteen years. This reflects the fact that few women attempt to become chief clerks by sitting the examination and many of them remain at Grade 4 even after many years of service. Figure 4.7 sets out the regular employees' eagerness for promotion. In contrast to male rank-and-file regulars, who tend to aspire to be a store manager or higher, only 13.7 per cent of their female counterparts aspire to the position of section head or above, with 36.9 per cent aiming at becoming a chief clerk. The number of female rank-and-file regulars who wish to stay where they are is as high as 49.2 per cent. Thus, there is a definite propensity in this stratum of female employees to preserve the status quo. In other words, female rank-and-file regulars show a strong tendency to stay in one store, to remain at Grade 4 even after many years of service and not to become a chief clerk. Among the female chief clerks in Figure 4.6, some have been promoted to this position after their successful attempt to advance to Grade 5 by passing an examination (52.9 per cent), but quite a few others have been appointed while still at Grade 4 without taking an examination (44.1 per cent). The majority of these chief clerks are quite negative (there are just over 30 per cent who are positive) about their appointment from among ranks of long-serving female rank-and-file regulars, a group which likes to maintain the status quo. Table 4.4 shows that thirteen out of fifteen female chief clerks have selected the store-specific path. This clearly indicates that they will remain at the chief clerk level and in fact they do not want 'to advance higher than a chief clerk' (Figure 4.7). The inclination to want to preserve the status quo seems to be a shared characteristic among female rank-and-file regulars and chief clerks. What are the differences between those who are appointed as chief clerks and those who remain rank-and-file regulars?

The role of a chief clerk

Let us now have a closer look at the role of chief clerks who are responsible for management at the very base of store work. 'Leadership' and 'customer orientation' are the 'abilities required' of chief clerks and section heads in Company X. Chief clerks and section heads are also required to demonstrate 'mentoring abilities' towards their subordinates, as is the case with store managers and section heads.

Figure 4.6: Qualifications of rank-and-file employees and chief clerks (Store A)

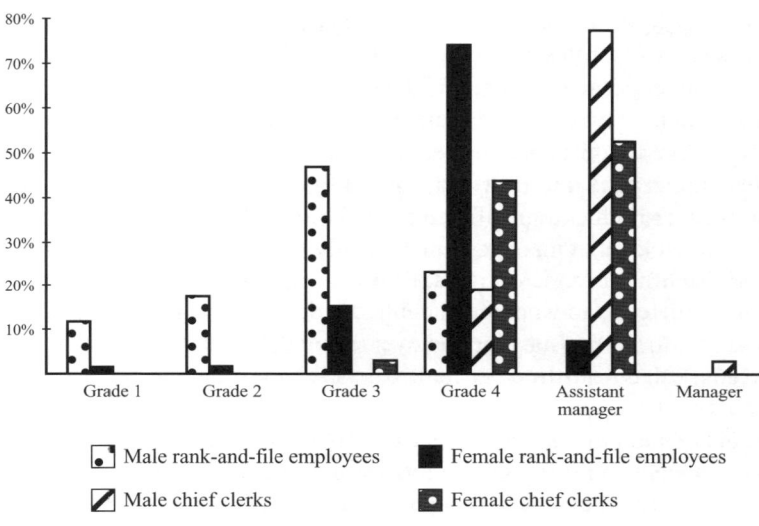

Figure 4.7: Aspirations for promotion of rank-and-file employees and chief clerks (Store A)

Source: Figures 4.6 and 4.7 are both based on a questionnaire survey of Store A

The two qualities set out as requirements solely for chief clerks are 'thoroughness' and the 'drive to achieve targets'. The former of the two refers to the ability to track an error or an omission thoroughly and to grasp the accurate information. The latter is the ability to interpret the store's strategies and policies and turn them into concrete targets at the level of the sales area. Chief clerks are expected to get closely involved in how the work is carried out by their subordinates in order to achieve the targets (source: Company X's internal information). They are expected to fulfil managerial functions at the bottom of the store and to achieve specific numerical targets. Chief clerks, who are the lowest level of management, are fully accountable for controlling and checking numerical targets. They are responsible for directing their subordinates as to what they should do, drawing up a work schedule and giving instructions for and overseeing the implementation of the schedule. It is up to the chief clerk to decide if the rank-and-file regulars and part-time employees need to be made aware of the numerical targets. The abilities of the chief clerk in each sales area have a decisive significance for the sales capacity of a store. According to the manager of the Merchandise Department in one Area Business Operations Division, it is essential for the sales section head to hold meetings with the chief clerks to ensure that they know where the focal products are to be displayed and how many of them are to be sold. The chief clerks in turn try to pass this information on to the rank-and-file regulars and part-time employees. The repetition of this process strengthens the store and this is ultimately reflected in the sales figures.

In the food section, the rank-and-file regulars place orders for standard items, while chief clerks are responsible for ordering the weekly specials and the specific products that are targeted for special promotions. The vegetable area of the food section in Store A is the only section in which part-time employees are not required to do the ordering. Generally speaking, it is more difficult to order fresh food compared to merchandise in other sections. Ordering is a stressful task, as is clear from the remarks of Part-Time Employee 3, who now no longer has to perform this task, '[after I stopped ordering], it got so much easier. Ordering was a burden. I had a nightmare – of being squashed under lettuces. I enjoy coming to work more now that it is not so stressful. I don't want to do the ordering any more.' Her remark gives us an insight into the heavy psychological burden she bore when the products she ordered didn't sell as well as she had expected. On the other hand, however, if one's ordering prediction proves right, then one can experience a great sense of achievement. With the exception of the vegetable area, the part-time employees are responsible for placing orders for the standard items and this role is a significant one. Chief clerks are responsible for giving instructions to the rank-and-file regulars and part-time employees. For Female Chief Clerk 2, who is the chief clerk at the checkout counter in the food section, one of her important jobs is to 'get a forecast each month from the section head of the expected number of customers and to prepare a work schedule [according to these figures]' so that the number of employees, including part-time employees, can be adjusted to respond to the cycle of busy and less busy times. At the same time, she needs to be on the alert to respond quickly when anomalous situations arise, for example, when queues at the checkout counter get much longer than expected. As they are handling cash, she also needs to stay vigilant and keep checking money amounts to avoid discrepancies. This is particularly important.

In the apparel section, chief clerks give instructions to the part-time employees and the rank-and-file regulars, ensure that all is as it ought to be on the sales floor, check merchandise and also work at the checkout counter to inspect and check money. Sometimes when the cashiers are busy, chief clerks themselves work as cashiers. Superiors constantly pressure the chief clerks regarding sales targets. Female Chief Clerk 3, a chief clerk for only six months, said, 'it's not easy to aim at the figures and carry out one's work duties. As she has a weighty responsibility she says, 'I can't just say "OK, that's enough" and go home. I get home at ten o'clock at night and I do nothing apart from eating the dinner prepared [by my mother-in-law] and go to bed. It's been like that for a while.' Female Chief Clerk 4 also in the apparel section, who has been in her position for six years, explained her situation as follows, 'I have a responsibility and I can't just leave it. If I stay until the end, it is very late when I get home. Sometimes all the family is asleep when I get home.' Female Rank-and-File Regular 3, who has experienced working as a chief clerk in the apparel section, said, 'I think it's so much easier now that I have returned to being a rank-and-file regular after having been a chief clerk. Chief clerks are sternly reminded about sales targets by their superiors – almost to the point of being driven to a nervous breakdown. Quite often I felt really low. Sometimes, it was necessary to scold my staff members.' Chief clerks tend to concentrate on the numerical targets that their bosses impose on them and inadvertently fail to pay attention to creating an attractive store or keeping an eye on merchandise and customers. Some chief clerks face scathing criticisms from part-time employees, as in the case of Part-Time Employee 1 who was told, 'chief clerks only manage the numerical targets, they don't understand the practical side of the sales floor.'

Therefore, among regular employees there is a palpable distinction between rank-and-file regulars and chief clerks in terms of the roles they perform. At the beginning of their appointment in particular, newly appointed chief clerks are required to have the determination to endure the long working hours needed to learn the job, as was the case for Female Chief Clerk 3. The section heads too are under pressure: as Male Section Head 2 put it, 'the talk from above is about nothing else but efficiency and gross profit'. The chief clerks are under the same pressure. Chief clerks are the chief executives in their sales areas and accountable for their own areas. As such, responsibility for meeting target figures is strictly imposed on chief clerks. In addition, we should not overlook the fact that many female chief clerks feel a heavy psychological burden as a result of their sudden promotion to the position of chief clerk. Female university graduates from the younger generation see themselves as eligible for promotion to chief clerk as soon as they join the company just like their male counterparts. Both Female Chief Clerks 6 (aged 26) and 7 (aged 24) became chief clerks after three years of service. The former said, 'I was very happy when I became a chief clerk.' Even so, she added that understandably 'the first six months were very hard, as I did not know at all how to do my new job.' We can easily imagine the heavy psychological burden felt by female chief clerks from the older generation when they suddenly find themselves appointed without the necessary preparation.

Female Chief Clerk 2 at the checkout counter in the food section said, 'all of a sudden a chief clerk [position] came down from above and landed on me.' Her appointment was a move to fill a position that had become vacant after her predecessor left the job. She 'didn't receive any formal training' and had to spend everyday 'constantly following the section head and getting instructions from him'. However, 'I started doing it on my own after six months when the section head was transferred.' Female Chief Clerk 3, who was promoted after sixteen years of service said, 'It was a surprise to me. I wondered why since I don't have the ability.' This promotion was a surprise because she was selected after just having finished working short hours under the child carers' work arrangement, after two successive periods of maternity leave. It came as a surprise also because she felt that she 'had fallen terribly behind' when she returned to work after her maternity leave to find that desktop computers had been introduced to the office. However, she was told to 'become a chief clerk' by the male section head, who recognised her ability. He declared, 'I will not let you be demoted as long as I am your section head'. She has accepted that 'he won't let me go back to a rank-and-file position' and as a result she has a stressful time at work.

The willingness of female chief clerks to be promoted

As mentioned earlier, the willingness for further promotion is not strong among female chief clerks. As seen earlier in Figure 4.7, only 31.4 per cent of male chief clerks think it 'OK to stay in our current positions' with the majority of them aspiring for promotion to section head or store manager. Some 65.7 per cent of the female chief clerks on the other hand want to stay in their current positions and only a small proportion hopes to attain positions of section head or above. Only one interviewee, Female Chief Clerk 1, aged 27, expressed her interest in a section head position. She said, 'I can't deny that there is a small part of me wanting to try being a section head' and so 'I would like to try different areas in the food section.' However, she also said, 'it's quite enough to be a chief clerk. This is the highest point you can reach within the store-specific path.' She wrote that she 'would like to advance to section head' in her self-assessment form that she submitted to the office. She wavered, however, saying, 'I would perhaps like to be a section head if there are enough staff and if I am not preoccupied with other things.'

Female Chief Clerk 2, on the other hand, said, 'It's so hard to hold onto the chief clerk's job. I might fail any time. I don't think I can handle anything more than being a chief clerk.' This is because she thinks that 'while I have children to take care of it's impossible for me to work as hard as the male section head', who is her immediate boss. Promotion is also difficult for her to imagine because 'I sometimes wonder why I keep working like this. I want to be more relaxed and also want to become an ordinary mother.' One of the reasons female chief clerks do not want a promotion to section head is their strong aversion to a position with added responsibility which in turn demands working longer hours. Female Chief Clerk 3 agrees, 'being a chief clerk is enough' because 'being rank-and-file regulars and therefore not accountable for figures and not having to give instructions to other people is so much easier'. Female chief clerks do not want to become section heads, as they envisage that the working hours would be longer and the responsibility weightier for a section head than for a chief clerk.

Female Chief Clerk 4 said, 'what is fascinating about being a chief clerk is that you can make sure that your staff do what you want them to. At any rate, it's just so fascinating to have people working for you.' She thinks that she 'would like to continue working as a chief clerk, but I do not think that I can become a section head.' This is because 'I don't have anything [ability] in terms of educational background and I don't think of myself getting advancement [to section head]. Rather, I think it would be better if I could nurture my staff and see them advance further. It would be very hard in many ways if I were to become a section head. This is because I'm not good with computers and I can't do data analysis. I am at a few levels below men in many ways. Another thing is that section heads have to have discussions on a par with the store manager and I can't do that.' The 'men' she is referring to here are the male university graduates. She closes the door on becoming a section head herself, thinking that she does not have the skills to use information technology as she is not a university graduate, and that it is impossible for her to work on an equal footing with the store manager, who is a male. During her 22 years of service, she witnessed for a long time only capable men – university graduates and even high school leavers – move up the career ladder. Therefore she is still amazed that she herself was chosen to become a chief clerk and is now in the middle of experiencing the challenge and fascination of the chief clerk job. In her narrative we can get a glimpse of the history of the workplace. Embedded in it was a fixed idea that men who got promotion were all university graduates and it was taken for granted that female high school leavers would remain as rank-and-file regulars. Educational background and gender were intertwined and acted decisively upon each other.

When we examine female chief clerks' views on promotion, we find that those women who have advanced smoothly to their position are willing to move up to section head but those who have been selected unexpectedly after working as rank-and-file regulars for some time tend to display a similar desire to female rank-and-file regulars to maintain the status quo. Chief clerks and rank-and-file regulars, however, bear entirely different day-to-day burdens of responsibility.

The view of chief clerks

How do rank-and-file regulars regard chief clerks? Most of the female rank-and-file regulars who have selected the store-specific path are negative about their own possibilities of becoming a chief clerk. Female Rank-and-File Regular 1, who has been working for six years, said, 'When I joined the company, I had a strong desire to become a chief clerk.' But now she professes, 'I don't want it at all.' Female Rank-and-File Regular 2, with nine years of service, did not want to say much, 'the chief clerk's job seems to be a hard one...'. Female Rank-and-File Regular 4, who has worked for as long as nineteen years, said, 'I don't want to take on any more pressure for achieving more sales, so I don't want to become a chief clerk.' As mentioned, Female Rank-and-File Regular 3, who has had experience working as a chief clerk in the past, said, 'it's so much easier now that I have gone back to being a rank-and-file regular employee.' The reasons for this are, 'I'm not sternly reminded about the sales targets by superiors. Also, I don't have to scold my staff members.' As the drive to promote women to chief clerk positions has reached a stage where female chief clerks are not uncommon, the issue of promotion has come closer to them as a real possibility. Also, they are witnessing women, who were until only recently their colleagues, get a promotion and then struggle as chief clerks in the same workplace.

In this environment, there is a discourse circulating that discriminates against female chief clerks. Female Chief Clerk 7, who became a chief clerk at the age of 23, says 'I was shocked to hear a colleague say to me "For you, a woman, to have become a chief clerk you must be hardhearted"'. Female Chief Clerk 4, who was promoted in her mid-thirties, said: 'the biggest shock was a remark made by a female colleague. She said to me "you used to be more friendly, but now that you are a chief clerk you are stern".' She said she was worried by this remark for a few months. Female Chief Clerk 2, who was promoted in her twenties, agreed: ' When I was promoted, a male chief clerk once told me "you are scary".' She said: 'Female chief clerks have to be stern. Otherwise they can't do the job. As a chief clerk, sometimes you have to give instructions to your subordinates or even scold them. Sometimes as a chief clerk, I have to play the role of a nasty boss. But the staff would understand me if I explain the reason why I am scolding them.' As the promotion of female employees to chief clerk positions becomes more of a reality, a discourse is being created that says 'stern women become chief clerks' and female chief clerks are now being viewed as quite different beings from the rank-and-file employees.

We should note the distress that female chief clerks themselves feel at their own role. They have to communicate their intentions to their subordinates, sometimes even by scolding them. It is distressing because the people they have to scold are those who used to be their colleagues. Part-time employees are also females and many of them have extensive work experience. They do not necessarily see the female chief clerks as having strong authority, as Part-Time Employee 4 put it, 'there are more female chief clerks and I think I can say anything to them. If the chief clerk thinks you are a troublemaker, you can still survive. But it may be more difficult if it is someone higher than that [a section head or above].' This is why 'some part-time employees don't listen to their chief clerk' (Part-Time Employee 1). On such occasions, female chief clerks might have no choice but to 'scold' their subordinates. Female Chief Clerk 7 said, 'It looks to me that how well the part-time employees work depends on whether the chief clerk is on the floor or not.' This means that the part-time employees do not necessarily feel they have to be particularly alert when they are with the female rank-and-file regulars. This suggests that appointment as a chief clerk removes one from the possibility of continuing to share 'the camaraderie' enjoyed among female regular employees who have chosen the store-specific path and whose only possible workplace is the same store for the time being. In this regard too, female rank-and-file regulars have drawn a clear line between themselves and the female chief clerks even though they are a fairly homogeneous group, as observed earlier.

The female rank-and-file regulars who have selected the store-specific path tend not to consider male chief clerks as part of their camaraderie group. This is shown in a remark made by Female Rank-and-File Regular 4, who works in the food section where the bulk of the employees are male regular employees and female part-time employees, 'when sales are slow, we discuss this with the [male] chief clerk and the part-time employees. But it is the part-time employees who have the good ideas. They tell me things like – "This type of product should sell well at this time of year." or "I saw that product in another store." And so I tend to ask the part-time employees [rather than the chief clerk] for advice [about work]. The part-time employees are far more dependable. It's the part-time employees who love the store. The [male] chief clerks are here for only three years and then they move on. But the part-time employees and I have been working here for a long time and we feel very attached to this store.' We can gather from this remark that the female rank-and-file employees have a strong feeling that they share the same fate with the part-time employees. Chief clerks, not uncommonly, stay in one position for only a short time and as a consequence, in practice, they do not have enough time to form a sense of camaraderie or trust with the employees. Part-Time Employee 2 in the food section pointed out, 'our current chief clerk has been here for three years. But earlier, chief clerks changed very frequently. It is easier for us if they stay longer. We can understand each other as we build up our relationship once we get used to each other.' The female rank-and-file regulars and part-time employees who work in a specific store seem to have a mentality that inevitably draws a line – based on one's degree of attachment to the store – between themselves and those who belong to the category of 'transient people', that is, the chief clerks and the younger university graduates of both sexes who do not work for one store only. This mentality can tentatively be called the sense of 'us' shared among the 'intransient people'. As mentioned earlier, the female chief clerk, once one of 'us' has been cut off from this harmonious group of comrades. The bottom layer of employees responsible for carrying out the practical aspects of store work draw complicated sets of lines of segregation that cannot be understood merely in terms of job segregation by gender. The section that follows will examine the meaning of these lines of segregation by looking at the world of 'us'.[10]

The world of 'us'

The lines of segregation between 'them and us'

The reaction of chief clerks to 'direct communication'
During the part of the interviews asking about responses to the 'direct communication' method, practised by the manager of Store A, there emerged a distinct sense of 'us'. This store manager is not one who has worked his way up from the sales floor. He spent a considerable time in the Personnel Department in a subsidiary company and in the Merchandise Development Department. Store A is his second posting as a store manager. During the two and a half years since he was appointed store manager to this store, he has emphasised communication with his staff members and has practised the following two methods. First, he communicates with individual employees including the part-time employees (but not those in the food section) via weekly reports which they submit to him. His boss is of the opinion that the reports should be daily rather than weekly, but he thinks it would be meaningless to ask for reports more often than is feasible for him to be able to provide feedback on them. He thinks that, 'it is essential to establish a system of promptly giving feedback [on the reports from

employees] in order to drive home one's responses.' Each section head gives written feedback or verbally communicates with employees and the reports come up to the store manager for him to look at. The other method is what he calls 'direct communication'. This means that the store manager talks directly to rank-and-file regular employees and part-time employees and gives them instructions without regard to the usual line of command on whatever he might have noticed while walking around the store. One of his reasons for practising such a meticulous management style was his view that Section Head 2 in the food section lacked communication skills. This is why he decided to give detailed instructions on the sales floor instead of leaving this to his section head.

The responses from chief clerks were mostly positive. Female Chief Clerk 1 in the food section was puzzled initially but soon understood the true intention of the store manager. She values the store manager's method and calmly observes the reactions of the employees, 'The store manager always looks at the store from the customers' perspective and then gives us detailed instructions. To tell the truth, it was really annoying at first and I thought it was bit of a nuisance. Some people don't like being told about small things. However, the store manager is saying what the section head [Section Head 2] should be saying. I think the store manager sees what kind of person the section head is and the store manager thinks he should be taking on the "thankless" role himself. I was very surprised at first when the store manager said all sorts of things directly to the part-time employees. But when I come to think of it, it is refreshing and often what he says is quite to the point. Part-time employees might feel that they are under pressure and find that annoying. I think the section head finds it frustrating; that is to say, the way the store manager handles things.'

Female Chief Clerk 2 in the food section values him, 'I submitted my opinion to the store manager as I wanted to eliminate the pricing errors [discrepancies between the displayed price and the price registered at the checkout] that were occurring. The store manager then told Section Head 2 to assume responsibility for this and to write a report on the cause each time a pricing error occurred. As a result, the number of errors was reduced. I think this is the only store where the store manager takes action to this extent.' Once again, when the store manager learned of the concerns of the chief clerks, he gave directions from above to Section Head 2 to change his ways. The chief clerks appreciated the true intentions of the store manager and with his help they improved the operation of sales floors.

The store manager commented, 'I am convinced that my actions have won me more supporters.' That seems to be true – at least at the chief clerk' level.

The reactions of the 'us' group

However, far from understanding the real intention of the store manager who took up a 'thankless role', the rank-and-file regulars and part-time employees blatantly express their defiance. Female Chief Clerk 1, as has just been mentioned, thought that the style of the store manager is such that the rank-and-file regulars and part-time employees 'might find it annoying'. Male Chief Clerk 5 in the food section said that 'when the store manager talks to them, the part-time employees, in particular, cower before him.' The reactions of the 'us' group, however, are much shrewder than this.

For example, Female Rank-and-File Regular 1 (food section) criticised the behaviour of the store manager as follows. 'The store manager comes directly to us and tells us many things. I sometimes wonder why he says these things, as he doesn't understand at all. Then I politely object. If he still insists then I give in, but I don't do what he tells me. If he tells me twice and it is still not done, he will give up most of the time. When there is a difference between what the store manager says and what the section head says, I would obey the section head. It should be written into the employee regulations that you have to follow your immediate boss.' This is how she indicated her strongly critical views. Female Rank-and-File Regular 4 (food section) joined her in criticising the fact that the employees were not the store manager's first consideration: 'Everyone feels that our current store manager puts the opinions of customers first.' Part-Time Employee 3 (food section) also stressed that 'the current store manager points out very small things. The former store manager was more tolerant. The current manager comes to say trivial things.' She gave an example of a decision on the freshness of the edible variety of chrysanthemums (*Chrysanthemum coronarium*). In her judgement, the chrysanthemums were still fresh as merchandise, even though they were a little bent after some force had been applied during transportation. The store manager, however, said 'they are old' and instructed her to remove them to the backroom. She spoke of her defiance: 'I took them out to the shelf later again as if nothing had happened. The store manger doesn't know enough about merchandise.' She has been working for six years as a part-timer and her sense of pride shows in this remark. Part-Time Employee 1, another part-time employee with six years of service said: 'I wish the store manager would come and work at the checkout counter just for a day. The store manager goes around the store and tells us to do this and that, but I wish he could experience the checkout counter himself. It is impossible to take out the merchandise from the storeroom while you are working at a cash register, but he comes around and says "this is not done" and "that is not done". It is really frustrating.'

What we can see behind the defiance of the female rank-and-file regulars and part-time employees is their strong sense of pride that it is them and not the managers who know the work at the floor level. At the same time, part-time employees experience complex feelings towards their bosses who move around the different stores. Part-Time Employee 1 said, 'the section heads don't understand that we, part-time employees, always have to do what they used to do when they first joined the company. "They" have forgotten about the past. Those who become section heads are really quick to get promotions. The quick ones become chief clerks only after one year and they have forgotten about the daily work [that the part-time employees do].' Her remark shows the vast distance that the part-time employees feel between themselves and 'the transient people'. As mentioned earlier, Female Rank-and-File Regular 4 with nineteen years of service emphasised this point, 'the part-time employees love this store. Chief clerks move ahead after three years. But the part-time employees and I have been working here for a long time and we are very attached to this store'. Female rank-and-file regulars draw a parallel between their circumstances and those of the part-time employees, who do not change stores to work. Her remark shows her wish to draw a line between 'us' and the 'transient people', a group including chief clerks, section heads and the store manager. We have to note here that no suggestion of defiance was made against female chief clerks, who also belong to the group of the 'intransient people'. This is due to their, previously noted, lack of authority, even with regard to part-time employees with the consequence that the latter do not see female chief clerks as a presence standing in opposition to the 'us' group. This state of affairs is also due to the deep 'attachment to the store' which both groups fully share.

Male Rank-and-file Regular 5 (store-specific path) observed, 'Female rank-and-file regulars and part-time employees get on very well without feeling dissociated from each other. Both of them have been working for this store for a long time and their passion and affection for the store are quite strong.' He gave an example that showed their strong attachment to the store: when the store organised a cleaning bee, they actively volunteered to do the cleaning. When we take these points into consideration, we see that the lines of segregation between 'them and us', drawn by the part-time employees and the long serving female rank-and-file regulars, is there for them to confirm where they stand and to assert their existence. They are at the very bottom of the work organisation. It is also an expression of their attachment to the store. An attachment felt by the long serving female rank-and-file regular and part-time employees, based on a sense of pride in the fact that the operation of the store depends on the skills that they have acquired by themselves. These employees feel a strong aversion to being dragged about by 'them' – those who come and go one after the other. The 'direct communication' approach introduced by the store manager of Store A upset the employees and resulted in their blatant defiance.[11]

The 'us' group's attitude to work

Tackling work

As mentioned earlier, Female Chief Clerk 3 said that the way rank-and-file regulars work makes 'it easier and more enjoyable to be a rank-and-file regular' because rank-and-file regulars are not accountable for numerical targets and they do not have to give instructions to staff members. How do they work? Let us look at the example of Female Rank-and-File Regular 4. She is in charge of cutting up fruit and making fruit platters (as hors d'oeuvres). She said: 'I might stay behind but I don't claim overtime. I am willing to stay behind because I want to make the sales figures. Some of the rank-and-file regulars are quite matter-of-fact about it and just claim overtime. Or some of them go home no matter what. But I really like it and I stay behind because I think the more one does it, the more sales one gets. It's good to achieve the sales objectives. The increasing figures keep me going, too. My challenge is to ensure the produce is fresh and also I have to have product knowledge.' She is working with autonomy and motivation. Rank-and-file Regular 3 works in electrical appliances sales in the household goods section and her duties are ordering products, handling paper work and dealing with customer complaints. She said, 'I tackle my work duties each day with a determination to sell. I want to achieve the target figures. It's hard to gain technical knowledge [about electrical appliances]. I have to study hard in order to keep up with the technical advances. I ask the representatives from the manufacturers or the male employees in the store who are capable [who have product knowledge]. I am trying hard and keeping up.' We can see that this employee keeps the achievement of sales volume and target figures in mind as she works.

Some part-time employees work in a fairly autonomous manner. Part-Time Employee 4, who works six hours a day and has 20 years of service behind her, runs the cosmetics area along with a regular employee. Her duties cover all aspects of serving customers in person, taking out merchandise from the storeroom, placing orders, serving at the cash desk and returning unwanted products. She talked about her work as follows, 'before I go home, I look around the sales floor and replenish the products that are running low. Otherwise, we "miss the opportunity to sell". I am particularly careful not to run short of "vitamin supplements" that customers like to handle and look at before buying them. I make sure the products are on the shelf so we don't miss out on the opportunity to sell. It would be no good to have products in stock in the backroom, if we can't take the opportunity to sell. I never go home without replenishing the shelves if there are any products that are not there, even if this means staying past my going home time. I am given a degree of autonomy on the sales floor and I am always conscious of the sales targets. It is fun to see that the more I put good ideas into practice, the better the sales figures in this area. I gain product knowledge by attending seminars [held by cosmetics manufacturers] of my own accord [without being paid]. Perhaps because I have been in the same area for a long time, the chief clerks let me do as I like'. There are areas in the store that are dependent on part-time employees who work in such an autonomous way.

Part-Time Employee 3 works six hours a day at the vegetable area of the food section. Each morning after she has looked at the produce left in the storeroom and the new produce that has arrived she cuts up the vegetables as she thinks best. If she is unsure as to how many vegetables to cut, she discusses it with other part-time employees and she makes a decision. The prices of bargain products can be reduced at the discretion of the part-time employees. As the part-time employees in the vegetable area are not involved in placing orders and therefore cannot grasp the total volume of the incoming products, they check with the chief clerk when they price and display the usual products. What she enjoys most is 'the moment just before the opening of the store when I have finished displaying the green vegetables quickly and neatly in the way I want.' She told us that she always shops in the store before going home, as she knows the produce is good there. She is a part-time employee and has worked for six years. She enjoys some autonomy and takes pride in her work.

Pride and resistance

The daily operation of the store depends on the skills of the rank-and-file regular and part-time employees who are familiar with their duties. Even part-time employees take pride in their work and they offer stiff resistance to bosses whose approach shows no regard for their pride. We ought to note that the actions of the part-time employee, whom we observed earlier pretending to follow the instruction of the store manager and then putting the edible chrysanthemums back onto the shelf, were based on her confidence in her own product knowledge.

Part-time employees sometimes resort to force against their bosses through 'bullying'. According to Part-Time Employee 3, 'the former chief clerk [male] was always scolding us and we couldn't put up with him. He would scold about the same thing over and over again and the part-time employees stopped talking to him altogether. He was transferred after six months.' 'Bullying' of female chief clerks also occurs. Female Chief Clerk 2 said, 'When I was promoted to chief clerk, I was bullied mainly by a part-time employee who had served for nine years.' She added, 'I studied hard and made sure I gave prompt work instructions. I repelled their bullying.' Part-time employees sometimes rebel and resort to acts of collective resistance, such as bullying. Their bullying is targeted at chief clerks who directly affect the way the part-time employees carry out their duties. Their resistance is also aimed at the chief clerks such as the one who 'scolded all the time', whom they could not bear, and also at chief clerks whose service with the company is shorter than that of the part-time employees and are helpless and powerless. The struggle with the male chief clerk ended when he was transferred, after the store manager concluded that he could not handle the resistance by the part-time employees. Female Chief Clerk 2 got over the bullying by showing the value of her presence as their boss. Once again, this shows that the part-time employees are not bullying their chief clerk for no reason at all. They expect their chief clerks to show that they value their presence. As Part-Time Employee 3 put it, 'The chief clerk has to give us clear instructions, because we are not educated.' We should note, however, that sometimes the part-time employees exercise power that results in the transfer of a chief clerk.

The attachment of the 'us' group to work and the workplace

We can certainly detect a strong sense of pride and confidence in the attitudes of the 'us' group to work. Figures 4.8.1, 4.8.2 and 4.8.3 show how both male and female rank-and-file regulars and part-time employees with more than five years of service view their work, on the basis of the questionnaire survey conducted in Store A. Figure 4.8.1 shows that 75 per cent of the male rank-and-file regulars – much higher than their female counterparts – agreed with the statement that 'complex knowledge and high skills are required at work'. This indicates that there is a difference in job allocation between genders among the rank-and-file regulars. Fewer part-time employees agreed with this statement, which indicates that the duties allocated to the part-time employees are relatively easy tasks. More than 50 per cent of both male and female rank-and-file regulars think that 'we can decide ourselves how we do the work,' while only around 30 per cent of part-time employees agree, suggesting that the rank-and-file regulars enjoy more autonomy than the part-time employees. However, 56 per cent and 60 per cent of the respective part-time employee groups (Figure 4.8.1 shows two groups of part-time employees: one group with service of over ten years and the other with five to ten years) agree with the statement that 'there is room for me to try out my ideas and plans at work'. This is a smaller proportion than the female rank-and-file regulars, of whom 80 per cent agree with the statement. The positive attitude of the part-time employees, who try to get involved in their work, is also demonstrated in Figure 4.8.2, which shows that about 50 per cent of them 'try to identify issues in my daily tasks' – not significantly fewer than the male and female rank-and-file regulars. There is little difference between the part-time employees and male and female rank-and-file regulars in agreeing with the statement that 'I implement my ideas and improvements in carrying out my daily tasks.' Over 70 per cent of all employees have this attitude to work. Part-time employees who have served more than ten years have the highest rates of agreement (about 65 per cent) with the statement 'I have a good understanding of what customers want.' A relatively small proportion of part-time employees say ' I make a point of telling my ideas and suggestions for improvements to my boss', while the majority of female rank-and-file regulars (76.2 per cent) do so confidently. Thus, there is a noticeable difference between the rank-and-file regulars and the part-time employees in terms of the degree of difficulty of their duties according to the jobs allocated to them and their status. There are differences in the degree of autonomy they have and the way they communicate with their bosses. In terms of the attitude towards work, the female rank-and-file regulars are outstanding in their positive way of tackling work and trying to put their ideas into practice, but part-time employees also are by no means passive in this regard.

Figure 4.8.3 clearly illustrates that female rank-and-file regulars and part-time employees get a strong sense of satisfaction from work.

Figure 4.8.1: Work perceptions 1 (Store A)

Source: Figures 4.8.1, 4.8.2 and 4.8.3 are based on a questionnaire survey of store A

Figure 4.8.2: Work perceptions 2 (Store A)

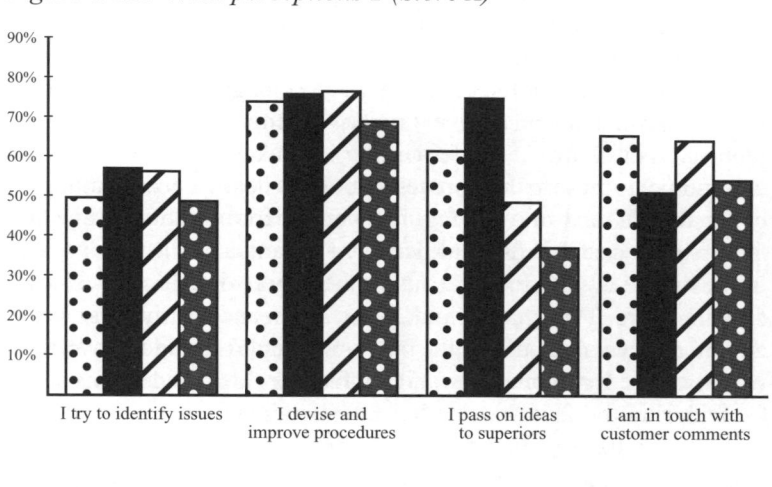

Almost 60 per cent agree with the statement that 'in general I am satisfied with my work at the moment.' Part-time employees are even more positive than female rank-and-file regulars in agreeing with the statement, 'I gain a sense of reward and achievement from work', with between 75 and 80 per cent of both groups agreeing. A great majority of part-time employees 'intend to continue working.' The fact that female rank-and-file regulars have fallen behind part-time employees in the rate of positive responses to questions except in the case of 'I am satisfied with my work' seems to be a reflection of the basic attributes of the respondents. Over 90 per cent of the part-time employees are in their forties or fifties and belong to the middle and older age groups. A little more than 90 per cent are married with children. As a result, they have a strong desire to continue working; they regard Store A as their only possible workplace and it seems that they provide their own 'sense of reward and achievement'. On the other hand, more than half of the female rank-and-file regulars are single and almost 60 per cent are in their twenties. Therefore, quite a few of them do not necessarily consider Store A their only workplace in view of the possibility of relocation when they get married in the future. Such differences in their basic attributes seem to explain the differences in their attitudes to work.

The data we have looked at clearly points to the fact that the part-time employees are far more attached to Store A as their only workplace. Many of the female rank-and-file regulars, however, share this attachment because, although they are single, they have selected the store-specific path and they consider Store A to be their only workplace, at least for the time being even though they might change in the future. They also have a positive attitude in that they try to identify issues, aim at implementing ideas and improvements and communicate these to their bosses. It looks as if, however, the attitudes of the female rank-and-file regulars vary according to their age and length of service. Let us recall Female Rank-and-File Regular 4 who, in the interviews at Store A, said, 'it is the part-time employees who love the store. The [male] chief clerks are here for only three years and then they move on. But the part-time employees and I have been working here for a long time and we feel very attached to this store.' Considering the fact that she has been working for nineteen years and is aged 40, it is hard for her to contemplate moving to another workplace or another area. Therefore, the relatively older and longer serving group of rank-and-file regulars, who consider the store to be their only workplace, seem to share the same strong attachment to the

Figure 4.8.3: Work perceptions 3 (Store A)

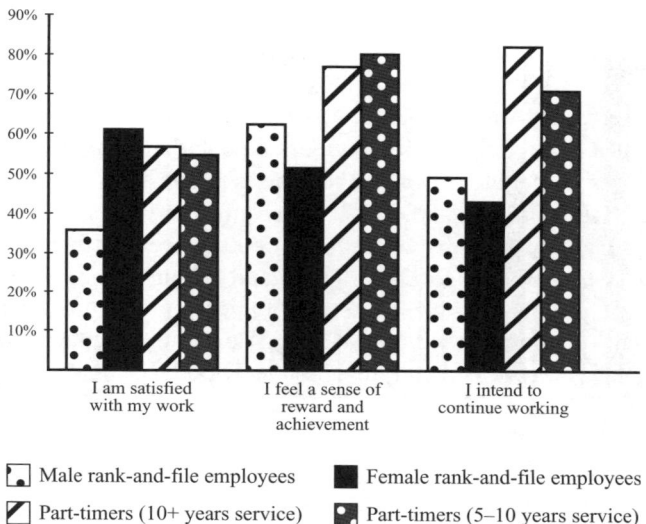

store as the part-time employees. Thus, the sense of 'us' is strongly maintained among the long-serving part-time employees and the married female rank-and-file regulars, who are similar in age to the part-time employees.

The sense of reward and achievement
When do women feel a sense of reward and achievement? Figure 4.9 shows the results of the questionnaire survey conducted among the male and female rank-and-file regulars and part-time employees in Company X's eight stores within the Area B Business Operations Division, which includes Store A. Those who answered 'yes' to the question 'Do you feel a sense of reward and achievement?' were asked to write freely on which occasions they might feel this way. Their responses have been compiled in Figure 4.9. The results clearly show that these occasions fall into a few specific groups, in spite of the fact that the responses were given freely by interviewees writing their own individual answers.[12]

Most of the male rank-and-file regulars said they felt rewarded 'when I achieved the target or when sales grew.' Nearly 70 per cent of male rank-and-file regulars gave the previous response together with 'when the merchandise for which I am responsible sells well'.

Figure 4.9: Occasions leading to a sense of reward and achievement (Area B Business Operations Department)

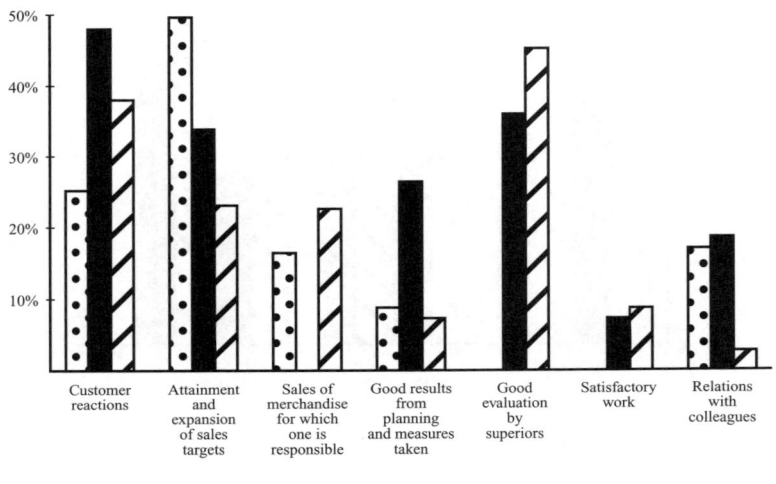

Source: Survey results in Area B Business Operations Department. Multiple responses given.

Conversely, the most important factor for female rank-and-file regulars is customer reaction. 'When I am thanked by customers', 'when shoppers appreciate it when I serve them' or 'when the same customer comes back again' were the rewarding moments that 47.6 per cent of female rank-and-file regulars chose to cite. These are followed by 'when I achieved the target and when the sales figures grew' (33.3 per cent) and 'when I got the job done as I wanted [planned]' (33.3 per cent). Individual examples of the latter include: 'when the products sell well after I have worked hard to devise a special display'; 'when the targeted work is completed as I planned'; 'when the job is done by the specified number of workers and within the hours specified and everyone finishes feeling satisfied'; ' at the cash register when there is a long queue which finally gets shorter as I really concentrate and work hard'; and 'when my estimates were correct and the amount of orders I placed turned out to be right'. They feel a sense of reward and achievement when dealing with customers and steadily carrying out the given work duties rather than achieving results in numerical terms. This trait is stronger among female rank-and-file regulars than among their male counterparts.

A female rank-and-file regular aged 38, with more than ten years' of service, works in the farm produce area of the food section. She has offered a long explanation. 'For outsiders my work may seem monotonous and repetitive. But I am working at my top speed within the time constraints. As I have been working for a long time, I feel attached to the products, too. I set a target each day and I try hard to achieve it. If I do something, I want to do it well. I discuss how best we can do the job with my colleagues and we will tell the boss our ideas.' We should note that at the end of her comments she added, 'I would like the boss to make sure it is easier for us staff to do our jobs.' She strongly expresses the pride she takes in the fact that 'it is not monotonous and repetitive work'. She works with pride and dedication. However, she expresses her dissatisfaction with her boss, who does not necessarily show respect and consideration for what she does.

One part-time employee, with three years service, works only two hours in the early morning taking out the produce from the storeroom in the food section. She wrote, 'If I could work longer hours, I would feel a sense of reward and achievement. But as it is now, when the time comes, I have to leave even though the job is not finished. When we are busy, I feel sorry for other people when I have to leave.' Her story tells us that if an employee is placed at work only for a short time and for a fixed task, then she is very unlikely to feel a sense of reward and achievement. If, on the other hand, a part-time employee works for longer hours and is assigned work duties with responsibility attached to them, she will be able to feel a sense of reward and achievement. Figure 4.9 shows that some 45 per cent of part-time employees – a bigger proportion than for female rank-and-file regulars – answered 'when I got my job done as I wanted'. As a further explanation of this answer, 30 per cent of these part-time employees said 'when I got my order prediction right.' As discussed earlier, the responsibility for placing orders is quite weighty. So much so that Part-Time Employee 3, as mentioned earlier, 'dreamed that I was being squashed under lettuces.' If one's results are good, however, this gives a strong sense of reward and achievement all the more because of the weight of responsibility. Quite a few respondents cited a strong sense of reward and achievement 'when the products I ordered and displayed were sold' and 'when the products for which I had exercised my judgement in ordering more than the usual quantity all sold as I had predicted.'

Other instances when female employees feel rewarded include: 'when I am able to complete the given task neatly'; 'when I can finish preparing my area within the time limit that I have set as my target

– I aim everyday to make a neat display at a certain speed'; 'when I have created a display that I think is effective and brings out the feeling of the season'; and 'when I have finally finished serving the customers at the cash register following a seemingly never ending queue.' The second most rewarding moment for part-time employees is related to 'responses from the customers' (37.7 per cent) and the individual examples are similar to those given by the rank-and-file regulars. Twenty-three per cent of part-time employees wrote about 'achieving the target and seeing the sales figures grow'. This is not in itself a considerable proportion but, in addition, 22.5 per cent say their satisfaction is related to the sales figures for products they are in charge of and also to the number of customers. Thus, we can see that quite a few part-time employees gain a sense of achievement through confirmation of the results of their own work.

A part-time employee, aged 47, who has served six years in the apparel section, considers that her work 'has depth'. She answered the survey question by writing, 'I feel quite close to the customers when I serve them. They ask me questions about the products or ask me for advice on various things. I feel very happy, too, when they come back and make a purchase. There are many difficult aspects in my work such as managing the stock and maintaining the stock level of the popular products. But as I learn more I realise the fun of it. This work has depth and that makes it worthwhile. So I think it is necessary for me to make an effort each day.' She realises the nature of her work duties are such that it cannot easily be learned and she aims to reap the rewards in the daily effort she makes. Another part-time employee, aged 56, who has ten years' service and works in the processed food area of the food section feels a sense of achievement 'when sales are up compared to last year and when we have achieved the sales target' and she cites the wide fluctuations that occur in her area as the reason behind her feelings. That is because 'there are big differences in sales volumes on different days. Weekdays, Saturdays, Sundays and public holidays all yield different sales figures from one another. Each season also has its different set of products. We have to predict the volume the customers will require and ensure we don't miss out on the chance of making a sale.' Thus, the high levels of complexity in her work duties are the reason why she feels a greater sense of achievement when things go well. A 56 year old part-time employee who has served for twelve years and who works for the seafood area in the food section wrote, 'preparing fish and sashimi used to be a job for regular employees. When it was decided that the part-time employees would take over this job, I was really worried and anxious about what was going to happen. But now that I have learned how to do the job, it is quite all right. When I see that the sashimi I prepared has sold, I think I have done my work well and feel satisfied. Perhaps this is what is called a sense of achievement.'

It was a history-making event when part-time employees also began placing orders and preparing the main lines of products. While this gave them heavier responsibilities, it also increased their opportunities for attaining a sense of reward and achievement. A 56 year old part-time employee in the apparel section who has served for nineteen years gave the following answers, 'when I have completed the day's scheduled tasks and achieved the sales targets for the day; when a new part-time employee has begun to manage to work on her own; when my boss has approved of my suggestions; and when my boss seems to enjoy working.' From what this long-serving part-time employee has written, we can sense her magnanimity. She takes responsibility for training new part-time employees and she watches her chief clerk, who is most likely to be younger and to have shorter years of service than herself, grow.[13]

The meaning of the lines of segregation and internal rifts

'Us' and management issues

As seen so far, the 'us' group display a positive attitude to and strong pride in their work. We can understand the strong opposition to the 'direct communication' used by the store manager in Store A as being based on this sense of 'us'. We must see the lines of segregation between 'them and us' as being charged with the desire of those at the very bottom of the work organisation to confirm their position and to assert their existence. At the heart of this is a pride in the fact that the daily operation of our store is dependent on the skills of the long-serving female rank-and-file regulars and part-time employees. Therefore, there is a strong aversion amongst them to the possibility of being made fools of by the members of the 'them' group who come and go one after the other. Although the part-time employees enjoy a degree of autonomy in running the sales floor, the work duties allocated to them are relatively easy. However, it is still possible to see that they themselves attach meaning to their work as they search for a sense of reward and achievement and tackle their jobs with zeal each day.

When we take these matters into consideration we can understand that their opposition to the store manager's approach, discussed earlier, arose from a feeling that this denied their positive attitude and sense of pride in their work. Likewise, the bullying of and resistance to chief clerks, as mentioned earlier, were not engaged in without cause. Rather, we can understand them as actions taken by the 'us' group in response to a feeling that their positive approach and pride had been infringed. At the same time, part-time employees are well aware of the boundaries within which they can mount their resistance. That is, 'you can manage somehow, even if your chief clerk thinks that you are nasty but this might be difficult if your boss is more senior than this [a section head or above]' (Part-Time Employee 4). The effectiveness of an individual's or a group's power varies according to their position within an organisation. Even a part-time employee, however, can sometimes exercise the sort of power that might prompt the transfer of a chief clerk, and higher management cannot ignore such resistance.

What part-time employees want in the relationship with their bosses is a relationship of trust and of appropriate guidance. Part-Time Employee 1, whose jobs are taking out merchandise and serving at the checkout counter in the book area of the household goods section, said that a chief clerk who is easy to get along with is 'a chief clerk who trusts me and leaves things with me'. For example, when she suggests ordering a new popular item, an ideal chief clerk would say: 'Thank you. Can you place an order?' On the other hand, 'a chief clerk who is particular and gives many instructions saying: 'Don't do this.' or 'Wait until you receive instructions from the chief clerk.' are difficult to get along with. In addition, the rank-and-file regulars who are easy to get along with are those who, for example, 'are willing to give support, with their product knowledge'. The relationship that part-time employees want to have with rank-and-file regulars and chief clerks is one in which the way they work is respected and where support is given as needed.

When we pay attention to these aspects, it becomes apparent that the 'us' constitute a delicate domain that should not be disregarded by the management in charge of employees in the store. In the interviews with part-time employees, chief clerks and section heads were criticised but not female rank-and-file regulars. They seem to manage to keep cordial relations with the 'us' group. A line of segregation clearly separates 'them' – those soon to be transferred – from 'us'. However, the female rank-and-file regulars – who form the lower echelons of the regular employees – are psychologically closer to the part-time employees, whom they respect and treat sympathetically. They would not do anything to upset the feelings of the part-time employees. It follows that management directives often fail to penetrate to the level of the long-serving female rank-and-file regulars within a work organisation such as company X, where those in the managerial positions keep moving after a short period of time. It is extremely difficult for those who move away after a short while to try to ensure that the management policies have permeated to the extremities of an organisation.

Internal rifts within the 'us' group
Lines of segregation, however, are not only drawn between 'them' and 'us'. There is a wide gap in objective terms between female rank-and-file regulars and female part-time employees, although both of them belong to the 'us' group and seem to share the same feelings. This gap is related, understandably, to differences in employment conditions based on different types of employment. The interviews unequivocally show that part-time employees are acutely aware of the wage and bonus differences separating them and rank-and-file regulars, notwithstanding the similarity of their work content. Their disappointment is especially intense on bonus days. This is because the biannual bonus for part-time employees is no more than between 30 and 50,000 yen. Part-Time Employee 1 said, 'the difference between part-time employees and regular employees comes home loud and clear on bonus day. All part-time employees are dissatisfied because it is like not getting any [bonus] at all. When I am paid the bonus, I really lose my motivation almost to the extent that I don't want to do the job any more. Whenever bonus time comes around, I get extremely annoyed and really want to quit.' This is because she feels that the amount of bonus she gets does not reflect the dedication she regularly shows – so much so that she does not mind staying behind. She adds, 'part-time employees can't leave work on time, either. Furthermore, we help people outside our area even in other sections by taking their merchandise out if they need help. [On bonus days] I feel stupid that I have to do the work for other sections.' This sentiment is shared by Part-Time Employee 4, 'the difference between part-time employees and regular employees is the difference in wages, especially bonuses, even though the work we do is nearly the same. There is hardly any bonus for the part-time employees. On bonus day, I wonder why there is so much difference and I get angry. I don't feel like working and I want to quit.'

It seems that awareness of difference is only reinforced by the measures implemented to support the female regular employees in

Company X. For example, the reduction of working hours arrangement for child-carers, introduced in 1995, made it possible for female regular employees to work only five-hour days for one year. These working hours are nearly as short as those of the part-time employees. Chief Clerk 3, who actually exercised this right, said, 'the part-time employees are envious because [regular employees] are entitled to have bonuses and holidays.' The privileged position of female regular employees compared to that of part-time employees was made apparent by this arrangement. Even so, part-time employees, who are placed at the bottom of the work organisation, do not take any action that might antagonise the rank-and-file regulars with whom they share a sense of 'us'. As we saw earlier, while they might criticise the chief clerks and section heads, they do not direct their criticism towards the female rank-and-file regulars.

As indicated in Figure 4.10, the type of work for which part-time employees are responsible has changed since they joined the company and now their work is similar to that of regular employees. They strongly feel, however, that they do not receive remuneration that matches the work they do and that they lack the necessary education and training. Part-time employees who have served more than ten years feel more dissatisfied than the ones with shorter periods of service. The reason for this can be sought in the recognition, not only by part-time employees themselves but also by both male and female rank-and-file regulars, that the work performed by part-time employees is equivalent to that of regular employees. Against this backdrop, between 40 and 45 per cent of part-time employees think, 'I would like to be allowed to be a regular employee if I want to' and between 60 and 70 per cent of them hope 'to be able to work longer hours if I want to' (Figure 4.10). Both of these wishes are stronger among the part-time employees who have served longer than ten years. When they started as part-time employees, it may only have been possible for them to work the hours of a part-time employee. As the years go by and their family members reach a different life stage, it may become possible for them to work longer hours. It is not surprising then that some of them, having seen the big gap in their remuneration, should want to become regular employees. Many of them actually already do work similar to that of regular employees and feel that they have developed the skills required for these positions.

Although no internal rifts within the 'us' group have surfaced yet as a result of the differences in remuneration, there is no doubt that this is a contradiction that has been growing in the depths of the work

Figure 4.10: Complaints and aspirations of part-timers (Store A)

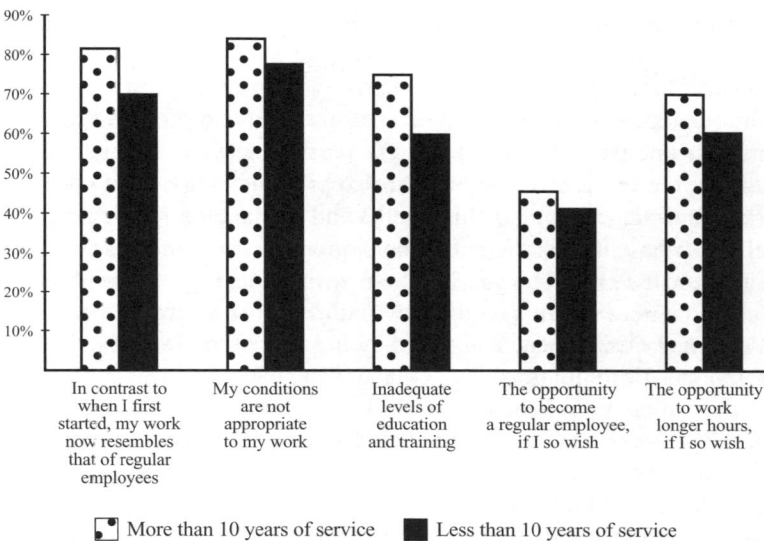

Figure 4.11: Part-timers' evaluation of their work performance (Store A)

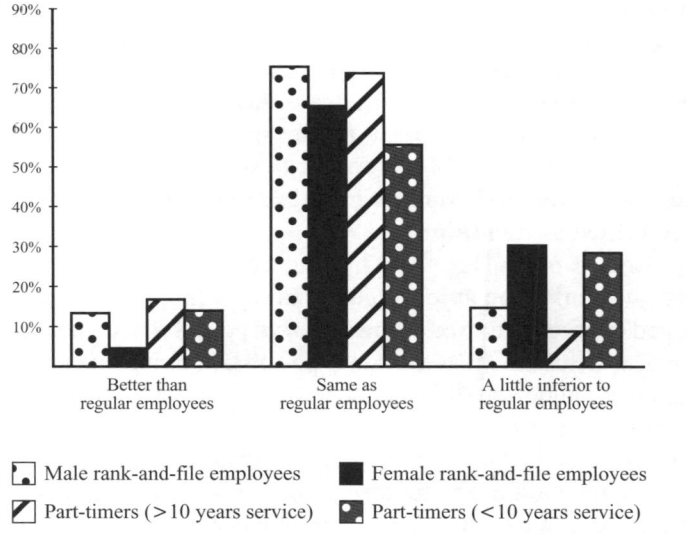

Note: both figures 4.10 and 4.11 are based on interview surveys conducted at Store A

organisation. In recent years, Company X has been actively promoting moves to turn part-time employees into chief clerks. Through this move, the company delegates management work to capable long-serving part-time employees and guarantees remuneration at a level closer to the starting salary of a high school leaver. This raises questions about the basis of existence of female rank-and-file regulars who remain in the same position over their long years of service. As mentioned earlier, there is a drive on one hand to promote long-serving female rank-and-file regulars to chief clerks and on the other to create chief clerks from amongst the part-time employees. How then can female rank-and-file regulars justify their position as regular employees, which is more advantageous than that of part-time employees? The Personnel Department said that they hear concerns from the female rank-and-file regulars asking, 'what will happen to us in the future?' If, in the future, more female chief clerks are created and more part-time employees are promoted to chief clerks, then the basis of existence of the female rank-and-file regulars will be even more constricted. The lines of segregation drawn within the organisation will possibly have to be re-drawn in a different manner, reflecting the changing situation within the organisation.

The mechanisms of segregation within an organisation

This chapter so far has examined segregation in the organisation by looking at what is actually happening within the work organisation. I have tried to examine not only job segregation between the genders but also the issues that arise at a deeper layer within the organisation. Let us now take a look at what these examinations have revealed.

The mechanisms through which job segregation by gender is maintained as 'tradition'

First, we must look at job segregation by gender, which has been shaped by practices based on management policies from the top. These practices determine how certain types of jobs or jobs in a particular section are allocated. It is true that the image of the food section as a 'difficult' workplace that requires heavy physical work and the 'dirty work' of preparing fresh food have contributed to the formation of the perception of the food section as a 'men's section'; and this perception is partly the reason why it has been avoided by female regular employees. In many cases, this was the explanation given.

But it is not enough. We must not overlook the mechanisms acting to alienate women during the process of forming their perceptions of the food section as a 'men's section'. The food section has been regarded as 'masculine' because it is 'more lively as the cycle of the merchandise is short'. Furthermore, the 'masculine' image of the food section is strengthened by the fact that the section has a large number of employees, including a higher proportion of part-time and casual workers than other areas, who need to be managed and therefore the section requires stronger leadership.

According to one man, who occupies a key position in the top management team of Company X, during the 1960s – the company's former period as a chain store – processed food achieved tremendous sales growth and those (men) who were in charge of the processed food area strutted about 'as if they were the ones carrying the whole company'. This was a time when processed foods, such as instant noodles, helped bring sweeping change to the nation's eating habits and supermarkets worked as the engine room driving this change. At that time, supermarkets were on the rise and offered new processed food items on a large scale (Kikkawa and Takaoka, 1997a). With these factors working together, the food section was positioned as the gateway to career advancement for men and it was prestigious to work there. Thus, it became historically a 'men's section'.[14] During this process, the checkout counter was specifically marked as a women's workplace. This is related to the fact that relatively young women were concentrated at the checkout counters at the time when general merchandise supermarkets started and these women were employed with the thought that they would resign when they got married. Thus, a women's workplace was formed, as if a world of its own, within the food section where a considerable accumulation of skill is required. When subsequently many part-time employees were posted to the checkout counters, its basic characteristic as a women's area was reinforced.

On the other hand, the process by which the apparel section became a 'women's section' cannot be explained in terms of women's role within the family – the idea that it is women who procure, mend and manage the clothing for the family. This is because the procurement and preparation of food is closely related to women's role within the family and as far as the nature of the group of products that a section deals in is concerned, the food section could easily have become a women's section. But, in fact, this is not what happened. It is clear that the respective reasons for the food section coming to be considered 'masculine' and the apparel section 'feminine' are not based on the same grounds. The process of determining gender ascription to different sections is not simply based on the nature of the merchandise or the need or otherwise for physical work but on a range of factors such as the gender composition of the labour force and the power relationship between the genders. This happened against the backdrop of the various historical conditions under which a new form of business, the general merchandise supermarket, was developed. Once a 'tradition' is formed, it is not easy to break the existing gender-based division between sections. The strength of a 'tradition' is such that, even after the grounds for its existence are removed, other grounds will be found and the tradition will be forcefully maintained. Company X's practice of placing women in the food section over recent years is the first step towards an attempt to change this tradition.

The domain of organisational culture

Secondly, there is the question of how we should understand the low level of interest in promotion among female rank-and-file regulars and female chief clerks. As has been discussed, nearly half of female rank-and-file regulars wish to remain rank-and-file regulars, with quite a few of them staying at the lower ranks of the status ranking system. Under the mobility path selection system, introduced in 1993, not only married women but also quite a few single women in their twenties have chosen the store-specific path. Most of the women who have been selected to become chief clerks wish to remain chief clerks. The desire of these women to maintain the status quo seems to be related to the long standing image that it is men, especially male graduates, who should climb up the career ladder in the work organisation. This sentiment was expressed by a female chief clerk who said, 'I don't want to become a section head.' Thus, a long history in the work organisation has been maintained in which women with many years of continuous service limit themselves to working in one store as rank-and-file regulars and continue to work there. Job segregation by gender has been established as a self-evident axiom according to which women are expected to ensure that routine work duties are completed each day and management positions belong to the male domain. Nobody finds it unusual that male graduates overtake women and advance to being a chief clerk and a section head only a few years after having joined the company. Even though men and women work under the same status ranking system, they have each built their own respective worlds within the work organisation.

Under these circumstances, sudden selection as a chief clerk came as a bolt from the blue for the women who were chosen in this way. They are beginning to discover the fun of working as part of management, but they do not intend to become section heads. The reason for their reluctance is that they believe that higher management requires a variety of skills that are easier to achieve for people with stronger educational backgrounds. Another concern for them is that the greater responsibility will mean a heavier workload and they want to avoid this. Men tend to accept as a matter of course the longer working hours that correspond to the heavier responsibility, while women tend to avoid them. The differences between men and women arise from their respective environments – men are in an environment in which they are expected to push on always aiming to climb higher up the career ladder within the organisation, whereas women are neither expected to or nurtured so as to be able to do this. The view that married women's strong inclination to maintain the status quo is due to their 'family responsibilities' is superficial. Job segregation by gender that has resulted from both gender and educational backgrounds is accompanied by a set of assumptions about which nobody has any doubt. This type of segregation is capable of making any behaviour based on these assumptions appear 'natural'. That is why even single women without any existing 'family responsibilities' select the store-specific path as a matter of course. The perception that it is a suitable path for women and that selecting it is the only 'natural' premise for women is shared within the organisation.

Segregation within the organisation formed around gender differences in the allocation of staff to different sections or different duties within a section, as well as around gender differences in transfers and promotions. This segregation has created the specific set of assumptions and behaviour patterns of the individual members of the organisation. In short, there is a contrast between the men who keep getting promotions and transfers on one hand and the women who keep working for the same store at the same status grade on the other. Even though they work within the same organisation, women and men are expected to follow completely different behaviour patterns. Indeed, the actual behaviours that they have accumulated conform to the expected patterns. The organisational culture, with its historical reasons for being, embraced into its fabric gender differences and differences in educational backgrounds. It is this culture that has a decisive influence on an individual's behaviour.

On this point, it is necessary to take a closer look at the relationships between the new personnel system, existing practices within the organisation and the organisational culture that supports these practices. As discussed earlier, the area-specific path was created with only the working conditions of the male employees in mind. Its original targets were male employees. It aimed at preventing the loss of motivation among male employees through an unwanted transfer to a larger area. For female rank-and-file regulars, there had been a practice in personnel management of trying to minimise their transfer between different stores even before such a system was established. The system of new paths was then added only to confirm this practice formally. The new system, however, resulted in the practice being legitimised in that it is possible for female rank-and-file regulars, if they so desire, to work in a specific store. Therefore, it is now possible for female rank-and-file regulars to select with certainty the store-specific path as their vested right, irrespective of their marital status. The influx of female rank-and-file regulars choosing this path in recent years has made the Personnel Department in Headquarters realise that this path was a system that would remove the flexibility of transfers and question the system that allows the selection of the area-specific path. In effect, the establishment of this system led to a reinforcement of segregation between the genders in stores. Single women, too, choose this path at an early stage and as a result exclude themselves from opportunities for transfers and promotions. When this system was created, the Personnel Department's intention was not to support female employees. Considering this development, we must not overlook the fact that while a system is capable of creating practices, a new system can also be interpreted according to existing practice and may be used to reinforce it. This is an indication of the strength of historically formed practices and of the organisational culture that accepts them.

Lines of segregation at the bottom
Thirdly, we must discuss the issue of the line of segregation between 'them and us'. As we have seen so far, the individual members within an organisation perform, in accordance with their status, the act of response-negotiation in the face of management policies and communication from the top. At times, this means an individual or collective resistance intended to neglect or disobey the intentions of their superiors. Collective resistance by part-time employees who are located at the very bottom of the organisation actually has the ability to bring about the transfer of a chief clerk. This particular act of resistance

was mobilised in response to actions by their boss that stifled the sense of pride and responsibility that they felt in their work. Female rank-and-file regulars who are at the bottom of the organisation together with part-time employees have set up a barrier and drawn a dividing line between 'them' who keep moving away and 'us'. The female rank-and-file regulars are operating from a standpoint in which they see their store as the one and only workplace for them for the time being. The grounds for drawing the line of segregation are their confidence and sense of pride based, firstly, on their realisation that there are areas that are dependent on the way they work – with a degree of autonomy – and, secondly, that daily routine tasks are carried out because of their high levels of achievement. Their attitude is not an obstinate one, one which on no account accepts management from the top. However, they vehemently oppose and resist when 'those' who will be leaving the store show behaviours that undervalue their own work, dampen their enthusiasm and injure their sense of pride.[15]

For the work organisation, this line of segregation means that an area is formed that is difficult for management to reach from the top. This difficulty arises from the psychological closeness between the part-time and female rank-and-file regulars – who are the bottom layer of the regular employees – especially those with relatively long years of service. The line of segregation between 'them' and 'us' is an attempt by part-time employees and rank-and-file regulars, who are, in fact, separated by widely divergent employment conditions, to confirm for themselves the idea that 'we are the ones who love this store' by closing ranks emotionally. If in the future, however, more of the female rank-and-file regulars and the part-time employees are made chief clerks, it is conceivable that the nature of this segregation will change.

It seems that the lines of segregation examined in this chapter tend to occur in work organisations where the frequent transfer of managers is inevitable. The important question is, however, how does management from above deal with this area that forms the base layer of the work organisation? If management is not aware of the existence of this area, or acts in a top-down manner, ignoring it altogether, then this could lead to conflict. Even though the problem may not surface as conflict, it might be internalised and result in a stagnant atmosphere. On the other hand, once the existence of such a delicate area has been acknowledged, it might be possible to adopt an approach that attaches more emphasis to the sense of reward and achievement felt by those working at this level of the organisation. Questions need to be asked about the company's management style. Chapter 5 will examine this issue more closely.

5 The Challenge of 'Creating Female Store Managers': Management Style and Gender

Continuing on from Chapter 4, this chapter will examine the case of Company X, a general merchandise supermarket. As mentioned previously, Company X has risen to the challenge of placing women in charge and also of throwing women into areas generally thought of as 'men's sections'. These steps have been part of the 'making positive use of women' (*josei katsuyō*) policy, adopted from the mid-1990s on. We can view this as the first step in reforming internal organisational segregation, of the kind discussed in the previous chapter. In this chapter, we turn our attention to the 'creation of female store managers', which is pivotal to the policy of 'making positive use of women' and also very significant in terms of the influence of this policy. Let us analyse the internal organisational changes ushered in by the 'creation of female store managers' – the organisational challenge which Company X set itself. In this analysis we will look at the aims of this policy; the process of putting it into practice; the career differences between male and female store managers; and the gender differences in the management styles of store managers.

The organisational challenge of 'creating female store managers'

Reactions to the 'creation of female store managers'

The challenge of 'creating female store managers'
Organisations set themselves various targets and tasks in order to revitalise themselves, and they also attempt to overcome any existing limitations. From amongst the various environmental conditions surrounding management, the organisation may select, for example, personnel cuts aimed at reducing costs; reform of the stock management system; or innovation of the ordering system. It is to be

expected that these actions will have a direct impact on the work site. 'Making positive use of women', the Company X policy referred to previously – particularly the 'creation of female store managers', is also one part of this organisational challenge.

Currently, these attempts are proceeding successfully and a succession of female store managers have been created – a number of these women leading the way, as they move on to their second store as store managers. The first female store manager was appointed in 1996, with a total of nine having been appointed by 1999. There has been a steady creation of female store managers from the year 2000 on, with their numbers reaching eighteen in 2002. We should note that this has occurred extremely smoothly and, moreover, that this policy is being pursued at an ever-increasing pace. For the purposes of the analysis contained in this chapter, I have labelled the nine female store managers, who had already appeared by 1999, the 'first generation' and I use data from interviews with all nine cases as my core source material. Of the nine who make up this 'first generation', five are single, three are married with children and one is separated with children. In addition, I also conducted interviews with three women from the 'second generation', those who became store managers after 2000. A summary of these cases is set out in Table 5.1. In order to provide a comparison with female store managers, I also carried out interviews with ten men who were, or had been, male store managers[1] (Table 5.2).

A chilly response

The 'creation of female store managers' made its way down through the whole company and the Personnel Department in Head Office urged the Personnel Departments of Area Operations Divisions to put this policy, devised by senior management, into practice. The 'creation of female store managers' policy certainly cannot be described as having won the endorsement of the whole organisation. The senior ranks of management regarded the low numbers of female managers, regardless of the ratio of male to female employees, as a problem and sought to bring about reform of the organisation via active efforts to 'make positive use of women'. Also, the Personnel Department in Head Office had this policy put into practice in every area even though they did not necessarily have confidence in female store managers. Ultimately, the implementation of this policy was left to the judgement of each Area Operations Division and the responses varied throughout these Divisions. Some areas selected suitable women

Table 5.1: Career characteristics of female store managers

	Store experience prior to becoming a store manager	Positions held outside the store	Education
First Generation			
Case 1	14 years	Full-time union official	Junior college*
Case 2	12 years	Merchandise Department	University
Case 3	15.5 years	Advertising Department	Junior college
Case 4	9 years	Private Secretary, Merchandise Department	Vocational school
Case 5	14 years	None	University
Case 6	3 years	Merchandise Department	University
Case 7	13 years	None	University
Case 8	12 years	Training Department	University*
Case 9	7 years	Training Department	Vocational school*
Second Generation			
Case 10	3 years	Staff Development Department	Junior college
Case 11	9 years	Personnel Department	Junior college
Case 12	12 years	Business Reform Department	University

Source: Interview surveys
* = joined halfway through career, and not as a recent graduate.

Table 5.2: Career characteristics of male store managers

	Store experience prior to becoming a store manager	Positions held outside the store	Education
Case 1	6 years	Merchandise Department, Processing Centre	University
Case 2	12 years	None	University
Case 3	3 years	Full-time union official	University
Case 4	0 years	Personnel Department, temporary transfer to subsidiary company	University
Case 5	19 years	Full-time union official	University
Case 6	7 years	Merchandise Department, Processing Centre	University
Case 7	8 years	Personnel Department	University
Case 8	6.5 years	Full-time union official	University
Case 9	18 years	None	University
Case 10	15 years	None	University

Source: Interview surveys
* = joined halfway through career, and not as a recent graduate.

immediately but others left matters to the passage of time, arguing that waiting a few years would lead to the cultivation of capable women. Alternatively, other Area Operations Divisions regarded it as a 'pity' to create just one female store manager, and sought to create two at once. According to the Head of the Personnel Department in Head Office, senior management had a very determined policy of 'creating female store managers': 'We think that, as a Personnel Department, we have done our best and produced results but those at the top are still not satisfied' (2001).

In the 1990s male store managers and male middle managers gave a cool response to these efforts by the senior ranks of management, greeting them with statements like 'This is nothing but ornamentation' and 'It will soon all come tumbling down'. There were also mutterings along the lines of 'Those female store managers are just a passing thing'. These comments were based on the confidently held expectation that female store managers would most likely fail when ultimately faced with long serving male subordinates, with whom they would find it difficult to get along. In the second half of the 1980s three women had actually been appointed, during the fanfare surrounding the 'creation of female store managers', but this exercise 'collapsed' after a short time. Because of the existence of these memories within the organisation practically everyone in it felt that this time too the attempt would collapse – sooner or later.

Female Store Manager 9 was aware of her male superior's frank views on the 'creation of female store managers', a policy which the men did not welcome and with which they did not agree. The head of the Area Operations Division (male), the person with overall responsibility for the area, told her at a dinner around the time that he was transferring to another area, 'You did not become a store manager because of any personal abilities but because of company policy! I decided to make you a female store manager when I knew that I myself would be leaving the area and would no longer be responsible for what happened here'. Let us consider her superior's reluctant compliance with company policy. In keeping with orders from above, the 'creation of female store managers' policy trickled down from top to bottom, but those on the receiving end gave it a lukewarm reception. The 'creation of female store managers', delivered as a decision of senior management, was, as we shall see later, an extremely radical policy which caused a stir in the existing operations of the organisation. In reality, however, this policy was put into practice without an adequate understanding of its true aims within the organisation. We can guess that there were various points of friction in the actual implementation process.

Support from the labour union and the state

The labour union was supportive of this company policy, publishing interviews with female store managers in its monthly magazine and setting up round table discussions with female store managers. The deputy chairman of the union (male and current chairman) came to realise, through listening to people on the sales floor, that the promotion of women was an important issue.

For example, when there are sales price errors, men, who are at the forefront of the store, shout at women on the registers, who are at the very bottom of the store hierarchy. In the majority of cases, however, it is not the women on the registers who cause these errors but incorrect price tags. However, because the Registers Department, to which only women are assigned, has a very weak voice in the organisation, moves to improve their situation are slow. When the deputy chairman of the labour union questioned a female rank-and-file regular, who had succeeded in her battle to eradicate sales price errors in a certain store, about the key to her success she replied, 'I seized the most prominent men in the store by their lapels and forced them to change all the price tags'. Unless they express their thoughts this forcefully no one will listen to these women who are at the very bottom of Company X's store. The deputy chairman of the union analyses this in the following way, 'Because male superiors make no effort to listen to the voices from below, they are unaware of the difficulties that exist and this hinders the development of any sense of interest in the lower ranks'. Consequently, he continues, the appearance of female store managers has made possible a management style which pays attention to the voices from below and which, 'gives encouragement to the whole store, from the bottom up, drawing out everyone's feelings and best efforts' (1999). The union supports the company's policy and accepts 'making positive use of women' as indispensable to the improvement of existing conditions in Company X.

We must not forget also that external legitimisation helped to make the organisational challenge, which had been thrown down in this way, an even more powerful trend. The former Ministry of Labour (*Rōdōshō*) commended Company X as a leading business in the area of Equal Employment Opportunities between Men and Women (2000). The response to this commendation by the person in charge of personnel in Head Office, which did not necessarily have confidence in this policy originally, was 'Our company is still at an embarrassing stage and therefore we must fight even harder from now on' (2001). The atmosphere at this time, when equal employment opportunity and the movement towards gender equality had become leading state policies, endowed the battle to 'make positive use of women' with legitimacy. If we take this point into consideration, we can see that the policy of 'making positive use of women' could not be easily dropped, even though there was a backlash and attempts to evade it inside the organisation.

The real motive behind the 'creation of female store managers'

The careers of female store managers and women middle managers

What kind of women went on to become female store managers under these conditions? Let us attempt to clarify the status of the 'creation of female store managers' policy in Company X's thinking by answering this question.

Table 5.1, referred to above, sets out the distinguishing characteristics, particularly store experience, in the careers of the nine female store managers who had been appointed by 1999. With the exception of Female Store Manager 6, who had the least experience (three years), it is clear that, generally, they all have long years of service. Even the shortest period of service is seven years, with the longest stretching to fifteen and a half years. Two of the nine (Female Store Managers 7 and 9) joined the company halfway through this survey and have only had in-store experience. Female Store Manager 6, with her extremely limited store experience, has worked continuously as a buyer in the Merchandise Department, following her three years of store experience after graduating from university and joining the company. It is clear from the above that most of the 'first generation' of female store managers were women with an abundance of store experience. Even in the case of the 'second generation' two women have extensive experience of around ten years each, although Female Store Manager 10 has only a short three years of store experience.

Incidentally, before the advent of the 'creation of female store managers' policy, there had been earnest efforts in the 1980s to foster women middle managers in Company X. The company strove to make 'positive use of women' by picking out able women from the store and putting them into the Merchandise Department in Area Operations Divisions and in Head Office. Under this system 'women middle managers' were those who had accumulated a certain level of continuous years of service and a rank above Level 7 in the status ranking system (see Table 4.1, Chapter 4). If we contrast the careers of these women middle managers and those of female store managers, we see considerable differences. Can we possibly detect the intentions behind the 'creation of female store managers' in these differences?

According to internal company records, in 1998 there were 58 women middle managers. The shortest serving female employee at the middle manager level is 33 (with eleven years of continuous service) and the longest serving (with 37 years of continuous service) is 56. Most women middle managers, however, are largely concentrated in the age range between the late thirties and early forties. When we look at their store experience, as shown in Table 5.3, we notice that most of them have scant store experience. A mere seven (12.1 per cent) have more than seven years of store experience. In contrast to this, there are as many as 33 (56.9 per cent) with less than three years of store experience. Of these women middle managers, 22 have never had any store experience, having been posted to areas such as General Affairs and Accounting immediately upon joining the company. Nine out of these 22 joined the company halfway through their careers and were immediately assigned to jobs outside the store because of the value placed on the experience they had gained in other companies. Looked at as a whole, those who joined halfway through are a minority: close to 80 per cent are newly employed university graduates and most of them are posted to the store immediately upon joining the company. This is because Company X's personnel policy ensures that new female employees begin by gaining experience in the store, which is in effect the 'basis of the business'. The majority of these women are characterised by substantial experience in postings outside the store, following their initial posting to the store. These other postings might include the Merchandise, Personnel, Publicity or Systems Development Departments of either Head Office or Area Operations Divisions. It is clear from this that most of the women who have become 'women middle managers', after accumulating many years of service, are to be found in either Head Office or Area Operations Division, with an emphasis on office work, and have been developing their careers as professionals in fields such as personnel and merchandising.

Because general merchandise supermarkets are characterised by their base of influential female customers, Company X realised – albeit a little belatedly – the necessity of securing competent and talented women. Their approach, however, was to pluck talented women, who were deemed to have prospects of a promising future, from the store

Table 5.3: Number of years of store experience of female middle managers, excluding store managers (1998)

	Number of years experience										
	None	1	2	3	4	5	6	7	8	9	10	Total
Joined as university graduates	13	3	0	8	4	4	8	1	2	1	2	46
Joined halfway through career	9	0	0	0	1	1	0	0	0	0	1	12
Total	22	3	0	8	5	5	8	1	2	1	3	58

Source: Internal company documents

and to assign them to staff departments. According to Female Store Manager 10, who became a store manager on the basis of experience accumulated through devising and implementing programmes for developing the abilities of employees as they gain a thorough knowledge of the sales floor, staff departments outside the store have the advantage that it is easier for women to continue working for longer in them than in the store. There are more long serving women with children in staff departments outside the store than in the store. This is because women in staff departments find it is easier to take time off to see to their children's needs and also because it is possible for them to adjust the nature of work itself more flexibly. Conversely, 'although there are long serving women in the store, it is difficult to find any who want to climb the career ladder'.

What does the fact that women with clearly different career characteristics from those held by the majority of women middle managers, namely women with abundant store experience, were the ones chosen as store managers tell us? Does it not imply that the work abilities resulting from the pattern of cultivating future women middle managers do not match the work duties of store managers? In other words, Company X achieved actual results in nurturing female professionals in the area of office work but we can surmise that the policy of 'creating female store managers' had its sights set on a goal that went beyond these results.

Women middle managers and the work of store managers
Company X's inherited view of store managers – one which excluded women – can help to explain the fact that the policy of 'making positive use of women' developed along the lines of making capable women with long years of service master specialist work in the Staff

Department. The image of a store manager was always that of a man and there was no notion of grooming capable women for this position. Alternatively, we can also see paternalistic attitudes towards women as the reason why they were kept away from store manager work – that is, because this was seen as men's work and hard – and also as the reason why they were instead steered towards training in specialist abilities.

A look at the career characteristics of the ten present and past male store managers in Table 5.2, above, shows that, with the exception of Male Store Manager 4, who has no store experience at all, and Male Store Manager 3, who has little store experience (three years), most of them have over six years of experience. Most of them also have some specialised experience, such as in the Merchandise or Personnel Departments or as a full-time labour union official. There are just three cases with no experience outside the store and these all became store managers after extremely lengthy periods of in-store experience – fifteen to eighteen years – but these are exceptional cases. I will analyse the careers of store managers in more detail later but men, despite some significant individual differences, basically build up their careers through experience in departments outside the store, while still making their store experience pivotal. Some of these men become the core middle management cadets as they build up a career pattern in which they, firstly, put into practice their sense of how the store works in Head Office and in Area Operations Divisions and also – conversely – secondly, implement the points which they have picked up in Head Office and in Area Operations Divisions in the store. Store manager work is a managerial position beyond the attainment of some men and is regarded by others as a dead end top managerial position. However, in the eyes of male core middle management cadets, store manager work itself is a stepping-stone to the gateway to success.

The cultivation of women middle managers has been conducted in a manner not even distantly resembling the pattern just described for cultivating core male middle managers. We can infer that there was no thought in this of women middle managers becoming store managers, let alone moving up to even higher levels. We can think of the 'creation of female store managers' as the result of the appearance amongst top management of a new problem consciousness and a desire to overcome this situation. Internal company documents (2000), state that, 'despite making positive use of women, we still have not reached a stage in which there are large numbers of female store managers. In three years' time we must have a situation in which women make up at least one out of every four of total middle managers'. This clearly goes beyond the nature of the former pattern for women middle managers and also demonstrates a will to nurture a core middle manager class amongst women. This implies a consciousness of the limitations of the former pattern for nurturing talented female employees and also the development of a consciousness of the importance of giving women the same store experience as men. What then were the limitations of the policy for women middle managers in the past?

The limitations of 'making positive use of women' to date
The head of the Food Department in the Merchandise Department of Head Office is critical of the format of 'making positive use of women' in this department, to date (1998). He says that large numbers of women, who are working well in chief clerk positions in the store, are selected to go off to the Merchandise Department at around 26 or 27 but that there are many cases of women around age 35 who have 'reached the top' without having been able to awaken any motivation or will regarding their work. He uses the term 'reach the top' in the sense of these women, 'losing their spirit of challenge, avoiding management and not wishing to hear any talk at all about becoming store managers'. He comments harshly that this is the result of, 'having little experience of dealing with human relations because they were selected as buyers at an early stage' and as a consequence, 'their extreme pride and narrowness as human beings results in them having difficulties in knowing how to deal with people'. He is critical of the situation saying, 'The problem is that in the interests of making positive use of women (women only) have been made into specialists early'. This is despite the adoption of a company-wide personnel management approach which emphasises the fostering of generalists and encourages men's career development via movement between the store and Head Office and the store and Area Operations Division.

At the time when I interviewed one of the small number of female buyers in the Product Development Department (1999), there was hardly any mention of topics suggesting a consciousness of cooperation with the 'work site', that is, the store. This buyer is one of the women who have achieved the highest status grade level amongst the female employees of Company X. Having built up her career as a buyer from 1984, within three to four years of having joined the company she had become a female chief clerk – an extremely rare phenomenon in the company at that time. She said that the work of buyer 'appeals' to her 'because it is easy to show results in the figures.

In stores results fluctuate because of factors unrelated to individual effort, for example store location, whereas in the Product Development Department figures will improve in response to the development of good products, making it easy to verify success. Also I am not the type of person who is very good at sales and thinking up ways of plugging the company's own brand'. These sentiments left me feeling that the head of the Food Department was accurate in his comments about these women whose superior he was. He commented on their lack of any spirit of challenge or a will to attempt management posts and also their assertion of self-regulation, in which they limit themselves according to what 'our own type' is good at or not good at.

However, rather than there being a substantial problem with these individual women, the essence of the problem is to be found in the trapping of women from the generation in which the trend towards long term continuous service appeared in specialist jobs and a situation with no prospects for nurturing talent. Senior management, who began to be aware of this point, also realised the necessity of overcoming the limitations of the existing 'women middle managers' policy in order to cultivate cadets for core female middle manager positions. The true motive behind the 'creation of female store managers' is to be found in this point, and as a result of this senior management emphasised store management, the 'basis of the business', and promoted the selection of female store managers. However in talking about staff departments, we should not forget that not all departments are equally distant from the store. The Product Development Department is closest to the store's products and customer feedback and seen in terms of its relations with the store, there is close cooperation with the people in charge – those with responsibility for specific product groups. However, there are no close relations with the work organisation inside the store or with store management. Others, such as the Education and Skills Development Departments, which are responsible for producing manuals on store work and implementing decisions on research and training plans, have very close relations with store work. Female Store Manager 10, who spent a long time in this type of staff department (three years of store experience), says that as the 'creation of female store managers' progressed, 'I thought that I would probably become a manager too at some time'. Because of her extremely strong sense of proximity to the store, her work in the Staff Department was to develop and put into practice a skills development programme, which took into account the actual conditions of store work. According to Female Store Manager 10, 'Because I was already doing work closely related to the store I embraced [the opportunity to become a store manager] but normally it is not possible to pick women out of staff departments to become store managers and if one were to try the woman in question would probably say "no". Alternatively, they would probably say, "In that case, I'll leave the company". I do not think that the Personnel Department would take that kind of risk.' Company X's paternalistic stance regarding women has resulted in a narrow approach to the nurturing of female employees and we should see this as having given rise to a tendency for women middle managers to exist comfortably within this situation. The 'creation of female store managers' was a policy designed to break down these limitations and to seek out and nurture talented female employees as the future core middle management cadets.

The status of female store managers: their management styles and careers

Store manager roles and management

The prerequisites for store managers as set out in company documents
How do the careers of female store managers – created as a matter of policy through the 'creation of female store managers', which was itself advanced as a result of the circumstances outlined above – differ from those of male store managers? If we take account of reported comments such as 'they are nothing but ornaments' and 'it will soon all come tumbling down', we can imagine that there are considerable disparities between the two. I will go on to consider these gender differences in the careers of store managers but first let us make clear the duties of store managers. The most critical work responsibility for store managers is listed in Company X's *Store Managers' Manual* as financial responsibility. Central to this is the calculation of sales figures, rough profit estimates and budgets for the store. In this regard, the manual also mentions having responsibility for store policy and sales activity and also running a vibrant store by promoting the training and utilisation of human resources within the store. In addition, store managers, as representatives of Company X in the region, also shoulder the roles of liasing on regional activities and of promoting co-prosperity and harmonious co-existence with tenant stores. In addition to being responsible for merchandising and sales activity, as the person in charge of the store and its management group and as the leader of the employees working in the store, the store manager, in his marketing capacity, is also expected to carry out research activity in

the business area. However, most store managers do not necessarily read this detailed, bulky and nearly 300 pages long *Store Managers' Manual*. According to the interview survey, upon first becoming store managers, there was no room for acting in accordance with this manual. Instead, store managers managed by relying on experience and knowledge, based on their careers to date, and by consulting with those below them. Because the financial responsibility assigned to store managers' work is the prime consideration in staff appraisals and has considerable influence on bonuses, all store managers act with this uppermost in mind.

The five selection criteria for store managers, given in company documents (1999), are: section head experience in the store; one's reputation regarding management skills; merit rating; status grade; and the will of the person concerned to do store manager work, assessed on the basis of a personal statement. There is also a natural assumption that store managers will have sales skills: they are expected to have a thorough knowledge of 'salesmanship' and 'sales floor arrangement'; to be able to carry out customer sales in all parts of the store; and also to know how to compete against rival stores. The main career path is referred to as the 'sales skills dominant type'. This is a promotion model in which one normally becomes store manager by progressing through chief clerk and then section head positions. First one must have experience of being a chief clerk in more than two widely divergent product areas; a level of business achievement that is above standard; and a favourable reputation in the Merchandise Department regarding sales floor arrangement and product knowledge. If all of these criteria are met, then one may be considered a worthy candidate for the position of section head. Furthermore, if one's business achievements as section head are of a high standard, then that person is recommended by the head of Area Operations Division as a candidate for store manager. Store managers who have travelled this career path have been judged to possess sales skills and management ability. In addition to this 'sales skills dominant type', there is another way of becoming a store manager without first having been a section head in the store. This could occur in cases where individuals have been judged to have a high standard of business results as either head of the Staff Department or manager of the Merchandise Department. However, because the sales skills and management abilities of this group are not known, they are required to undertake Off-The-Job study and training. In practice, these cases form a minority and the 'sales skills dominant type' is the main route to the store manager position.

The realities of the store manager role

The roles of store managers, referred to above, vary according to the ranking of a store. Stores are classified on the basis of sales floor area and sales volume, with five gradations separating the lowest and highest ranking stores. New store managers are often assigned to low-ranking stores and they progressively make their way up to higher ranking stores. According to the Personnel Department, there is not necessarily any correlation between degree of management difficulty and store ranking. This is clear from the experience of Male Store Manager 3. He suddenly became a store manager, in a large store, after long years of experience as a full-time labour union official. When he asked the Personnel Department, 'Am I up to being store manager in such a large store?' he was told, 'On the contrary, you would be no good as the manager of a small store. You can do it precisely because it is a large store.' It is possible to be an effective store manager in high-ranking stores, even without business abilities in the area of sales skills, because the section heads in each of the sales sections have a vast reserve of experience and training. In contrast with this, small-scale stores with a low ranking look for 'adroit businessman-type store managers' who have excellent sales skills. As the former head of personnel in the company says, 'store managers of small-scale stores need to be people of ability, with a thorough product knowledge, and who have normally been chief clerks and section heads but the type of management required by large-scale stores is different from this; simply being an "adroit businessman" is not enough'. Qualitatively different management abilities from those of the 'adroit businessmen' are required in large-scale stores.

Male Store Manager 3, as store manager in a large-scale store, was expected to be able to put to use the management skills, which he had built up during his period as chairman of the labour union. Although this type of appointment of new store managers to large-scale stores can occur when people are suddenly selected to become store managers from areas such as the Staff Department or the labour union, these are unusual cases. In most cases in which people progress smoothly to the position of store manager on the basis of accumulated store experience, they start off in a small-scale store and gradually move up to stores of higher ranking. In this sense, small-scale stores are regarded as 'training stores' for new store managers. Small-scale stores are also assigned the same status with regard to new chief clerks and new section heads and, given this, there is a greater need for 'businessman' leadership ability in these stores.

The basic daily work duties of the store manager are understanding the sales policy each week at weekly store manager meetings; passing this on to the section heads and chief clerks and putting it into practice in a manner corresponding to the actual conditions of the store; and, ultimately, achieving numerical targets whilst keeping a watch over the sales process. Those responsible for putting policies into practice (in practical terms, displaying promotional sales goods, changing the number of shelves and other similar aspects of sales floor layout) are the chief clerks posted to the various product groups. As mentioned also in the previous chapter, chief clerks, whilst respecting the decisions of section heads – their direct superiors – implement policies by spurring on general rank-and-file employees and part-time employees. I will come back to this again later but, once regular employees have been assigned to a specific department within the store, such as food or clothing, they then move around the department or the store, basically along the lines of the initial assignment. Usually these moves are limited to within the section. Consequently, chief clerks are well informed about the products in each area and each day's business basically progresses along the section head-chief clerk line. 'Wandering around (*hottsuki aruku*) the store during the day' (Male Store Manager 7) while looking out over the whole store, is an important part of the store manager's work. Both male and female store managers are allocated one working hour per day for this 'wandering around'.

According to an interview survey (1999) of store managers in one particular Area Operations Division, a store manager's daily work time is divided up as per Table 5.4. That is, 50.7 per cent of time is spent on the sales floor, where the store manager gives instructions to employees, engages in selling, or carries out checks of each area. For 34.5 per cent of the time the store manager is in the store office in meetings or checking data and preparing documents. The remaining 11.7 per cent is devoted to surveys of rival stores and outside negotiations. When we look at the answers to questions about 'your ideal use of time as a store manager' in this same table, we see that the respondents wished to decrease their work in the office and increase substantially time spent on the sales floor and in outside negotiations. I have heard it said that in the past some store managers stayed trapped in their offices but, their numerical results were unsatisfactory and the company has come to realise that it is precisely 'wandering around' the store which is important in the role of store manager.

Table 5.4: *Breakdown of daily work hours of store managers (Area C Operations Department)*

Work content	Actual (%)	Ideal (%)
1. On the sales floor		
Giving instructions to employees	17.8	21.6
Devoting oneself to sales	14.3	12.9
Conducting checks of the shop floor (includes communicating with tenant stores)	18.6	21.4
Sub-total	50.7	55.9
2. In the store office		
Meetings	12.5	10.4
Checking and analysing sales data	10.1	8.8
Preparing various documents	11.9	6.8
Sub-total	34.5	26.0
3. Outside the store		
Surveys of rival stores	5.8	7.3
Negotiations with the region	2.7	4.5
External negotiations	3.2	3.7
Sub-total	11.7	15.5
4. Other		
Store manager conferences, dealing with complaints	3.1	2.6

Source: Internal company documents (1999)

The benefits of 'wandering around'

At the time when Honda Kazunari carried out his research survey into the development of human resources in chain stores, he emphasised 'dealing with change' and 'dealing with the extraordinary' – two approaches thrown up by research into careers in manufacturing industry. Honda lists the skills of store managers in the following way. 'Dealing with change' is making decisions, in keeping with the special characteristics of any particular store, on modifying shelf divisions and lowering prices. In relation to 'dealing with the extraordinary', Honda mentions countermeasures aimed at rival stores, responding to unforeseen bad conditions in the distribution of goods and dealing appropriately with claims from customers and suppliers (Honda, 2002: 11–12). I continue to have doubts regarding the question of whether manufacturing work and store work in supermarkets can be analysed from the same angle. Retail research in Europe, regards ready recourse to the manufacturing model as, at the very least, doubtful and is striving to find a research method based on the difficulty of estimating consumer buying activity in retail industry, for use in comparisons with manufacturing industry (Dawson, 1999a; 1999b). Even viewed from the realities of the store manager's role, which have emerged from the interview surveys in this book, this can be seen as too superficial, if only in terms of understanding the capacity to respond to 'changes' and the 'extraordinary' and the knowledge and skills which make this possible. To begin with, store work has a character which is significantly influenced by factors such as the weather, the actions of rival stores and the holding of events in the area. Responding to the realities of 'change' and the 'extraordinary' must itself be seen as the very stuff of everyday work in the store. The capacity to respond in this type of remarkably changing environment is consequently not something confined solely to the store manager. It exists not merely in the section heads and chief clerks but also in the accumulated capacity to respond amongst rank-and-file regular employees and part timers. It is naturally the store manager who bears the responsibility for making the final decision in times of crisis but how to draw out of one's subordinates the ability to respond rapidly to semi-normalised change whilst getting on with daily business, is the most critical aspect of management. Precisely for this reason, we ought not to overlook the importance of close communication abilities with subordinates. It is in practising store management that 'wandering around' is valuable.

Male Store Manager 7, who used the term 'wandering around', elaborated, 'It is extremely important to chat with part time and casual workers while wandering around the store. Part-time employees, in particular, by virtue of being local residents are also important sources of local information. When a store manager chats with part-time employees, there is a very real impact on sales.' It becomes possible, he says, to gain hints about the arrangement of products by seizing on the strong reactions to products by customers in the area around the store. But that is not all, by talking to general rank-and-file employees and part timers the store manager has a direct impact on creating a spirit of 'let's sell' in them. 'Because the store manager is a unique presence in the store – in a sense a star – sales increase to a surprising extent when he talks to them [rank-and-file regular employees and part timers]. This is because simply having been able to talk to the store manager brings out a will to work and because when [a store manager] listens carefully to the intentions and requests of part-time employees, these provide feedback, which can lead an even greater sense of wanting to work.' In this respect, wandering around the store is extremely important for store managers. The communication that occurs in the course of 'wandering around' is linked to awakening, in those at the very bottom of the store, a work attitude of attempting to exercise their ingenuity, from a customer's perspective. This results from the 'wandering around' talks awakening in them a sense that they are not simply 'workers', but rather 'the very people responsible for sales'.

As might be expected, this role of store managers varies according to the status and scale of the store. In large-scale stores, the store manager while 'wandering around' checks on the section head-chief clerk lines within the section and area and, where necessary, makes appropriate corrections to these. Moreover, this chatting with people at the bottom of the store makes smooth management – the patching up of gaps – possible. In the case of store managers in small-scale stores, while 'wandering around' they can, in an appropriate way, give practical leadership and hints on smooth business practice regarding sales methods and sales floor layout, on floors which they feel are experiencing problems. Also, by stepping in and helping out with work which is running behind or by giving practical directions for any delays, it is possible for the store manager to create a sense of the existence of a leader who 'works with others'.

The resistance of those at the bottom of the store to the 'direct communication' that went on during the 'wandering around' of the store manager in Store A, Company X, cited in Chapter 4, must be seen as arising from the fact that Store A is a large-scale store. That is to say, the resistance of the women was directed at the fact that despite the premise that section head-chief clerk lines in large-scale stores are relatively securely constructed, the store manager overstepped these lines and personally issued detailed instructions to rank-and-file regular employees and part timers. As mentioned previously, the true motive of the store manager in Store A was that he felt that there were problems with the management abilities of one section head and that is why he adopted this approach but, this was not understood by the 'us' group at the bottom of the store in Chapter 4 and the result was simply one of resistance. The communication that arises as a result of 'wandering around' primarily provides opportunities to encourage a 'will to work' rather than 'resistance' and it was in failing to do this that the 'direct communication' of the store manager in Store A was not a success.

The importance of aligned vectors
The head of the Food Department in the Merchandise Department of Head Office, mentioned before, also turns his attention to this 'will to

act' on the part of those at the bottom of the store. He points out that Company X was characterised by high levels of personal discretion on the work site because the operations set up is not sufficiently built up yet (1999). As a result of this, 'the will to act on the part of those at the bottom of the store, particularly chief clerks and part timers, is very influential'. He gives the example of the tofu counter, where the part timers who bring out the product attempt to sell off the lot and by shouting out 'this tofu is excellent' to customers they can sell out. This is because not all customers set off for the supermarket having already planned their menus. Individual sales attitudes, born of a united will to 'sell out', are important. When the store manager-section head-chief clerk vectors are aligned, then their intentions are conveyed to those at the bottom as well. He says that, 'when these slip out of place, discord arises and stagnation follows'. As mentioned earlier, chief clerks, in particular, are proficient in the selling of specific groups of products in the department and they usually have no superior to whom they can turn for advice on these matters in the store. Consequently, there is a tendency to respect staff in the Merchandise Department as seniors who can be relied on. In recognition of this point, store managers are seeking 'an alignment of vectors', which encompasses section heads.

According, again, to the head of the Food Department in the Merchandise Department of a certain Area Operations Division, the 'strength of a store', fundamentally, lies in the head of the sales section gathering together the chief clerks and holding meetings; stating accurately 'which are the priority products and how many should be sold'; and then chief clerks passing this on down to part timers (2001). In other words, he sees the factors which determine the 'strength of a store' as being clear instructions from the section head based on a sales plan; chief clerks putting forth schemes adapted to the product group for which they are responsible, while following the section head's instructions; and, furthermore, drawing on the abilities of part timers. This situation in which the section head-chief clerk line vector and the store manager are aligned in the same direction is the ideal.

As we can gather from the above indications, the store manager plays an extremely large role in the store's sales. The store manager is the linchpin in communications inside the organisation. This is particularly the case in terms of developing a united will in the management line and then making this reach down to those at the bottom of the store and also of drawing out the 'will to act' in those who work at the very bottom of the store through 'wandering around'.

The management styles of store managers

There are, however, differences in the management styles of store managers. The differences in style which I am discussing here are those found amongst male store managers. This is because, owing to the passage of only a short time since the appearance of female store managers, discussions during the interviews were entirely about management differences between male store managers. According to the head of the Food Department of the Merchandise Department in Head Office quoted above, there are various types of store managers, with the worst being the 'controlling type'. He gives the example of the type who places stringent demands, regarding matters such as cost cutting and thorough cleaning, on his subordinates and says that he is unlikely to be, 'the type who is capable of stirring up enthusiasm for selling whatever the circumstances'. This is because tying up one's subordinates on small points cannot produce any 'enthusiasm from below'. At the opposite pole from this 'controlling type' is the 'over-zealous' type. This type issues orders haphazardly and promotes selling uncompromisingly. This same head of the Food Department points out that, 'unintelligent enthusiasm is extremely dangerous and that this type causes confusion on the work site through decisions not based in reality. The ability to test hypotheses based on fact is an indispensable quality for store managers. Their capacity, simultaneously, to communicate in such a way as to align vectors with their subordinates is also important.'

Other interviewees, although expressing it in different ways, also pointed out the same thing. The head of the Food Department mentioned above, says that whilst there are various types of store managers, the majority belong to the 'on the offensive type'. He says that this type 'thinks only of sales at all times' and is skilled at financial management. In addition to this form of 'on the offensive' management, 'store manager types vary widely according to whether they really nurture their subordinates or not'. That is to say, it is entirely natural for store managers to make financial achievements their prime consideration. However, they are classified into types on the basis of the methods they use in the attempt to realise this end – whether or not they can pursue this end in a manner balanced with the need to nurture the talents of subordinates.

The head of the Personnel Department in one particular Area Operations Division, who views this from precisely this same point of view, says that store managers can be classified according to 'whether they are or are not interested in and concerned about their employees' (2001). What the Personnel Department considers to be a 'good store manager' is 'a store manager who takes an interest in his individual subordinates and is enthusiastic about nurturing their talents'. At the opposite pole from this 'is the store manager who is not interested in his subordinates and who, by exercising close supervision over them and through 'over-zealous management', tries to make everything redound to his credit in a short time'. Because the latter lacks the perspective of nurturing subordinates, this type shows not the least interest in taking capable subordinates under the wing or in the career development of subordinates. According to this interviewee, there are few of this latter type amongst store managers in large-scale stores. This is because those who have risen up to the level of store manager in large-scale stores are people who know that one cannot get on through this latter type of behaviour alone. He says that the 'over-zealous' type attempts to make his subordinates work hard to fulfil his unreasonable demands but that if he works them relentlessly in this way, the strain will continue to build up in his subordinates and will eventually be reflected in the sales figures.

As seen above, the management styles of store managers can be classified from precisely the same perspective whether one is in the Merchandise Department or the Personnel Department. The points separating store managers are the presence or absence of 'an interest in subordinates', a perspective on 'the nurturing of subordinates' and a calm decision-making capacity. Uncompromising 'over-zealous' types and types who are merely concerned with their own feats, are regarded as not likely to last long-term, even though they may improve their results temporarily.

As mentioned previously, what is particularly important amongst the duties of store managers is achieving numerical targets but we can appreciate that there are differences in the management styles employed to this end. Even though it may have been possible to achieve the figures by making unreasonable demands on the people working in a store for a short period of time, this can by no means continue in the long term. It is important that both the Personnel Department and Products Department recognise this. The qualities sought in store managers are the ability to communicate appropriately with the people at the very bottom of the store and also a calm decision-making capacity, which takes into account the nurturing of subordinates. However, according to the head of the Personnel Department mentioned before from one particular Area Operations Division, whether one is a store manager devoted to 'being on the offensive' or, alternatively, the 'over-zealous' type of store manager depends on the actual personal cases of success experienced by these store managers in the course of their own career development. Store managers who have built up personal experiences of success under 'offensive' type superiors will inevitably, he argues, be apt to employ the same type of management. Put another way, there is also the fact that they know only this type of one-pattern management style. We may say that the point of divergence in management styles lies in the issue of how a store manager himself was nurtured and under what kind of superior.

The gender differences evident in the career development of store managers

The special characteristics of the careers of store managers

In reality, what is the appropriate career development path to equip one for the store manager duties described above? According to the head of the Personnel Department in Head Office (1998), the experience gained by moving between Head Office and the store has come to be seen as the most desirable path and has been the mainstream approach hitherto. The second path has been to become a specialist assigned to the staff and the third path is to join the company halfway through one's career and be assigned to the Staff Department as a specialist. This third pattern would, for example, see someone join the Merchandise Department from a maker of household electrical goods and then be nurtured as a buyer. With the exception of those who have joined the company halfway through – and in keeping with the 'most ideal' career development described by the head of the Personnel Department – practically all new employees are initially assigned to the store. As we shall see later, most store managers possess the experience of having moved between the store and posts outside the store.

Let us look then at the actual process of development of a store manager's career. Table 5.5 records the presence or absence of experience outside the store for those in store manager positions in May 2002, by year of entry. Those joining the company halfway through have been excluded.[2] Out of a total of 199 new graduate (all university graduates) employees, those without any experience outside the store, in either Area Operations Divisions or Head Office, are limited to a mere 30 (15.1 per cent). As suggested by the comments of the Head of the Personnel Department in Head Office, quoted above, close to 70 per cent of people have had experience outside the store

Gender and Japanese Management

Figure 5.1: In-store careers of store managers by year of entry into the company (183 people)

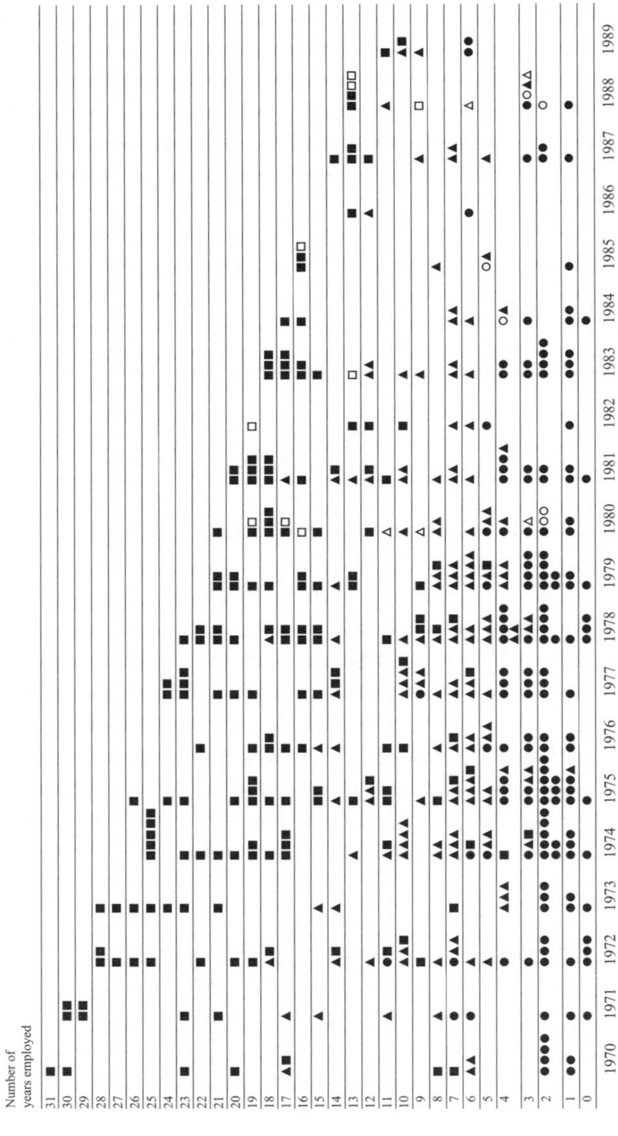

Notes: 1. Symbols are not necessarily of equal value as the year of promotion is unknown in some cases.
2. Cases of demotion to Department Manager and also of joining the company halfway through one's career are not included.

Source: Internal company documents

before becoming store managers. Due to the severe personnel changes – resembling the scattering of billiard balls – which accompanied the previously mentioned opening up of new stores and the scrapping of old ones by chain stores, most regular employees, if they are not on the 'store specific path', keep moving around the store once every two to three years. At the shortest, there is even a case of this happening after less than one year. Also, those with some experience outside the store before becoming store managers numbered 40 (69.0 per cent) in the case of people joining the company in the first half of the 1970s and 52 (64.2 per cent) in the second half of the 1970s but went on to reach 34 (79.1 per cent) in the first half of the 1980s. Because there are still very few employees who joined the company from the second half of the 1980s on who have become store managers, I will leave this discussion here. It is, however, at least clear that there is a growth in the number of those following the 'most ideal' path of career development amongst those joining the company in the first half of the 1980s compared to those who joined in the 1970s. If we turn our attention to this point, it is possible to see that since the middle of the 1990s, when those joining the company in the 1980s started becoming store managers, there has been a move towards a situation conducive to this 'desirable' pattern.

Figure 5.1 has been compiled from internal company documents, using the promotion records of those who became store mangers in 2002.[3] I describe the in-store careers of 183 people, omitting those who joined the company halfway through and also those whose details are uncertain. According to these figures there are considerable disparities between individuals regarding the number of years of service required to become a store manager in any given year. There is a case of someone having been promoted to chief clerk within a year of joining the company but there are also cases of this having taken six to seven years. The situation is similar regarding store managers – whilst some who joined the company in the first half of the 1970s were appointed as store managers after three to four and six to seven years, one appointment occurred after around 30 years. These disparities occur because in the past a great variety of stores existed side-by-side, separated by considerable differences in scale and ranking. Although we are now at a stage where the scale of stores has been standardised to a certain extent as a result of the scrapping and rebuilding of stores, there is still a considerable difference between ultra-small and ultra-large stores. Nevertheless, taken as a trend, the disparities between individuals regarding the number of years of

Table 5.5: *Store managers' experience outside the store*

Year of entry into company	Experience outside the store			Total
	None	Some		
		Pre-store manager	Post-store manager	
1970–1974	6	40	12	58
1975–1979	12	52 (3)	17	81
1980–1984	7	34	2 (1)	43
1985–1989	7	11	1	17
Total	30	137	32	199

Source: Internal company documents.
Note: numbers in ( ) indicate full-time union officials.

Table 5.6: *Number of years taken to reach each occupational position, by store managers' years of entry*

Year of entry	Chief clerk	Section head	Store manager
1970–1974	2.3	9.2	20.4
1975–1979	2.5	7.4	16.1
1980–1984	2.3	7.8	16.6
1985–1989	2.9	7.0	12.8
Total	2.4	7.9	17.2

Source: Internal company documents.

service required to become a store manager were considerable amongst those joining the company in the 1970s: displaying a widening of the gap between the speediest and the slowest cases of promotion to store manager. However, when we look at those joining the company in the first half of the 1980s, we detect a tendency towards a considerable reduction in these individual differences.

Furthermore, Figure 5.1 is clearly uneven and reveals that, in general, the length of service required to become a store manager is decreasing with the years. In order to verify this, let us look at the average length of service that it takes to become a chief clerk, section head and store manager, as given by year of entry in Table 5.6. According to this, the average length of service required to become a chief clerk does not vary greatly over the decades; the figure is two years. However, when we compare the situation for section heads and store managers joining the company in the first and second halves of the 1970s, we detect a declining trend. Compared with the situation for those who joined in the first half of the 1970s, when it took 9.2 years to become a section head and 20.4 years to become a store manager, since the second half of the 1970s the number of years required to become a section head has fallen by over a year and for store managers by more than three years. We can cite the increase in the number of stores as a factor influencing this shortened cultivation period. As we can see from Figure 5.2, the number of new stores has increased rapidly since 1992 and this has resulted in a corresponding attempt to speed up the creation of store managers. We can see the early cultivation of talented individuals who could become section heads and store managers as being pursued towards this end. According to the Personnel Department, in the second half of the 1990s one needs to have a career spanning at least seventeen years in order to become the store manager of a large-scale store. This might be achievable in just fifteen years for a 'vigorous, outstanding talent'. If we consider that those joining the company in the first half of the 1970s needed to have worked there for an average of 20.4 years in order to become a new store manager, then we can clearly see that the number of years required to become a store manager of a large-scale store, for which one is supposed to have first had experience in a small-scale store, has fallen. However, we must take note of the fact that, even in these cases, there has not necessarily been any decrease in the number of years needed to become a chief clerk. We need to acknowledge that even in the midst of a period of rapid store creation, the decrease in

Figure 5.2: Changes in the number of stores (Company X)

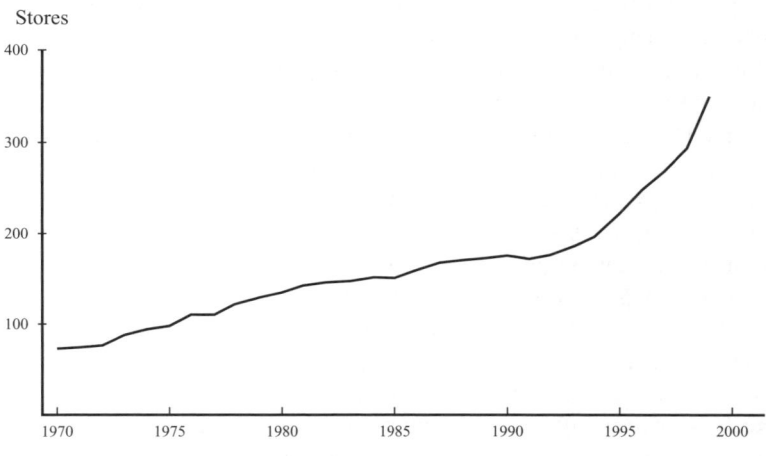

Source: Internal company documents

the set number of years required for the cultivation of chief clerks, who occupy an important position over and above being the foundation on which sales floors are built, has been modest.

We must first acknowledge that the individual differences in career development are, as above, still as large as in the past. This is because it is an extremely difficult task to create a standard promotion route amidst the process of tremendous personnel changes brought about in response to the scrapping and building of stores. Even so, we detect a tendency towards the reduction of individual differences for those who joined the company in the 1980s, as they all head towards fast-track promotion to section head and store manager.

Gender differences in store manager careers – The case of employees who joined in the 1980s

How then should we understand the gender differences in store managers' careers? Were female store managers' careers quite a strain when it came to store manager work, as was anticipated in strong criticisms such as, 'you are merely ornaments' and 'it will all soon come tumbling down'? As is clear from Figure 5.1, mentioned above, the first female store manager to be appointed was from the 1980s intake of employees and female store managers have continued to appear in steady succession since that time. Let us look now at the career details, up until the store manager level, of three 'first generation' female store managers produced from the 1980 intake of employees. Table 5.7 sets out the career development of eight employees from the 1980 intake who had become store managers as of May 2002, excluding cases where these details were uncertain. When we look at the length of service at the time of becoming a store manager, we can see that women certainly took on store manager work rather early: Female Store Manager A after sixteen and a half years, B eighteen years and C seventeen and a half years. Male store managers took 21 and a half years at the longest (E) and sixteen and a half years at he shortest (G). In this sense it may be argued that this reflects the fact that female store managers were consciously promoted early through senior management's policy of 'creating female store managers'.

However, if we look carefully at the career details, then we realise that we cannot necessarily say that this is all there was to it. Firstly, in the case of male store managers, compared with G and H, who have accumulated mainly in-store experience, D, E and F have as much as eight and a half to eleven and a half years of experience outside the store. However, both became chief clerks after starting with experience inside the store. Also, if D is excluded, then both were promoted to store manager after gaining experience outside the store and becoming section heads. In D's case, after having reached the level of section head, he then affiliated himself with the Financial Control Department and the Merchandise Department over an eleven and a half year period, after which he became a store manager. Even D is similar to the other male store managers in that he has become a store manager after copious experience as a section head in the store.

Comparing this with female store managers, B could be seen as quite peculiar in her lack of experience as a chief clerk but neither A or C display any significant departure from the male store manager career: they both have had the usual chief clerk and section head experience and, furthermore, have come back to the store after two to two and a half years' experience outside the store. Female Store Manager B, was assigned to office work as a secretary in the Operations Department immediately after graduating from college and has not had the store experience normally expected of new employees in Company X. However, as secretarial work was not so busy she sometimes undertook sales promotion work in the Merchandise Department, becoming a clothing buyer with her formal move to this department in her sixth year of employment. Following this she became a section head after one and a half years in her first store assignment and without ever having been a chief clerk. She had an irregular posting when she first joined the company but we cannot necessarily say that her career development was far removed from that of male store managers given that she became a store manager after seven and a half years' experience as a section head in the store.

There are many kinds of section head in the store, not simply head of the Sales Department – there are also heads of departments not directly connected with sales such as General Affairs and Customer Service. Female Store Manager C only has experience as a section head in Customer Service and Male Store Manager D only in the General Affairs Department but all the other store managers have been section heads in the Sales Department. If, in the interests of checking, we pick out those with experience as section head in the Sales Department from amongst the people who became store managers in 2002, we end up with the results in Table 5.8. The overwhelming majority (83.3 per cent) of men have abundant experience as head of the Sales Department. Amongst the women, three out of five cases have considerable experience as head of the Sales Department and the remaining two have none.

Table 5.7: Career development of store managers (8 cases taken from the 1980 intake into the company)

Female A		**Female B**		**Female C***		**Male D***		**Male E**		**Male F**		**Male G**		**Male H**	
Store 1	½ year	*Out of store 1*	1½ years	*Store 1*	1½ years	*Store 1*	1 year	*Store 1*	3 years	*Store 1*	1 year	*Store 1*	1½ years	*Store 1*	½ year
Store 2	1½ years	*Out of store 2*	½ year	*Store 2* Chief clerk	3½ years	*Store 2* Chief clerk	1½ years	*Store 2* Chief clerk	1½ years	*Store 2*	1 year	*Store 2* Chief clerk	1½ years	*Store 2*	1 year
Store 2 Chief clerk	1½ years	*Out of store 1*	2½ years	*Store 3* Chief clerk	2 years	*Store 3* Chief clerk	½ year	*Out of store 1*	5 years	*Store 3*	3 years	*Store 1* Chief clerk	2½ years	*Store 3*	2½ years
Store 2 Section head	2 years	*Out of store 3*	½ year	*Store 4* Chief clerk	1 year	*Store 4* Chief clerk	1 year	*Out of store 2*	3½ years	*Store 4* Chief clerk	1 year	*Out of store 1*	4 years	*Store 4* Chief clerk	½ year
Out of store 1	2½ years	*Out of store 4*	4 years	*Store 4* Section head	½ year	*Store 5* Section head	1½ years	*Store 3* Section head	2 years	*Store 5* Section head	2½ years	*Store 3* Section head	1 year	*Store 5* Chief clerk	3 years
Store 2 Section head	5 years	*Store 1*	1½ years	*Store 5* Deputy Section head	1 year	*Out of store 1*	1 year	*Store 4* Section head	2 years	*Out of store*	9 years	*Store 4* Section head	4½ years	*Store 6* Section head	4 years
Out of store 1	2½ years	*Store 1* Section head	2½ years	*Store 5* Chief clerk	2 years	*Out of store 2*	1½ years	*Store 5* Section head	2 years	*Store 6* Section head	1½ years	*Store 5* Section head	1½ years	*Store 7* Section head	2 years
Store 3 Section head	1 year	*Store 2* Section head	½ year	*Out of store 1*	2 years	*Out of store 3*	3½ years	*Store 6* Section head	2½ years	*Store 8* Store manager	1½ years	*Store 6* Store manager	2 years	*Out of store 1*	1 year
Store 4 Store manager	3 years	*Store 3* Section head	4½ years	*Store 6* Chief clerk	3 years	*Out of store 4*	5½ years	*Store 7* Store manager	1 year	*Store 9* Store manager	2 years	*Store 7* Store manager	3 years	*Store 8* Section head	½ year
Store 2 Store manager	4 years	*Store 4* Store manager	3 years	*Store 6* Section head	1 year	*Store 4* Store manager	3½ years							*Store 9* Section head	2 years
				Store 7 Store manager	3 years	*Store 6* Store manager	½ year							*Store 10* Store manager	1½ years
				Store 1 Store manager	2 years									*Store 11* Store manager	2½ years
	(16.5)		(18)		(17.5)		(17)		(21.5)		(19)		(16.5)		(17)

Source: Internal company documents.

Notes: ( ) indicates length of service upon first becoming store manager. * denotes those cases without experience as Section Heads in sales. I have adjusted the number of months of experience. I have not recorded the managerial positions held outside the stores because these differ from those in the stores. The numbers (for example,1 2 3) following Store or Out of store, are used to show the individuals' moves between stores. The relationship to the Case numbers used in Table 5.1 are A: Case 2, B: Case 4, C: Case 3.

Table 5.8: Presence or absence of section head experience in sales

	Males		Females
Some	120	(83.3%)	3
None	24	(16.7%)	2
Total	144	(100.0%)	5

Source: Internal company documents. Unclear cases excluded.
Those listed under 'None' were, for example, Section heads of General Affairs and Customer Service.

This may be seen as resulting from the frequency with which women are selected for section head jobs, in the area of customer service, in acknowledgement of the preponderance of female customers. Possibly, this is the reason why women differ from the mainstream 'sales skills dominant pattern' and why, compared with men, they tend more often to become store managers with no experience as head of the Sales Department. There are certainly differences on this point but we cannot presume that women's careers are completely different from those of their contemporary male store managers. Two of the three female store managers from the 1980 intake of employees actually have experience as head of the Sales Department.

The tendency for women to remain at the same status grade
Next, let us examine Figure 5.3 and the process of increases in status, based on rank in the status ranking system, of the eight store managers referred to above, who joined the company in 1980. As mentioned briefly with reference to Figure 4.1 in Chapter 4, university graduates can generally expect to be able to reach Grade 4 but promotion to Grade 5 and above is dependent on the results of personnel assessments by superiors and on passing exams. In short, the motivation to be promoted, which depends on appraisals by superiors, and the results of exams taken by the individuals concerned must all be favourable.

In Figure 5.3 we see that the rise in rank to Grade 5 on the part of Female Store Manager A was more rapid than that of any of her male peers from the same intake group. However, she remained at Grade 6 for as long as twelve years and was considerably outstripped by the male store managers when she eventually moved on from that position. According to the interview survey, this period was, in fact, one when she also had and raised two children. Female Store Manager B took the longest to reach Grade 4 but she then also spent twelve whole years on Grade 5. This occurred primarily as a result of the peculiarity of

Figure 5.3: Store manager promotions (8 cases who joined the company in 1980)

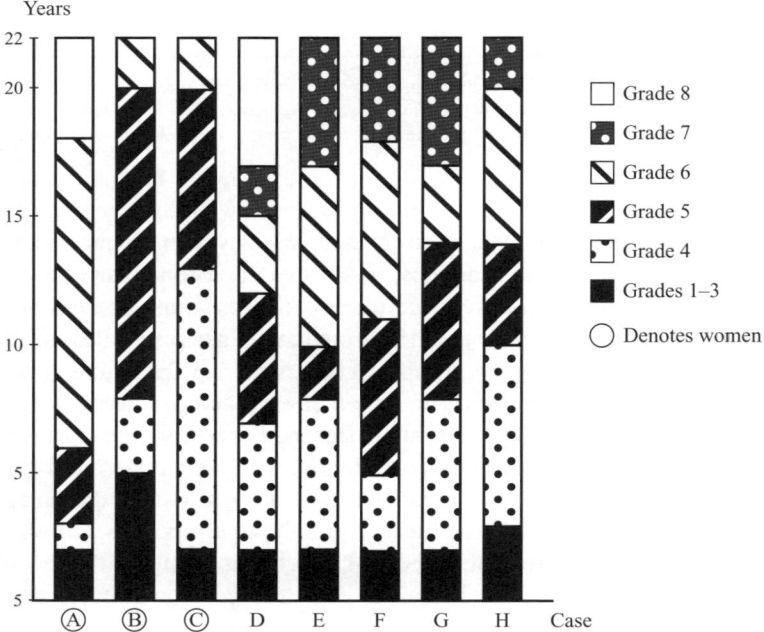

Source: Internal company documents. There are slight discrepancies with current occupational ranks (Table 4.1) because of changes to the system.

the post to which she was assigned at the beginning of her career, as discussed previously, and the changes in status which followed from this – her unique career building process. That is not all, however, as in this period she also had and cared for two children. Female Store Manager C has, as we saw earlier, a background in store work, which is in no way inferior to those of male store managers, but a look at her status grade reveals that she spent a longer period than anyone else at Grade 4. This is because although she reached Grade 4 comparatively early – at a speed comparable with men – it was difficult for her to want to put up her hand to move beyond Grade 4 and on to Grade 5. According to Female Store Manager C, the 1980s 'were a period in which women quit work after three years' and she says that in this environment she also began experiencing endless worries at work about resisting transfers. However, at the time of the second round of personnel changes for chief clerks her superior kindly told her, 'you are the only one I would consider' and with that she decided to make a positive attempt at developing her career.

As we can appreciate from these three cases, they paint a picture of female regular employees sometimes following a pattern different from that of male employees, right from their initial posting. These women themselves tend not to attempt to improve their status grade and those around them accept this, giving rise to a tendency for them to spend comparatively longer than is the case for men at the one same grade in the status ranking system. Two of the cases cited above have also included childbirth and child rearing in this period. However, as we see from the case of Female Store Manager C, even when there are none of the practical career limitations imposed by child rearing, both the woman concerned and her superior held back from any increases in rank. If we take note of this point, then we see the need for caution in interpreting these women's periods of not moving beyond their current level by simply relating this to childbirth and child rearing. Why then have they had to spend relatively long periods of time at the one grade? We can probably think of this as being bound up with the circumstances of the era in which it was widely held that 'female employees are going to quit after three years'. We can speculate that in this context, even when there were female employees who had gradually accumulated four or five years of service, those around them probably thought, 'they will be quitting anytime now'. Because of this, women have not stood out in any conspicuous manner or challenged themselves by enthusiastically attempting exams with the result that women's movement up the status grades has tended to stagnate. This is attributable to the widespread nature of practices encouraging male superiors to 'think' that there is no need to challenge their female subordinates to achieve higher status grades and managerial positions.[4]

Female Store Manager A, looking back on the twelve years that she spent on Grade 6, waiting to move up to Grade 7, says, 'it was a period in which I was unhappily marking time, while being steadily overtaken by the men'. Female university graduates were dissatisfied with the treatment of women in Company A and they quit the workplace one by one. Witnessing the fate of these female university graduates she was seized with anxieties such as, 'I have not been to even one of my child's sports days. Is this career worth having gone so far as to sacrifice my family, even having my parents look after my child for me?' When we turn our attention to issues of this type, then the interpretation of the tendency for women to stay at one grade as 'a problem inextricably linked with home duties and child rearing' appears one-dimensional. We also ought not to overlook the aspect that this interpretation lacks a woman's view regarding whether women can be put to positive use inside this organisation and whether it is an organisation in which women can perform valuable work. This, as will be analysed in detail later, is closely bound up with the problems of an androcentric organisational culture.

However, even though we can discern a tendency for women to stay at the one grade, what we must acknowledge here is the fact that, as we saw previously, these three women, who joined the company in 1980, have not had a store career which is vastly different from that of their male peers. Viewed from this perspective, we can see that there is no basis to remarks such as 'This is merely ornamentation' and 'it will all soon come tumbling down'. Instead, we can think of this chilly reception as perhaps having been based on the belief that 'it is not to be expected that female employees have been nurtured in ways which make them capable of store manager work'. It is a grim historical fact that in Company X the practice of superiors, in reality, excluding women from 'consideration' as candidates for the nurturing of 'talented people' has continued, as has the view that store manager work is the monopoly of men. This situation has spurred on the impression that the careers of men and women who have been promoted to the store manager level are decidedly different and has also created an atmosphere in which senior management's 'creation of female store managers' policy was viewed as an unnecessarily risky venture.

'Just ornamentation?'

In comparisons such as the above we do not see any sizeable gaps in the careers of the men and women from the 1980 intake who became store managers. Looking at the careers of the 'first generation' of store managers, we see that most of them, with the odd exception, had over ten years of solid store experience, as per Table 5.1. Only Female Store Manager 6, with eleven years' experience as a buyer in the Merchandise Department, had extremely short store experience of three years. Furthermore, Female Store Manager 9, with only seven years of store experience, is a rare case in that she became a store manager in her ninth year after having joined the company halfway through her career. There is no other case of this type to be found amongst either male or female store managers. For two of her nine years with the company she worked in the Personnel Department. For the remaining seven years, she was assigned to the store, becoming a chief clerk and section head within an extremely short period of time. This was a case of fast track promotion, in acknowledgement of her real abilities, before the advent of the 'creation of female store managers' policy. Consequently, with the exception of the lengthy experience of Female Store Manager 6 in the Merchandise Department, all the other cases of female store managers have experience as section heads in stores. These types of exceptional cases also certainly exist when we look at male store managers (Table 5.2); there is Male Store Manager 4 without any store experience at all and Male Store Manager 3 who abruptly became a store manager, with only three years of store experience, after specialising in the union. Also, of the eight cases of male store managers, excluding these particular cases, there are four who fall short of ten years of store experience. We certainly cannot regard only female store managers as being short on years of store experience.

Consequently, we can by no means say that the 'first generation' of female store managers experienced radically divergent career development from that of male store managers. Nevertheless, just as male store managers continued repeatedly whispering to women, at the time of their appointments, 'This is just ornamentation' and 'it will all soon come tumbling down', there were certainly also women amongst the female store managers themselves, and I will refer to this later, who felt that 'I became a store manager because I am a woman'. Those who had spent a relatively long part of their store experience as section heads took up store manager work positively. Female Store Manager 1 says, 'I decided to take it on, without hesitation, because I had built up considerable experience and it was a natural step at my age, and also because of the growth of a sense of being a role model serving to encourage the appearance of more striving women'. Female Store Manager 2 had consciously built up her career in the store with a view to becoming a store manager and felt no 'hesitation'. Female Store Manager 5 says, 'I felt very honoured when I heard the unofficial announcement. I thought that I had to do my best in order to forge a path for those [women] coming after me who might aspire [to be store managers].' Female Store Manager 3 states, 'I was not at all confident but I thought that I would try it out for the time being and that I would quit if it did not work out. What is more, I thought that if I was no good at it, then the company which had selected me was also no good.' We can infer a positive stance from these statements.

However, notwithstanding the deficiencies in their careers as store managers which resulted from the 'creation of female store managers' policy, there were also some women with a self-awareness of having gained the store manager's position early. Female Store Manager 7, with thirteen years store experience after having joined the company halfway through her career, says, 'Given that there were people (men) who had been section heads in sales for longer than I had and were still not store managers, I am aware of the fact that the reason why only I became a store manager early is because I am a woman.' Female Store Manager 6, with only three years of store experience, was called in by the head of the Personnel Department at Head Office and told, 'We will work with you in all regards. We are all going to back you up'. She felt that, 'This sort of thing happened, despite their being many men who were more suitable than I, because of the senior ranks' policy of creating female store managers. It is inconceivable that a male store manager would be called to Head Office and encouraged in the way that I was.' Female Store Manager 4 (nine years in the store) who, after her initial irregular posting, has had experience both in the Merchandise Department and the store, says, 'when I was the Head of the Sales Department in a store, I received a written appointment to the position of store manager. It came from nowhere. [Becoming a store manager] had not been part of my own career plan so everything went black and I said to my superior, "Please overturn that order." But in the end I thought that I could quit anytime.' Female Store Manager 9 received her written appointment as store manager in her ninth year with the company and when her superior whispered the news in her ear, she said, 'I have decided to resign'. She says, 'the company's policy of forcibly creating female store managers, even when [the person concerned had] no real ability, was too blatant. While men made it [to store manager] after spending 20 years making their way through a fierce battle zone, I was a mere novice. As I was told that company policy could not be recalled, in the end I took it on defiantly.' Female Store Manager 10, belonging to the 'second generation' and with three years of store experience, says 'I became a store manager because I wore a skirt.'

As we see above, women who had managed career development comparable with that of male store managers felt 'honoured' and displayed a positive attitude. However, in cases where women had followed a comparatively unusual career pattern they had a strong sense of 'I was nominated to be a store manager under the ['creating female store managers'] policy because I am a woman'.

As mentioned previously, there are cases of male store managers, albeit rarely, becoming store managers despite only short periods of store experience. The women's experience should have been the same as that of these male store managers but when these men were selected as store managers, they were not told that they were 'nothing but ornaments'. We can also see female store managers' responses of 'I became a store manager because I am a woman' as resulting from these women themselves becoming caught up in the understanding inside Company X that in spite of everything store manager work naturally belongs to men. As seen previously, all male store managers, individually, have achieved widely divergent career development without attaching any particular importance to this individuality: the image that '[male] store managers are proficient in sales skills' permeated the whole of Company X. Consequently, the words 'creation of female store managers', convinced considerable numbers of people that women with inadequate careers behind them were recklessly being appointed. A significant number of women were also convinced that store manager work was hard, required high levels of proficiency and was for men, and that it was a managerial position beyond their reach.

However, female store managers betray this general supposition and are developing positive practices whilst either confronting, or simply putting up with, remarks around them such as 'nothing but ornaments'. Next, let us explore the characteristics of their management.

The challenge of female store managers and their management styles

The battle against androcentrism

Androcentrism as seen in the rules surrounding job transfers
As mentioned previously, the differences in management styles between male store managers are to be found in how they themselves have been nurtured and under what type of superior. We can also see the differing management styles amongst female store managers as corresponding to the type of nurturing process which they have undergone. Let us look firstly at the type of organisational culture in which female store managers have built up their careers. To pre-empt the conclusion of this investigation: the organisational culture, through which female store managers have come, was permeated by an androcentric value system.

As mentioned earlier, the national expansion of general merchandise supermarkets gives rise to frequent and large-scale personnel changes. These types of personnel moves simultaneously become an important opportunity for considering upward career moves for each individual but in Company X at these times, only male employees have been considered 'talented people' equal to these moves and have, consequently, been selected as the future middle management cadets. Women have not counted in terms of these 'talented people' and women with long years of service have been pegged to specific duties in a specific store and to the resultant low rank. As I mentioned earlier, this (low rank) has itself come to be viewed as a 'consideration' of women's household responsibilities. It is clear that this type of 'consideration' occurs because women, in fact, do not form part of the 'talented people', of whom something is to be expected, and also that the personnel management system itself is operating in an androcentric manner.

Female Store Manager 2 states, '[They] are not nurturing the talent of women. [They] have always used [women] as stop gaps, without attempting to give them a share in the normal career development cycle.' She says that when she wanted to move from being in charge of personnel in the store to the sales sections in the store, after having been with the company for a year, 'I appealed directly to my superior but it turned into a big quarrel'. Her superior claimed that 'since female university graduates only stay in the workplace for two years, it is useless to put them on the sales floors'. She ended up being assigned to the Clothing Department after earnest requests saying, 'I absolutely will not quit after two years'. She relates 'I was shocked by my superior's lack of feelings of trust towards female university graduates'. Female Store Manager 8, on the basis of her experience of having minutely observed the footsteps of her female seniors, is critical of the state of female personnel (matters) in Company X saying, 'excellent women are quickly singled out by staff from the Area Operations Division only to be abruptly returned to the sales sections in the store and scrapped'. Upon hearing the head of the Area Operations Division's indiscreet remark, 'we do not elevate the likes of women' she defiantly beat a path to a career in the store, remaining hopeful at every opportunity. Female Store Manager 9, looking back on her own history of moves, says, 'I was frequently in a whirl as I was sent from one section to another and one area to another'. Because the method adopted when it was time for personnel moves was one in which men were moved first, and if this did not yield sufficient numbers, then capable women were hastily moved, she always found herself with a change of posting when she was not anticipating one. She says, 'when I became aware of this, I thought that it was pitiful so I admonished myself saying, do not let them make a display of you, try something new!' Female Store Manager 3 says, when my transfer orders arrived I conceived of the order in my own way. I convinced myself that I was deemed essential for this move (by the company).'

Precisely identical questions about their record of moves were thrown at both male and female store managers but, generally, the narratives of the career history of female store managers were longer and with more profound contents than those of male store managers. A common feature of all of their accounts was that the female store managers spoke in detail about how they had come through on the occasion of each move, with anguish and while trying to motivate themselves. As a result of being treated as 'secondary talent', women could not let themselves be lacking in motivation and, in cases where they have wanted to become store managers, they have also had to cultivate their careers by being prepared not to shy away from quarrelling with their superiors in order to continue gaining experience on the sales floor of the store. In contrast to this, there were no statements from the men about having 'convinced oneself' or having motivated oneself. As we saw previously, the pattern of moves for male employees is also diverse and there may well have been cases of moves resulting in a loss of bearings for the individuals concerned. However, men can hold on to the feeling of assurance that the Personnel Department is concerning itself with organising the moves that will enable them to proceed normally up the career ladder. Even if they provisionally end up with a move which does not suit them, they can think of it as merely one point along the way. This is because they accept the androcentric use of the personnel management system as a natural premise. In this case, however, specifying that this is a 'capable men'-centrism may be more in keeping with reality.

Androcentrism as seen in the speech and behaviour of superiors

Androcentrism, which regards men alone as capable, has not only penetrated formal personnel policies and practices, it is also embedded in the organisational culture of the workplace and is apparent in the everyday speech and behaviour of superiors. According to Female Store Manager 8, there was a male superior who began whispering, 'When are you going to quit?' to female regular employees from the first day of their arrival at their posts. This same male superior also 'muttered,

"When are you going to quit?"' to a woman who had just become a chief clerk 'when she was trying to do her best while feeling flustered. He ended up crushing the female chief clerk'. She also said that there are male superiors who hold male only morning meetings and then fail to pass on any information to female employees. She had also come across a male section head who held a 'men's meeting' as soon as anything came up and she would have to hold direct talks with him and ask him to call a meeting of everyone, not only men. As a result male only meetings stopped. We can detect in this the male superior's explicit stance of regarding female employees solely in terms of the likelihood that they will resign early and of never seeing the capacities of female employees in the workplace. The problem, rather than being one of male superiors harassing their female employees, results from the fact that these women are, from the outset, 'invisible' in the male superiors' eyes. These very same attitudes are found in the Personnel Department which – when it is struggling to put together personnel moves – blots out all female employees, as if this were entirely natural, treating them as if they 'were absent even though they are present'.

Other cases of male superiors' widely divergent words and actions with regard to men and women are too numerous to mention. Male Store Manager 6, for example, frequently gathers together seven or eight subordinates and holds a drinking session for a short period of time outside the workplace, calling these 'evening management'. He says, however, 'I occasionally invite women but their going home late is a worry so I basically do not invite them'. Male Store Manager 9, whilst considering himself to be someone who treats his subordinates equally, says 'Where men are concerned, I think that since they will probably keep working with the company, I speak sternly to them, even if I sound a little harsh, as it will yield something, it will be of benefit to the person concerned. However, when it comes to women, there is a strong sense that they regard work as a makeshift activity, that they will quit the workplace when they marry and that as a result not too much can be expected of them. I do give them some guidance but...', he mumbles. There is nothing at all strange about new female employees – who are introduced into this daily workplace atmosphere, and who have had driven home to them the fact that they are human resources of whom nothing is expected – thinking of pulling out. Similarly, there is nothing strange in this situation about women who continue simplifying matters (for themselves) in various circumstances by attempting to get silently on with routine work. This is because there is practically no effort by superiors to expect anything of them or to nurture them.

The women who are persevering positively within this organisational culture reprimand their male superiors for their stance. Female Store Manager 2 says, 'For several years after joining the company I made proposal after proposal but they were all rejected'. For example, even when I identified a hot-selling line of goods through a data analysis of sales and merchandise the male section head shouted at me, 'Don't tease the chief clerk! Just how much teasing of the chief clerk will satisfy you?' The male section head shielded the male chief clerk who was too inexperienced to adopt new ideas from subordinates. She says that this section head told her 'If you want to be accepted like the men in this company, then work like a dog!' According to Female Store Manager 2, when she joined the company at the beginning of the 1980s, new employees consisted of approximately equal numbers of male and female university graduates but significant numbers of female university graduates had resigned out of disappointment with this organisation.

Resistance to androcentrism
We need to acknowledge that the personnel management system, which sees men as the only valid 'talent', is influencing the speech and behaviour of superiors. We can think of this as having come about through the intervention of processes which strengthen stereotypical views of women, rather than seeing the exclusion of women as one of the original intentions of this type of personnel management system. In the past, it came to be believed that the ways of viewing women such as 'a sense of being temporary' and 'lacking any spirit of advancement', corresponded to reality. For example, even cases of women quitting the company out of a sense of despair with the organisation are understood as conforming to the experience of women being 'temporary'. The androcentric bias keeps being strengthened by the fact that all events are grasped and interpreted as an extension of the view that women regard work as a makeshift phase and will quit the workplace when they marry. However, there are also some male store managers, who have built up experience on the work site of the store, who are considering the subject of the nurturing of women. Male Store Manager 2 says, 'despite the fact that it is women who work the hardest when they first join the company, for some reason, after the passage of a year or two, one feels men do work hard don't they?' He points out that if women 'are given more responsibility for work and their status grade and work are elevated, then they come to see that the work can be interesting'. There are some male superiors who, in

this way, are aware of the importance of consciously nurturing and motivating women in their workplaces, but they do not go as far as posing the problem in terms of challenging the practices surrounding personnel management, which have built up inside the organisation, and which allow androcentrism to survive.

Within this setting, the very act of women building up their careers whilst continuing to motivate themselves was itself a struggle of resistance against androcentrism. Female Store Manager 2, who kept experiencing the unreasonable rejection of her proposals – made in a positive spirit – when she was a newcomer, says 'I realised that unless I increased my own status grade, I would not be able to carry my point'. These are weighty words. She points out that inside the organisation 'the problem lies in the fact that men are held together by a group principle in which fellow men stand side by side, and, even though women are selected for a variety of posts, the men around them constantly use the expression "women are nothing but ornaments"'. This is a problem because it serves to diminish women's will and, in situations of failure or difficulty, drives them to the negative thought 'Maybe I am, in fact, nothing but an ornament'. Overcoming this is itself a big test for women.

It took some time for Female Store Manager 8 to act when she spoke directly to a male section head in the habit of giving orders for 'exclusively male meetings' and prevailed on him to stop doing this. She waited until 'the stage when I had acquired a voice' and then she questioned the male section head about the basis for his varying treatment of men and women. This section head maintained that he could not treat men and women equally because 'women have inferior physical strength. They work in an emotional way', but she says 'I insisted strongly on individual not gender differences and got him to change'. This is an actual example of having challenged a superior directly to a battle of words with the result that she made him stop his practice of holding 'exclusively male meetings'. We ought not to overlook the point that resisting an organisational culture of androcentrism and struggles against it are woven into the career development process of female store managers.

The performance of female store managers

Their reception by male store managers
Rosabeth Moss Kanter, who was one of the first to carry out empirical research into the work organisation and gender relations, came up with

the analysis, on the basis of research into one company organisation in the 1970s, that because women are extremely scarce in management and specialist positions they become 'tokens' representing all women. In other words, she held that women become the object of attention because of their scarcity, they are put under performance pressure, they end up being isolated as a result of having much made of the differences between them and men, who are in the majority, and are confined within the role of a stereotyped woman (Kanter, 1977=1995). Just what type of conditions did female store managers in Company X find themselves in before assuming their positions as store managers? On this question, let us look at how the 'first generation' was accepted within the organisation.

Firstly, all female store managers say that male store managers treated them 'kindly' at the store manager meetings, which were weekly gatherings of store managers in every Area Operations Division. Female Store Manager 5 says 'Many gave me kind looks at the all male store manager meetings. They were all kind.' In particular, a male store manager, her former superior, gave her advice on various matters. At the same time, however, she states 'I at times felt that that they were too easy on women at store manager meetings. Where men would earn a scolding, for example, women got away with "What about trying this?" There was clearly a difference.' At this stage, when there were at the most only one or two female store managers in all Area Operations Divisions, and owing to the prevalence of the relatively sympathetic view that they were 'simply ornaments', those around female store managers responded 'kindly' to them. In 1998 the personnel manager in a certain area asserted that 'At this time, there is no sign of men's morale falling as a result of selecting women to be store managers in this way. On the contrary, they kindly keep watch over them, worrying about whether they will make it up to a higher-level store. At this stage they were not at all seen as rivals to male store managers, rather, the male store managers were sympathetic to them and watched over them kindly.

What was the reaction at the store level? Male Store Manager 6 says 'What made it difficult for female store managers was the prevailing atmosphere of making fools of women in the store. There are times when store managers need to take the initiative and prove themselves [to their subordinates] by, for example, showing that they can carry heavy loads or by suggesting faster ways of getting things done. Male [subordinates] make fools of women because they [physically] cannot manage some of these things. You can say that it is unavoidable that an atmosphere of "[female] store managers are just all talk, they cannot do anything" hangs in the air in the Food Products Department, the epitome of intensive work. Male Store Manager 1 also points out that '[relations between] members of a single sex group are stormy'. This is because, given the fact that women, beginning with part timers, form a majority in the store, a store manager will be seen as not being up to the position if he does not have the backing of his female subordinates. Consequently, he says, 'I am unable to shed my feelings of unease regarding the posting of women to higher positions'. To put this in everyday language, this is the view that 'woman is woman's enemy'. Male store managers were forecasting that women would not be able to take the initiative and carry out physical work and also that it would be difficult for women to demonstrate leadership in the store with its high proportion of women. These items were both discussed at the time of the 1999 interview.

The ordeals undergone by female store managers

However, in reality, the majority of female store managers have not encountered difficulties that have brought them to a standstill as store managers. Rather, many of them have been welcomed as women. Female Store Manager 9 relates that she became a store manager in her ninth year, after joining the company halfway through her career, and that when she was newly appointed as store manager, in a store containing many of the female colleagues with whom she had previously been working, these former colleagues 'felt sorry because a novice, like them, was constrained to become a store manager and they helped me'. Female Store Manager 7 says that, like Female Store Manager 9, she was newly appointed as store manager in a store in which there were former colleagues with whom she had once worked and that 'the part-time employees all welcomed me calling "Welcome Back!"' Only Female Store Manager 5 is experiencing some disagreeableness from fellow female subordinates. She says that there was the case of one part time worker who wrote to Head Office slandering her store manager manner. This matter was, for the most part, attributable to envy towards a woman from the same generation. Although her own appropriate responses, and those of Head Office, settled the matter, she says 'I fell to thinking that it is women who thwart other women'.

There were also actual cases of male subordinates who found it difficult to accept female superiors. Female Store Manager 2 says 'both part-time employees and female employees accepted me quite

The Challenge of 'Creating Female Store Managers'

naturally. Men in their twenties and thirties initially had some difficulty accepting me. However, as I went on achieving results as a store manager, they recognised my abilities and accepted me.' In contrast to this, Female Store Manager 8 underwent some fairly strenuous ordeals, due, in part, to the fact that she became a store manager in her thirties. According to this store manager, a male superior had had a word to her, saying that she would find management difficult in this store because it contained part-time employees who had been working in it for over 20 years before her recent appointment. However, 'the part-time employees had fiery temperaments but once I clearly set out [my policy as store manager] they turned out to be my allies'. More so than women with lengthy years of service, it was men who had hurdles to overcome on the issue of accepting her as a store manager. This was because 'when I arrived at my post, there was bewilderment amongst the male managers, along the lines of "we have a store manager who does not know very much". It was a male in his mid-forties, who had stood still at the chief clerk level, who was responsible for this atmosphere; he habitually asked, 'Why is it that women become store managers?' She said that once he realised that she was competent in her managerial position he changed tack, declaring that 'a life of work alone is not much of a life'. The problem was resolved when a month later the head of the Area Operations Division had this man moved to another store. The bewildered chief clerks gradually came to recognise the abilities of Female Store Manager 8 and ended up having confidence in her. However, she had to deal with a male section head in sales, in his mid-forties, who kept repeating that 'the company treats men and women differently'. She is in a difficult relationship with him because he was once her superior and also because she overtook him to become store manager. She thinks that there is no alternative but for her to weather the situation as best she can.

As this shows, accepting women as superiors is likely to present difficulties for male subordinates where there is an organisational culture of androcentrism, of the kind we saw previously. A male employee in the Personnel Department of Head Office said, 'When female store managers first appeared they were given special personnel consideration along the lines of having younger section heads appointed under them. This type of special personnel consideration was limited, however, to the initial period after the appearance of female store managers. There were thus also those who saw female store managers as likely to fail, sooner or later, once they encountered older subordinates – the old timers.' The advent of younger female store managers, in particular, can be seen as problematic for male subordinates. However, the youngest male store manager, who became a store manager after early promotion, is also experiencing something similar. According to the interview with Mr Y, who became a store manager in his early thirties, 'When I became the youngest store manager some of my past superiors were still stuck in the section head class and some fairly unpleasant things were said to me'. This was because the older male subordinates regarded him as a mere 'stripling'. It is unclear whether the feelings of opposition towards young employees who become store managers are stronger in the case of men or women. When Female Store Manager 9 became a store manager in her ninth year of service Mr Y says that he himself complained muttering 'Why has someone whose status grade is one grade lower than our own become a store manager? "We men could do it and yet", "Why is it that we cannot be store managers? What is wrong with us?" However, we stopped complaining when we heard that she was achieving good results'. The younger males at least were finally won over once she displayed her leadership as a store manager, even though they had started off feeling that a female store manager was difficult to accept. This attitude in itself is not an insurmountable difficulty.

In this regard, the 'old timers', who had begun to feel that there were limits to their promotion prospects within the organisation, were at times also a difficult presence for male store managers. In one sense, the androcentrism in Company X is based on the hegemonic masculinity (Connell, 1987=1993) of male store managers, which we must see as driving the subordinate masculinity of the 'old timers'. However, although the male generation referred to as 'old timers' also harass young female store managers, their behaviour does not hinder the accomplishment of work duties. These 'old timers' will continue to be a problem with which female store managers must deal, in the same way that male store managers have had to deal with them.

Looked at in above fashion, whatever the ordeals stemming from the feelings of resistance towards female store managers, these did not present insurmountable problems. For the most part, in fact, women store managers have been accepted without problem in the workplace.[5]

Alternative management styles
In any case, at the end of 2002 not only has not a single female store manager from the 'first generation' deserted, some have even

moved on to their second store while others have been appointed to department manager positions in Head Office, following their store manager experience. Some of these female store managers have even moved abruptly from large-scale stores to being store managers of ultra-large stores. Female store managers have begun winning the annual outstanding store managers' prizes, with one going on to receive the most outstanding store manager award. As mentioned previously, the appointment of 'second generation' female store managers has also progressed further. The reason why these women, who were told that the creation of female store managers was 'nothing but ornamentation', have been able to work smoothly in this way can be found in the appropriateness of the strategies adopted by them and their performance on the basis of these strategies.

As we saw in the previous detailed analysis of the career development process, included amongst these women were some who had steadily built up their careers and consciously reserved their energies with the aim of becoming store managers. Their own efforts made it unnecessary to make particular mention of the 'creation of female store managers'. Even those who had not particularly aimed to become store managers had built up careers which were in no way inferior to those of male store managers. Female Store Manager 2, from this first group, is consciously seeking an approach which is different from the management style which men are apt to adopt. She explains that in contrast to 'men's attempts to achieve the numerical targets' she has been practising 'management which stresses communication with my subordinates and trying to put myself in the position of ordinary citizens and consumers'. She has 'suffered under', the androcentric organisational culture and sees it as 'oppressive management'. She has consciously been trying to seek out an alternative form of management. The point of this alternative is to find a state of affairs favourable to communication with her subordinates. What Female Store Manager 3 has also endeavoured to do is to patrol the store 'assuming the perspective of customers, over half of whom are women', 'listening to the discontents, which part-time employees whisper to the chief clerks' and talking with those in charge in order to effect improvements.

On the other hand, the people in the second group, who feel that their store manager careers are inadequate, in the sense that their store experience has been relatively slight, as we saw previously, uniformly thought 'My rapid rise to store manager was due to being a woman'. This group are also attempting to make use of the problem consciousness cultivated in them by their work experience to date.

Female Store Manager 9, who became a store manager after nine years with the company, is making repeated attempts to gain entrance into the workplaces at the very bottom of the store. She is persisting with this because she thinks that under conditions in which she cannot avoid tough rivalry with competitor stores, 'since I have no technique at all...I will defiantly tackle it as a complete amateur'. She is also motivated by the thought that 'it is important for a leader to take away any suffering in the workplace and the individual pain of part-time employees'. She thinks 'there are some male store managers who misunderstand leadership and who constantly roar at subordinates but some day I would like to speak out clearly and say that this is a mistake'. We can evince in this a sense of backlash against the androcentric organisational culture. After becoming a store manager, Female Store Manager 4, who had irregular postings from the time of joining the company, also endeavoured to 'listen to the difficulties of part-time employees', 'be aware of their feelings as they worked' and 'in any case to go out onto the sales floor and listen to both the customers and the part-time employees'. As a result of this, within a short time of moving to her new appointment she was able to find a way of discovering that a section head, who struggled to achieve his sales figures, was abusing rank-and-file employees and part timers, calling them 'dull-witted', and rendering personal relations awkward.

Female Store Manager 6, who had spent a long time in the Merchandise Department and had only three years of store experience, realised that she had not had any opportunity to master the management skills needed for being a store manager, and wondered exactly what resources she did possess herself. Whereupon she reached the conclusion that 'if there was a single area in which, as a female store manager, I did differ from men, it was in that female employees and part-time employees found it easy to talk to me. There was nothing for it but to think of a management approach which would make positive use of this.' She also stresses communication with her subordinates. 'Those around me [male store managers]' say that 'I must have the authority of a store manager'. However, thinking that in circumstances where one is short-handed 'people will not stir simply as a result of authority', she started listening to her subordinates' talk and helping out with work like bringing out stock.

Thus, even female store managers with widely divergent career patterns unexpectedly display similarities to each other through striving to communicate with female part timers and rank-and-file regulars and tackling a bottom up form of management that leads to an enhanced will to work on the part of these women. Actually, most of these female store managers were initially assigned to small-scale stores and because the vast majority of the 'us' group in these stores were part-time employees they started off by listening to these part-time employees. It is a way of doing things which consists of chatting with one's subordinates whilst 'wandering around' inside the store. Part-time employees often tell Female Store Manager 7 'we like female store managers because they listen to what we say' and they do, in fact, often call out to her to stop and have long conversations with her. She says that thanks to this 'these women' can gain a sense of 'working together [with me]'.

It is necessary to make clear that this way of doing things, which stresses communication, is completely different from the 'direct communication' intended by Store A's male store manager, encountered in Chapter Four. The female store managers' way of doing things is not to give instruction after instruction to subordinates but an approach which listens to subordinates and tries to keep alive the idea of an 'us' group inside the store. As we saw in the previous chapter, the 'us' group is made up of people who continue to work in the same store for many years and who embrace a strong sense of 'our store'. Behind this approach towards women subordinates, adopted by female store managers who have consciously developed their careers inside the one store, is repulsion towards the type of management which 'stresses results and figures' and 'shouts' at people. For female store managers who have become conscious of a personal lack of management skills, their enthusiasm for attempting to meet the challenge – by mobilising, at any cost, the resources that they have acquired in the course of life as a woman – explains the choice of a bottom up type of management. They report that because, as women, they have certainly been in the vanguard of career development in the store they have up until now 'always felt the pressure of never being able to fail at anything because of our unique and rare existence' (Female Store Manager 6). However, their performances overcome the arguments of Rosabeth Moss Kanter and are instead powerful and strategic. The fact that one woman who is aware of the deficiencies in her career as store manager is amongst those nominated for store manager excellence awards is evidence of this.

The deputy chairman of the labour union (male), mentioned previously, also pays attention to the bottom up style of management practised by female store managers. He thinks that what is lacking in the whole of Company X is bottom up management. He points out that the 'able people [males]' in the company or alternatively those (males) who have reached the top, in due course, by climbing up the stages of promotion 'have largely practised top down management and are hindering the development of a sense of reward amongst their subordinates because they do not listen to the voices of those at the bottom'. The head of the Personnel Department in a particular Area Operations Division says that 'In daily store management they commonly pay no heed at all to the views of their part-time employees. I think that they need to change and begin listening even to the views of people in the lowest positions.' We could say that if Company X were to listen to this statement, then the management style of female store managers, one which has striven for communication with the women in the store, has already laid the foundations for an alternative leading management style in the company.

The significance of bottom up management

I touched previously on the view, pointed out by Female Store Manager 2, that 'Male store managers attempt to meet the targets and figures before them '. Female Store Manager 9, similarly, argues that 'Male store managers are inclined towards business results and figures'. During the interviews with female store managers, the management style of male store managers was described as 'oppressive' and the point was repeatedly made that 'there are some male store managers who misunderstand leadership and who constantly roar at subordinates'. In contrast to this, female store managers emphasise the point that they 'stress communication' and 'listen to subordinates'. Naturally, the bottom up type of management, which I have been discussing, does not imply a lack of numerical responsibility. This is because, as I specified earlier, the most significant aspect of a store manager's role lies in this. Female Store Manager 2 recalls that when she became a store manager, 'I made up my mind that I would definitely reach the numerical targets' and 'take an unyielding stance in making sales'. If there are differences, then these are whether to concentrate on 'short term numerical targets' or on numerical targets as a whole, whilst keeping an eye on the sense of achievement and growth of one's subordinates.

How are these polar opposites in images of store managers perceived by subordinates? Female Chief Clerk 6 (aged 26), with experience of working under both male and female store managers, has the following to say about the gender differences between store managers. She notes that male store managers 'have a strong perspective of emphasising results. They both praised and scolded us regarding figures.' In short, male store managers are apt to exercise strong control over their subordinates regarding numerical targets. 'When confronted with this kind of male store manager, even though his "grumbles [Show results in the figures!]" get to you with the result that you end up thinking "I suppose I'll try to attain the numerical targets", this is hardly a feeling which "shows an interest" in one's work'. In contrast to this, a female store manager 'makes me feel more like working because even if I make a mistake she will watch out for me after having a brief word with me. If I approach her with "I would like to try this", she replies, "by all means, please do" therefore I can, in the true sense of the word, "show an interest" in my work.' Chief Clerk 6 also says 'I can feel a thoughtfulness to details' in her way of attending to subordinates. When she says 'I feel that there is a difference between men and women in management', her words carry more weight all the more because of the solid sense of her personal experience. In reality, the differences between management undertaken by women and men have various manifestations and subordinates accept these.

However, how can we account for these gender differences in management? Or alternatively, is it, in reality, possible to generalise these differences in terms of 'male type management' and female type management'? I think that we need to be cautious about arguments claiming direct links between the premise of gender differences in socialisation processes and gender differences found in management styles. These arguments claim that socialisation processes make it easy for girls to cultivate communication abilities in the rearing process which they undergo in the home and at school, whilst giving boys extremely few opportunities of this kind. The problem we need to address here is rather a question of what men and women inside an androcentric organisational culture learn during their respective career development processes. Many female store managers, on the basis of their own experiences of suffering under androcentrism, have tried to find management methods which are different from those they have experienced. Female store managers attempt to display their 'strength' – that is being the same sex as the 'us' who form the bottom of the work organisation – in order to offset deficiencies in their management skills. It is quite possible that the strategies employed by these female store managers appeal to the state in which part-time employees find themselves, thus leading this group to welcome and draw near to the female store managers because they are 'easy to talk to'. Female Store Manager 9, who joined the company halfway through her career, in accordance with her own experience of the lowest social stratum declares 'part-time employees are really seeking a feeling of achievement. They really want to do work for which they can get a thank you from the customers.' Her management beliefs are based on the ideas that 'It is to be expected that there is a link between pursuing this and results in the figures' and also on 'gaining entrance into their group and understanding and alleviating their workplace suffering'. This is backed up by her personal experience of coming into close contact with the 'us' group in the course of her own career history. It is as a result of these types of ideas that she received the most outstanding store manager award.[6]

Incidentally, I was able to grasp an unexpected aspect from the interview with Male Store Manager 6, in his capacity as a representative of 'male type' management. According to the Personnel Department, he is a store manager who practises a 'hard' type of management. His words were that, in reality, his approach towards his subordinates was 'to spur them on'; 'if they do not change their ways even after I have spoken to them calmly once or twice, then I have to say something high-handed to them'; I scold and shout at them, telling them that they must not be amateurish'; 'I do take them for a drink and appease them but I also use coercive management'. He uttered these words many times during his interview. At the same time, he spoke frankly saying, 'In order to ensure that numerical targets are met, the power to command the sort of loyalty capable of stirring the whole organisation to action instantly is indispensable. I probably use these management methods because I have no leeway. I have no choice but to use hard management. As a result of this I end up giving inadequate directions to my subordinates and there are sometimes failures which give rise to misunderstandings.' It might be possible to regard management which 'shouts' at subordinates as effective but it is also a fact that he himself is not necessarily partial to this shouting type of management, with 'no leeway' and 'inadequate words'. Seen from another viewpoint, this 'coercive' management takes on the aspect of being nothing more than immature management, used in order to 'command the loyalty of the organisation instantly' in conditions in which there is a lack of any latitude. If 'coercive' orders, to which subordinates find it difficult to agree, continue, then they end up giving subordinates the sense that the only reason for stirring themselves is in order to achieve results for the store manager.

The bottom up type management, which the 'first generation' female store managers have endeavoured to put into practice, was, in fact, undoubtedly a challenge to the leading management style then at work in Company X.

Careers and management styles within the organisation

We must, however, at this point be mindful of the fact that there are also some male store managers who are undertaking a bottom up type of management style. Male Store Manager1 says 'I try to make a point of talking to part-time employees, including engaging in silly banter with them'. One reason for this is that 'it is meaningful as an antenna for gathering information, working from the premise that a sales floor not supported by the part-time employees is no good'. That is not all. He says 'I also do this for the purpose of understanding whether my instructions and orders are making their way to the very bottom of the store, as they should, and also whether chief clerks are communicating effectively with part-time employees'. He points out his considerable experience of 'replenishing stock myself and making sales myself' in the Merchandise Department but that it was only when he became a store manager that he savoured for the first time 'the important experience' of 'nurturing subordinates'. He says that opening one's eyes to 'the magnificence of this' is the starting point of management. Male Store Manager 8, who spent a long period as a full-time labour union official following his six and a half years of store experience, keenly felt his lack of store manager management skills and as a consequence faced his management duties with a determination to attempt to display his communication abilities, which he had cultivated during his labour union period. In practice, he conducts interviews with his part-time employees almost every day. This interview lasts only a short amount of time but it is a time for touching on the problems troubling each individual part time worker and also their enthusiasm. He says that he plans to introduce interviews with employees following those with part-time employees. His starting line and the strategies he has adopted as a store manager are in accordance with those of female store managers who were keenly aware of their career deficiencies.

There are also cases of male store managers who, because of the type of nurturing process they have undergone within the organisation, are moving towards the bottom up type of management. There is a high probability that where one has learnt only under a top down type superior (male), then this will produce a store manager with a 'hard' management style. Would it not be easy – particularly in the case of men who have overtaken their colleagues, and in some circumstances even their superiors, and been promoted to the level of store manager

– to adopt methods such as making use of their authority and influence to issue high-handed orders or bring ideals of numerical control to the fore and force this on their subordinates in order to bounce back from the contemptuous view of themselves as mere 'striplings'? Perhaps this is the reason why the 'hard' management style is the leading one. In contrast to this, in cases where one's career development unexpectedly leads to becoming a store manager, those without this type of model behind them, even men, can adopt a style which is different from the mainstream. The experiences of women who have suffered under the mainstream management style are also linked to the conscious pursuit of a new management style. We need to see management styles as differing in response to how one has been nurtured and to one's accumulated experiences within the organisation.

However, we should not forget that this type of management style is also variable. A male section head, (early forties) from Store A, makes a very interesting point regarding changes in styles. He used to be the type that shouted at subordinates but he says that he 'changed completely' following his experiences in a small-scale (about 20 people) store. He says of this store, 'Thanks to the fact that successive store managers had securely strengthened the store it had an extremely good atmosphere. There was unity amongst the employees and an atmosphere of thinking beyond the department and getting on with work as one united body.' Having gained his section head experience in this place he says 'In this store I learnt and switched to a style (without shouting) of first thinking about the reasons behind subordinates becoming concerned and failing'. As we see in this case, coming into contact with a variety of superiors during the career development process is very significant in terms of the maturity of one's management. Looked at in this way, female store managers, who have climbed up the career ladder inside an organisation incapable of seeing them as anything more than 'ornaments', had no choice but to take on the challenge of seeking alternative management styles, based on their career histories. These were careers which had not trodden the path of fusing with mainstream organisational culture. We can see their attempts in this regard as being sufficiently powerful to command the loyalty of the organisation.

The impact of female store managers

Finally, on the basis of the above considerations, I will summarise the influence on the organisation of senior management's resolution to 'create female store managers' and then draw some brief conclusions about the present phase of the organisational challenge facing Company X.

The actual practice of 'creating female store managers'

Firstly, we can sum up the meaning of the actual practice of 'creating female store managers' as follows. The resolution of the senior ranks of top management was an attempt to go beyond the existing policy on women middle managers and aim for the full-scale nurturing of core women middle managers. The Personnel Departments in each Area Operations Division, entrusted with the selection of suitable people to this end, consequently, chose section heads with considerable store experience as being suitable candidates. What is important here is the fact that talented females who accorded with this selection viewpoint were being steadily nurtured inside Company X. The very fact that these talented people managed to improve their abilities and survive inside an androcentric organisational culture – which regards women as invisible or cannot treat them as talented people of whom something might be expected, both at the time of personnel changes and in the daily speech and behaviour of male superiors – is the most important point in forecasting the success or failure of 'the creation of female store managers'. These women joined the company during and after the 1980s, a period when women were regarded as likely to remain at work for two or three years. They survived a period, which could be described as lacking practically any critical awareness of consciously nurturing talented females in the normal course of store experience, and became talented people able to respond to the 'creation of female store managers' policy.

The comments, made mainly by male store managers, describing these efforts as 'simply ornamental' and 'they will soon all come tumbling down', can be said to be precisely the reaction of an androcentric organisational culture. Most male store managers did not think that women with the talent to be able to withstand store manager work had been nurtured within Company X and took the policy to be nothing more than the futile production of female store managers lacking in competence. Consequently, this was not a viewpoint based on concern about the appearance of 'rivals' who would threaten male territory; rather, 'sympathetic' looks predominated.

In any case, if we look at the career development of men and women before they reach store manager, the most striking feature is that of individual differences. This is, in part, the inevitable outcome of severe personnel changes during the scrap and build style of development accompanying the development of chain stores – opening new, large stores and closing unprofitable stores. This is because it is extremely difficult to construct a stable path for promotions. However, operating on an androcentric premise, personnel changes conceive of men as the effective talented people and, therefore, as the primary objects of these changes. Women are nothing more than chess pieces there to plug any gaps left after this process has been completed. Even so, there is no significant difference between the careers of the majority of women selected as store managers and those of male store managers in terms of adequate store experience. There are also rare cases of male store managers with shallow store experience having been selected but these men were not told they were 'simply ornamental'. In contrast to this, female store managers who felt that they had career deficiencies came up with their own responses as a result of thinking, 'I am only a store manager because I am a woman'. This situation arose because treading the path to the position of store manager conferred authority on men who had accumulated management skills and this was the gateway to success. The very entrance of women onto this hallowed path was full of epochal meaning for the organisation. The 'creation of female store managers' was, objectively, an extremely radical move, which eroded the perception that 'store manager work is for men'.

The alternative strategies of female store managers

Secondly, we need to look at the significance of the strategic performance adopted by female store managers. The career patterns of 'first generation' female store managers can be broadly divided into two groups but these share the common thread of the universal adoption of bottom up management, irrespective of the career pattern. The first group is composed of those people who were likely to become store managers soon, needless to say because of the 'creation of female store managers' – people whose careers are in no way inferior to those of male store managers. These women have suffered under the androcentric organisational culture, and as a consequence of their determination never to adopt a male management style they are making a point of developing an approach which will activate the enthusiasm of the lowest social stratum in the store – the female general rank-and-file regular employees and the part-time employees (in other words, the

The Challenge of 'Creating Female Store Managers'

'us' of Chapter 4). The second group are those women who think that they ended up being nominated as store managers because they are women and despite the fact that they have insufficient store experience and are lacking management skills. Because they saw themselves in these terms, this group of women thought of relying on the 'us' group, the ones with a thorough knowledge of the store in question, to teach them. Alternatively, they thought that they were expected to turn the fact that they themselves were women into an advantage in a work organisation where most people were women; or, that unless they did this, there would be no way of being able to cover up the deficiencies in their management skills. Although there are differences between these groups of female store managers, as a result of discrepancies in career patterns, in the very context and logic by which all of these women have found their way to bottom up management styles, both groups ended up striving for something different from the mainstream management style.

However, it would not be appropriate to refer to bottom up management as 'women's-style' and the type of management which seeks to command the loyalty of the organisation instantly from above in order to achieve numerical targets as 'men's-style'. This is because there are actually also some male store managers who are practising bottom up management. I was able to gather, from interviews with the Personnel and Merchandise Departments, that the 'over-zealous' style of management is, however, probably quite prevalent in the management styles of male store managers in Company X. We can see this as probably being connected with the practice of achieving results in a short period of time as a store manager. Store managers who attempt to achieve good results within two to three years in a system dogged by extreme personnel changes, which reach up to the highest ranks of managerial positions in a store, are unlikely to create a scenario in which capable subordinates are sent off to a store which will become the next step in their cultivation as talented people. Instead, it is probably difficult for these store managers to avoid tending to keep capable subordinates readily at their disposal whenever possible. Was it not more likely, in a world consisting solely of male store managers, that rough management, in which one produced results in a short time without choosing the means for doing this, would be prized? The successive progression of people, once they had become store managers, to the position of store managers of large-scale stores and then to even higher managerial positions, by appealing, in this manner, to 'the merit of vitality' and 'competence', can be seen as the mainstream approach to the formation of core middle managers. However, within this process, lurks the opportunity to learn that there are limitations in binding oneself to this type of experience of success. When one is appointed the store manager of a large-scale store one learns that there are limits to the approach in which subordinates are unreasonably forced to make a show of instant spontaneity and one cannot help but become proficient in a management style which takes a broader view of things, including the nurturing of talented people.

The management strategies adopted by female store managers in this environment pointed, in fact, to alternative management styles. In that sense, we can even say that as a result of its efforts, Company X was able to gain the chance to take stock and to reconsider its existing mainstream management style, as well as gaining the possibility for organisational change. It is, however, unlikely that senior management's vision in its 'creation of female store managers' policy extended as far as this point.

Gender differences in management styles

Thirdly, we need to see differences in management styles as reflecting the type of position held and the type of nurturing experienced by individual store managers inside the organisation and also in terms of what each individual has learnt from the organisational culture. It is also essential that we understand gender differences in management as being a fundamental extension of this. The absence, until now, of female store managers and the organisational failure to nurture women, as talented people of whom something might be expected, are historical facts in Company X. We can comprehend that the 'first generation' of female store managers, who appeared under these conditions, had no choice from their standpoint as the so-called 'peripheral' group in the organisation but to adopt a style different from mainstream management. These women had no choice but to undergo a set period of stagnation, even if they displayed efforts equal to those of men, and they were also compelled to resign themselves to unparalleled career changes, 'being moved frequently from one section to another'. They have inhabited a 'peripheral' world inside an organisation steeped in androcentrism. Inside this, they began to appreciate that the mainstream management style, against which they inevitably collided in their career development process, was a 'male-type' and they had to seek out an alternative style. On the other hand, because they were a 'peripheral' group, at the time when they became keenly aware of their career deficiencies they had no choice but to build up a strategy mobilising what few resources they had – 'the fact that they were women'. The emphasising of gender differences, in this way by female store managers, is itself inherently dangerous as they are themselves bringing gender stereotypes into the management domain. However, we cannot fail to notice the point that in the early stages of attempting to achieve prominence in a new field of challenge, inside an organisation permeated by androcentrism, the stressing of femininity, and confronting masculinity, can suffice as one strategy for women. We can identify it as a strategy emphasising 'the fact of being a woman' in a period of excesses aimed at removing the androcentrism of the prevailing management style.

On the other hand, whilst a group of male store managers has adopted the management style developed by female store managers, this has been recognised within the organisation as a 'female-type' management style. This is expressed straightforwardly in the words of a member of the Personnel Department in Head Office who said 'Female store managers are particularly good at communication with part-time employees'. This amounts to understanding this management style not as a way of operating, which is being strategically selected by women, but rather as stemming from women's 'intrinsic characteristics'. This is linked with thinking which bundles together all ways of operating displayed by female store managers as being of a 'female-type'.

What we need to affirm here is the significance of the ways of operating adopted by female store managers. This is a style actually also being used by a group of men; a style which is acquired as one matures as a store manager; one which stands at the opposite pole from the 'over-zealous' type; and a management style which rigorously maintains points of contact with the 'us' group at the bottom of the store and attempts to reduce the distance between the 'us' and management. Do we limit ourselves to the level of confining and acknowledging this simply as a 'female-type' or do we attempt to keep our gaze on its significance in challenging the former mainstream management style in Company X? How is Company X recognising the value of this and attempting to give it life within the company strategy? This management style, which is increasingly gaining approval through female store managers, can be seen as raising important questions for Company X.[7]

Reactions to the 'creation of female store managers' – young women

In 2002 the 'creation of female store managers' continues to be promoted in Company X, but it still has not reached the ten percent level and we cannot say that it is having a decisive impact on the whole organisation. However, the atmosphere is gradually changing. Because female store managers, far from and contrary to expectations that they would soon fail, have performed well as store managers and one of them has even been nominated for the most outstanding store manager award, views of them are changing. The company was coming to grips with 'making positive use of women' in the same period in which it was grappling with the 'creation of female store managers'. The injection of women into so-called 'male sections', whilst happening little by little, was measurable and the company had also started coming to grips with the appointment of chief clerks from amongst female rank-and-file regular employees and part-time employees with long periods of continuous service. 'Making positive use of women' has produced a steady undercurrent inside the organisation. Because this movement progressed alongside the delivery and implementation of the radical personnel policy of the 'creation of female store managers', it came to be recognised not simply as an undercurrent but as a trend which could not be ignored, and it engendered a variety of changes and reactions.

The first of these reactions occurred as a result of the opening up of the path to store manager positions to women also. There are cases of female chief clerks, who have observed the activities of female store managers beginning to burn with the desire, 'I want to be a store manager too'. 'There has also been an increase in the number of women who had previously thought that women reached a dead end as chief clerks but who have now been inspired by the appearance of female store managers to think "Being a store manager looks difficult but I would not mind trying to get as far as section head"' (Female Store Manager 3). There is an increasing tendency for female employees to possess a desire to attempt higher managerial positions. The female store managers belonging to the 'second generation' came to appreciate that it might be their turn next, as they paid close attention to the increasing shouts of encouragement accompanying the 'creation of female store managers'. The responses vary – 'I hated being made to go on the store managers' course because I was a woman' (Female Store Manager 12); 'It will be awful if I am made a store manager next' (Female Store Manager 11); and 'I too will probably become a store manager, in due course' (Female Store Manager 10). However, store manager work, including the necessary mental preparation and resolve, has taken its place in their career outlooks.

Compared to the era of the 'first generation', when the company spent a lot of time carefully scouting for talented people who had been reared inside the organisation, this 'second generation' was produced in half the time. One result of this has been an age shift into the thirties. Also, from 2000, the time of the initial appointments of members of this 'second generation', there had been an appreciation of the results produced by the 'first generation' and the growth of a company-wide atmosphere of backing up female store managers. In the midst of these types of trends, the looks being cast at female store managers by male store managers are said to have changed. The situation was one in which 'There were probably male store managers who were appalled and who really wanted to say, "What is someone like that (a 30 year-old woman) doing as a store manager?" but [conscious of the policy and atmosphere in the company] never said so openly' (Female Store Manager 10). We can infer that the looks being given by male store managers were shifting away from the 'sympathetic'.

In this type of atmosphere, in which depending on one's view, one might even suspect 'preferential treatment for women', rumours spread like wild fire that it was easier for women than men in the company to pass the exams for section head and chief clerk jobs. These remarks about 'preferential treatment for women' and 'special treatment for women' continue to torment the relatively highly motivated, young, female employees. One female chief clerk (early twenties, three years' service) states 'Do we need women to attract the customers? Is that why they are taking chances and forcing through promotions simply because someone is a woman, even though she has no ability? The strange appeal to the company of these appointments [of women] is irritating!' A section head from the Personnel Department of a particular Area Operations Division also says 'As women become increasingly successful at passing status grade exams, some of them are coming to the Personnel Department to ask "Did I pass because I am a woman?"' A backlash is developing, amongst young women, against this 'special regard' 'because we are women'. The thinking of these women, who have the possibility of succeeding the 'first generation' and the 'second generation', is 'We do not want this [special treatment], we want men and women to be nurtured in the same way'.

Reactions to the 'creation of female store managers' – male middle managers

We cannot overlook the point that the shift in the tenor of men's remarks away from 'sympathy' for the 'first generation', based on their actions, has brought about this bewilderment and backlash amongst young women regarding their 'preferential treatment' and 'special treatment'. The responses of young men, and those men who face the inevitability of having reached the upper limits of their promotion prospects, are taking on the form of bewilderment and casual mutterings, as a result of the fact that it is difficult for them to accept female superiors, who as in the case of the 'first generation' of female store managers, have already run the gauntlet. The reactions of a segment of male store managers and core male middle managers higher up are being expressed in the form of even more distinct remarks. The distinctive feature of these reactions is straightforwardly expressed in statements, which could be taken as apparent pleas for egalitarianism – 'If women, in particular, are singled out for any more preferential treatment than this, then this would amount to reverse discrimination'. According to Female Store Manager 3, as the numbers of female store managers have increased, male store managers have changed their comments to utterances such as 'Why are there still female store managers around?' and 'Why are they able to move on to managing their second stores?' Finally, comments have moved away from the viewpoint that 'It is [not whether one is a man or a woman but] the contents of the work that one does that ought to be decisive' to voices being heard here and there saying 'Cultivating women exclusively is reverse discrimination' and 'This is no longer a time for talking about [distinctions between] men and women'. These types of statements are also openly made by a segment of senior management.

Some people are also making comments like 'that is the right sort of store for a female store manager'. This statement by a section head in a certain Area Operations Division (2002), carries the implication that this is a small-scale store, where there is not a high level of expectation on the part of the company, and one in which the store manager has only to maintain good communication with subordinates for the store to be able to keep going, on its own. This is a statement which attempts to draw a distinction with large-scale stores, which face rival stores in their neighbourhoods and which require high level decision making ability and strong leadership ability. Not surprisingly, from the viewpoint of the indispensability of high-level management skills, it is men who are seen as best suited to this latter type of store.

As seen above, during the seven years since the appearance of female store managers, statements about them have changed in character. We should note that, particularly in recent years, core male middle managers have been making statements such as 'We ought to treat men and women identically from now on' and 'Preferential treatment exclusively for women is reverse discrimination'. The 'creation of female store managers' has only just begun. In numerical terms they still only make up less than ten percent of all store managers and the situation is still a long way off from the stated targets of senior management ('In 2003 one quarter of all middle manager positions must be held by women'). Nonetheless, we can perhaps imagine some feelings of confusion behind statements of this kind. They acknowledge and value the fact that the 'first generation' has not readily failed but gone on to produce sound performances. Furthermore, given the fact that women have moved beyond being the object of the organisation's (in reality, men's) 'sympathy' and 'consideration', is it not possible that perhaps these men are at a loss as to the best stance to take from now on regarding their views of women and the treatment of women? In this type of situation it is common for people to say 'From now on we should not give preferential treatment exclusively to women'. However, if we consider the brevity of the battle for the 'creation of female store managers', then we can muse that there might well have been a different response to this one. That is, a more positive reception upon encountering the steadfastness and endurance of the 'first generation'. In other words, a positive reception openly rejoicing at the fact that women had won positions as store managers and demonstrated their abilities; making it possible, thereafter, by scouting for and nurturing even more talented women, for them to be seen as precious assets for Company X; which would provide expanded business opportunities. We can read into the inability of even the male middle managers who formed the core of management to take this position the ingrained nature of androcentrism in the organisational culture.

It is to be expected that a variety of reactions will continue to circulate inside the organisation well into the future. However, at present there is nothing to hold up Company X's 'creation of female store managers'. If this were to be promoted even more, then the personnel policy would inevitably need to give even stronger concrete form to the issue of consciously nurturing talented women. The question for the future will be: How will male middle managers move beyond the narrow mindedness of 'consideration' and 'sympathy' to take this on as their own task? This, in turn, inevitably leads to the task of reforming the organisational culture. In this lies the possibility for the opening up of a path which would realise the fervently held wish of young women for nurturing to occur without distinction as to men or women.

Conclusion: Getting Closer to the Realities of the Work Organisation

This book has been structured around themes suggested by case studies which analyse gender within the work organisation – on the basis of an examination of the historical literature of women's labour studies – and has attempted to respond to these themes. I have chosen as the objects of these case studies department stores and general merchandise supermarkets, which are highly reliant on female labour and which, moreover, have in place a status ranking system with the same fundamental conditions and treatment for men and women. I would like to conclude this work by mentioning a number of points, which need to be emphasised.

Work organisation analysis as methodology

The first point in need of emphasis is the methodology which I have employed throughout this book. The concern of this book has been a thoroughgoing 'interpretation of gender within the very labour process itself', with particular effort being made to carry out the case studies at the practical and concrete level of the work organisation. This analytical standpoint was an attempt to take note of the process of segregation from below, which occurs at a deep level of the work organisation, and to grasp internal organisational divisions in their entirety, even whilst seeing the main cause of gender-based job segregation primarily in terms of the orthodoxy of work distribution from above. The aim of this was to attempt to draw close to the reality of the work organisation, by giving meaning to the individual and collective resistance within the organisation and to organisational challenges.

This analysis, firstly, revealed the complexity of internal organisational divisions. Gender and educational background have an affect on these divisions, as do various other factors such as whether or not people move on to other stores and higher positions. Positions within organisations also develop images as being 'men's sections' or 'women's sections' and each individual's hopes with regard to these sections are based on and develop along these lines. 'Men's sections' are generally high prestige positions which act as gateways to successful careers and also to high profits. There is a strong tendency, on the other hand, for 'women's sections' to consist of light work, to be in non-core areas, without requirements for high skill levels and posts which leave one with a weak voice in the organisation. This type of segregation does originate initially from the way in which jobs are handed out from above and from the approach to the necessity of fostering talent, which has put men at the centre. However, members of an organisation, simultaneously, create and give meaning to these images, independently creating and supplying the logic which assents to these segregations. This logic is applied through the mobilisation of various primary factors, and not necessarily particularly logically. Even so, once some sort of logic to the patterns of segregation does emerge it commonly comes to be seen as fixed and is not easily done away with. However, this logic itself is not immutable and can shift its borders as a result of various conditions. What is of particular significance for a work organisation is the posting of women in male areas as a result of changes in personnel policy.

Secondly, there is also the issue of the thinking of each individual within an organisation – each on the basis of the position they hold within it – regarding the stand they will take as they respond to the decisions coming down from above. They interpret the organisational culture and make decisions, both at the individual and collective level, regarding the appropriate response to make. For example, it is possible for even those at the very bottom, who have extremely little power within the organisation, to use their power to effect changes in the lower managerial positions of the organisation. We can detect in this the workings of an identity born variously from pride in the mastery of one's work and an attachment to the workplace. What has emerged from my analysis is the point that there are, within work organisations with complex lines of segregation, areas which are difficult for top down management to reach. Thinking will remain forever at the most superficial level of know how on the question of effective management styles unless we look for answers from an analysis which penetrates deep down into the work organisation, in the manner attempted by this present work.

It will be necessary to keep perfecting the methodologies of work organisation analysis henceforth but it is now at least certain that each individual within the organisation, according to his or her position within it, has a variety of associations and dealings with the organisational culture, be they accommodation or resistance. We should not overlook the point that the work organisation itself is daily constructed by this variety of response-negotiation relations. If grasped in this way, then needless to say that labour research lacking the analytical viewpoint of gender – the most fundamental basis of the diversity of each individual's experiences within the organisation – is meaningless.

The problem of androcentrism

The second problem that we need to look at is that of androcentrism in Japanese work organisations. As has been repeatedly pointed out by many researchers, most Japanese work organisations have to date remained extremely obstinate in their view that it is only men who are 'talented (or capable) human resources'. Even in the firms selected for this book, which are highly reliant on women's labour, androcentric personnel management and work practices are dominant. The case of department store A shows that even though women have strengthened the trend towards longer years of continuous service and even though they are being selected for low level managerial positions, still the type of organisational structure just described remains quite difficult to reform. This is because of the industrial predisposition of Company A and the predisposition of the entire industry, which instead of attempting to carry out self-reform, has remained reliant on the sales and distribution network established following the Second World War. This is also linked to a reliance on the system of dispatched salespeople (*haken hanbaiin*). Company A still holds on to a 'view of women' buried deep within its personnel system, (that is, that female regular employees will ultimately 'go off to marry' and also the fundamental premise that, by contrast, only men can serve as a long term labour force). In the midst of all this, female regular employees have been largely assigned to positions with scant discretionary power, on the assumption that they will ultimately be resigning, thus placing them in a clearly distinct position from both men and dispatched salespeople. The deep fissures present in internal organisational segregation have become apparent as a result of this. Whilst inhabiting the same workplace, female regular employees and female dispatched salespeople mutually regard each other as 'aliens' and they also constitute a separate world from men. Even the appearance of the trend towards the long-term employment of women, which has occurred since the establishment of this 'view of women', has had, at most, limited results, with women being selected for assistant roles without any radical readjustment of the personnel system or practices. We must understand from this that the internal incentives for 'making positive use of women' in a true sense are extremely weak in Company A. We need to ascertain just how female university graduates, the ones who experienced and learned the most from the contradictions of the job segregation described above, will put their views to practical use within the company strategy as it grapples with exposure to future developments in the competitive marketplace.

In the case of general merchandise supermarket X also, an androcentric personnel system and its corollary an androcentric organisational culture, have become firmly entrenched as a result of the long period of no attention having been paid to nurturing female talent. The usual practices of personnel management and the daily words and actions of male superiors have actively discouraged women, relegating them to an invisible existence and to being treated as people of whom nothing could be expected. However, Company X did not have the same view of women as Company A, it attempted to select 'capable' women for office work in the staff department and for specialist work. Company X wrestled with personnel selections of this kind, with a view to 'making positive use of women', whilst safeguarding store management as the sacred preserve of men. However, the company is becoming conscious of the limitations of this approach as a result of the lack of career development prospects for women: women find themselves confined to posts segregated, and patently different, from the course followed by core men in middle management.

Although, as seen above, Companies A and X differ from one another in this regard, it is clear that their practices of personnel management are premised on a particular type of 'view of women'. Despite the fact that women were resigning because of the lack of prospects within the organisation, the personnel department persisted in seeing this simply in terms of women 'naturally' resigning for reasons of marriage or childbirth. Women are seen merely as resigning to suit their own convenience, regardless of working in a gender-neutral personnel system and personnel management practices and regardless of 'consideration' upon 'consideration' having been shown to them. There is no attempt whatsoever to look at the problems of an organisational culture which discourages women; the absence of means for distributing work duties or motivating women; or the problem of the attitudes of male superiors. We can see that it is an extremely difficult thing for the male work organisation to become aware of the impact on women of an androcentric organisational culture and the practices within it. The women who have come up through the career ladder inside the organisation whilst enduring these conditions are valuable witnesses to these problems. There are also some men who are aware of the situation but it is difficult to make androcentrism visible in the organisation without the help of the women who have come up through the career ladder.

Because even the people responsible for personnel policy and its practices are unaware of the organisational culture, they are immediately inclined to think about childcare support policies when 'making positive use of women' is mentioned. These types of policies deserve further serious consideration but without a simultaneous rethinking of the very distribution of work duties within the work organisation and without the introduction of policies and motivations with some degree of career development prospects for women, 'making positive use of women' will not happen. Even if the only measure taken is the introduction of a childcare support policy, unless subjects are bred who will use this and attempt to aid their own career development, this valuable system too will be meaningless. What must be stressed in particular here is the need to revise attitudes which interpret everything in terms of the domestic and child rearing roles of women. Having realised this we should also take a hard look at areas which have been neglected – areas of serious problems inside work organisations. It can be said that that the way of thinking which regards women resigning or continuing to stay in a set managerial position for an extended period of time as an inevitable 'natural' phenomenon, prescribed by women's household roles, has played a role in maintaining androcentrism. We need to face up to the fact that the application of the personnel management system and its very practices have favoured androcentrism and we also need to recognise that a gender bias lies deeply embedded in personnel management.

The significance of the organisational challenge pursued by Company X

The third point which needs to be emphasised is the impact of the practice of 'the creation of female store managers' in Company X. This decision, taken by senior management in Company X – in conjunction with gradual steps by the organisation to appoint women chief clerks – has clearly pointed the way for organisational change. The significance of this decision to select women and to keep nurturing them as far as senior management is considerable. The main reaction of male store managers when this was first instituted was chilly, with comments such as 'they are mere ornaments' and 'they will soon fail' but within seven years the remarks changed from 'sympathetic' expressions to 'the exclusive cultivation of women is reverse discrimination' and 'this is no longer a time for talking about (distinctions between) men and women'. We can sense in this the signs of a developing sense of 'rivalry' towards the 'first generation' of female store managers, who displayed unanticipated levels of determination. We can infer the ingrained nature of androcentrism from the very fact that at the stage where female store managers are still merely less than ten per cent, the reaction is not to try to expand the active stage for women but rather to declare, 'from now on there will be no consideration or sympathy extended because you are a woman'. This reaction results from the beginnings of a realisation that the existence of female store managers may violate the male domain. If the 'creation of female store managers' progresses even more in the future, then men's sense of 'rivalry' may surface even more plainly.

However, we ought to note the fact that every time women break through each of the lines of segregation which have been established between men and women, the nature of the utterances heard within the organisation changes character. When a female chief clerk was selected, there were murmurs of 'they will choose a virago'. When female section heads first appeared, female chief clerks said 'a female superior would never do all that shouting (like a male section head)'. As the numbers of female store managers increased little by little comments such as 'that is the right sort of store for a female store manager' deliberately attempted to discriminate between the management abilities of men and women. As women break through existing boundaries and progress on to a variety of posts and managerial positions, new statements are produced reflecting these moves. As this happens the old statements are forgotten. Statements based on an understanding that women could not become chief clerks, in a period when there was not a single female chief clerk, are no longer in use today. These were next replaced by comments regarding the difficulties of women becoming section heads or store managers but once again these comments also lose their soul as they are overtaken by reality.

Another point to note is that the changes in these comments appear via the process of organisational reform. We can take it that in the midst of all this the organisational culture itself also changes. An organisational culture which has modelled itself on androcnetrism is difficult to change but we can think that it will gradually change if this process of change is linked to practical steps which will transform, one by one, the 'views of women' which have come to be embedded within the organisation.

Women as organisational innovators

The 'creation of female store managers' in Company X was brought about as a result of a decision taken by senior management. However, it was the very existence inside the organisation of women who responded to and took up this policy in Company X which led to its success. These women, whilst being used as players in an organisational challenge engineered by company policy, put this opportunity to good use and appeared on the stage as subjects developing their own strategic performance. The significance of the fact that the strategy adopted by them ended up attracting the attention of the whole company, as it moved beyond its 'ornamental' aims, is considerable. We can assume that there are likely to be significant numbers of women, in other work organisations today, who are building up their abilities as they wait for the arrival of opportunities for action. It is possible that although they are as yet excluded from decision-making, women are lying dormant within organisations, building up the abilities which would enable them to grapple with organisational challenges, should they have the opportunity. These women are able to play the role of innovators for the organisation and as such there is profound value in the existence of these women.

What we must be wary of here is the certain likelihood that labels such as 'feminine' (*joseiteki*) or 'female-type' (*joseikei*) will appear at the stage where women first begin to be active. In fact, there are strong influences at work attempting to stereotype the management of female store managers in Company X as 'female-type'. Even members of the personnel department say of female store managers, 'they can give detailed instructions'. They are very good at customer service. Their communication skills are excellent.' This type of thinking is linked to essentialism or an essentialist understanding of gender differences in management. In other words, it is an understanding which directly links the differences between the management styles of men and women to the differences in their respective socialisation processes. This is encountered, for example, in the argument that women are intrinsically good communicators, team players and abounding in cooperativeness whilst men, being authoritarian, are capable of a tougher management style. This grasp of things has the result of contributing to perpetuation of the gender-based segregation and re-segregation of management roles. Female store managers themselves seized upon both 'male-type management' and 'female-type management' comparing and contrasting them, in an attempt to give meaning to their own practices. This kind of strategy is undeniably effective in the very early stages of women assuming greater prominence. However, continuing to adhere to this type of dichotomy indefinitely is also dangerous. This is because it renders them incapable of taking part in any re-segregation themselves.

We need to take a close and careful look at the idea that the strategic performance of female store mangers is something which they learned from the organisational culture. It is, in fact, a strategy which their consciousness of being far from the organisational mainstream and the experience of their careers coming up against androcentrism drove them to choose. Alternatively, it is a challenge by a 'peripheral' group – women – who could not help but be conscious of being in a position which differed from the way in which men were being nurtured. The management style employed by them in these conditions is intentionally clearly different from the mainstream style. In this sense, female store managers have instituted an alternative to the mainstream. The above can be said of the 'first generation' of female store managers. Because the 'second generation' and 'third generation' would have a completely different experience of being a 'peripheral' group within the organisation than was the case for the pioneering 'first generation', we can imagine that they would also develop their own, different management styles.

Finally, we need to establish two points regarding the impact on the work organisation of the pioneering steps carved out by this 'first generation'. The first point is that the direction of organisational change being pointed by these women is towards reducing the distance between the top and bottom of the organisation. That is, a management style striving to get closer to the 'us' (female rank-and-file regular employees and female part-timers) found at the bottom of the store. As we saw in detail in Chapter 4, this 'us' group had a positive work consciousness and keenly sought a sense of reward and achievement. It is possible to demonstrate the effectiveness of this style of management, which does not lead to the loss of the can-do spirit of these women employees. It is a style of management which corresponds closely to the special characteristics of the work organisation. This management style would, furthermore, be of a type closely bound up with a decentralisation policy respecting the various individual conditions of the store's location.

The second point concerns the significance embodied in the experience not only of the appearance of female store managers eroding men's sacred territory but also of gaining entry into an area which had previously been held to be impossible for women. As touched on previously, the breaking through, one by one, of barriers by women leads to the old discourse disappearing and a new one coming into being. The disappearance of one discourse occurs as a result of women clearing another boundary and this experience of clearing cannot be turned back. We can detect in this the possibility for the unstoppable creation of new values. There is the possibility that the 'second generation', and the new generations of women and men coming after them, will grasp the meaning of the practices of the 'first generation' of female store managers, accepting and giving form to these values and devising a new code. Unearthing real cases of the process of accumulation of these new values over time is a task for researchers who introduce a gender viewpoint and attempt to develop it in empirical research. This is also a task of searching for clues to disconnect the chain of 'cyclical processes' which keeps reproducing the 'gender order' (Ehara, 2001).

An eye to future research

Finally, I would like to raise the angle of the efficiency of the work organisation. Generally, there are numerous cases in which there is a gap between the efficiency of the organisation and management's profits on the one hand and changes aimed at achieving gender equality in the work organisation's internal order. There are also cases of mutual contradiction. However, as has emerged from this book, we cannot possibly say that an organisational culture which confines talented women with concealed possibilities to live in obscurity inside the organisation and drives them to resign is superior in the area of organisational efficiency. There are also actual cases in which organisational efficiency is being lost as a result of the weak voice of the female areas into which only women are thrown. As seen in Chapter 4, we cannot say that all register errors were due to the lack of attentiveness of the women assigned to the registers; there were many cases in which there were problems with the position of the product price tag. Considered from this aspect it is clear that 'making positive use of women' has a very important meaning from the viewpoint of organisational efficiency. Seen also from the perspective of the work system, a situation in which one is unable to address an error despite being able to specify the cause because one has a weak voice will become a major cause of frustration for the people working there and will also lead to a loss of their will to work. I think that there is sufficient value in attempting to rethink androcentric organisational culture from the viewpoint of addressing inefficiencies.

In future we need to pursue the dual viewpoints of gender fairness and efficiency. As stated in the Introduction, the realities surrounding women's labour are complex and intricate. Under present economic circumstances, 'arguments that we ought to' emphasise only gender fairness cannot have any persuasive power. In order to aim for solid progress in gender fairness in every individual workplace, it is necessary to construct a logic with the power to persuade – one based on the actual state of individual workplaces and which regards the recognition of gender fairness at the state level, as represented by the Basic Law for a Gender-Equal Society, favourably. For this purpose, both the raising of actual problems by reviewing work organisations, which have become rigid as a result of being so deeply steeped in androcentrism, and also some means of simultaneously introducing a gender fairness perspective into the work organisation will be important.

Notes

Chapter 1

1. In this book, I use the term, 'Marxist-Feminism' although some scholars prefer the term 'Socialist-Feminism,' and others 'Materialist-Feminism' (Furuta, 1994). Although there are a variety of works in regard to women's labour, the works with which this chapter deals are limited to those approached from a women's studies perspective or a gender perspective. Works that merely *describe* labour phenomena in regard to women are excluded.
2. For empirical research on the structure of relationships in company society and families in Japan, one should refer to Section III in Kimoto (1995a), which is based on a survey of male workers in the Toyota Motor Company Ltd. in the 1980s. This period may well be considered the period of maturity of the company society in Japan (Kimoto, 2002b).
3. One of the few examples is an analysis by Masami Nomura of the baseboard assembly process of a general electrical manufacturer. Job segregation by gender, brought about by automation in this division, is considered from three perspectives: (1) job segregation between the television factory and the contract companies; (2) job segregation within the factory between the regular employed workers and the peripheral labour force; and (3) job segregation among the regular workers. The study shows that a clear line of segregation is drawn between the genders. The divisions among male workers assume a vague and flexible appearance when contrasted to the fact that female workers, who form a peripheral labour force, are fully mobilised in labour intensive, simple manufacturing processes. Nomura says that this fact points to the need for gender sensitive labour research (1993).
4. Shimazu's work (1978) is an example of this.
5. Molineux (1979) gives details of this debate. In addition, see Vogel (1981), Donovan (1985), Sargent (1981) and Beechey (1987). For introductions to the debate in Japan, see Kuba (1979), Mizuta (1980), Takenaka (1989a), Duden and von Werlhof (edited and translated by Maruyama Masato (1986)), Ueno (1990) and Furuta (1994; 1997).
6. The major points of the debate are reproduced in Ueno (1982).
7. Ueno (1990) was originally serialised in *Shisō no Kagaku* (The Science of Thought) from March 1986 to January 1988. At about the same time, many

translations were published including Kuhn and Wolpe (1978=1984), Sokoloff (1980=1987), Sargent (1981=1991) and Beechey (1987=1993). Thus, European and American debates in Marxist-Feminism were introduced to Japan after the 1980s.
8   This study, however, was first published in 1985.
9   See Chapter 3 of Kimoto (1995a) for a critical analysis of Marxist discussions of the family which continue on from Chitose Shimazu's study of the family.
10 I would like to expand on Beechey, whose 1978 study Takenaka (1989a, 4) quotes regarding 'the specificity of the position of female wage labour' (Beechey, 1978=1984,195). Beechey used the term 'specificity' in the original (1978, 195), but subsequently deleted this term when she published her work in 1987. This indicates that Beechey was still considering the 'specificity' of women's labour at the time when she was committed to the domestic labour debate, but she criticises her own arguments and proposes a new method for analysing women's paid work from a gender perspective, which I shall discuss later. The path taken by Beechey reveals the major shift in the focus of the argument that took place during the late 1970s and 1980s.
11 The concept of unpaid work arises from a critical awareness of questions about how one can position the various forms of employment identified by studies in developing countries in Latin America, Asia and Africa in the 1970s (Furuta, 1996). These forms include seasonal employment, casual employment, peddling, subsistence farming, familial labour and employment as a family worker in a self-sustaining household. For an overview of these studies of unpaid work, see *Josei no anpeido wāku: kokusaiteki chōsa kenkyū bunken risuto (Women's Unpaid Work: International Research Bibliography)* 1995 and Kawasaki and Nakamura (2000).
12 For a discussion of these types of theoretical trends in feminist economics in the 1990s see Kuba (2002).
13 This is another reason why an analysis of internal class and social differences amongst female employees is essential. See Hashimoto (2001,2003), Chapter 2.
14 This criticism has been made since the mid 1980s. It has been levelled at the fact that existing feminist theory and the concept of gender were built by middle class white women as if their interests represented those of women as a whole, despite the fact that the construction of these theories was heavily biased as a result of the egocentrism of this group. This criticism of arguments that take the experiences of white women as their natural premise inherently raises questions about the difficulties of organising 'neutral knowledge' (Collins 1998). For example, although the family is the source of oppression for white feminists, black feminists cannot but see this as a source of solidarity, necessary to their survival in a society that discriminates against

black people. The pursuit of a professional career and the achievement of economic independence by white women are dependent on the low wages of black domestic workers. Not surprisingly, the views of black feminists seem to suggest that the domestic labour debate of the 1970s – insofar as it posited the housewife as being responsible for domestic labour – was, in fact, taking a narrow view of things.

15 In response to my argument (Kimoto, 2000a), Emiko Takenaka, in her recent work, despite accusing me of 'misunderstanding', expressed her agreement with the matters most strongly stressed in my writing. In regard to my observation (2000a, 9) that emphasising unpaid work in discussing women's labour might result in disregarding the analysis of the mechanisms within the labour process, Takenaka says: 'That there is a propensity for such a danger certainly cannot be denied altogether' (Takenaka, 2002, 150).

16 On the labour process debate, see Thompson (1983=1990), Naruse (1990) and Kyōtani (1993). The commitment to the debate by feminists is detailed in Thompson (1983=1990), Chapter 7.

17 For details about the idea of a 'family wage' see Kimoto (1995a), Chapter 4. Attention to the idea of a 'family wage' was incorporated as an essential gender perspective in critical analyses of social policy and the welfare state (See Sainsbury, 1996, Chapter 3 and Fukasawa (2002)). The study by Kazuko Fukasawa (2000b) succeeded in fully incorporating the relationship between women's labour and social policy.

18 The labour process debate, which originates from a suggestion by Braverman, prompted the establishment of the International Labour Process Conference, in which the gender perspective was given an important place from the beginning. At its second conference (1984) 'Gender at Work' was the topic of discussion (Knights and Willmott, 1986).

19 Beechey herself conducted a detailed survey with Tessa Perkins on the demand for part-time labour in manufacturing industry and the public service sector in Coventry. Beechey and Perkins, in total opposition to existing theories which see part-time work as a 'natural' by-product created by the gender-based division of labour in the family, aimed to position part-time employment in an analysis of restructuring the labour force. Survey results show that the strategy of employers in regard to gender plays an important role. In other words, part-time labour is used by employers as a strategy to gain flexibility in structuring the labour force, and is due neither to deskilling nor the segmented labour market. The employers' gender ideology and occupational segregation by gender are closely related. Members of trade unions have particular hypotheses as to what type of work is suitable for women or as to why married women work on a part-time basis. These, intertwined with the employers' strategies, are helping to shape part-time employment. Furthermore, part-time work

manifests itself differently depending on what sort of gender ideology is presupposed by state policy; especially if the policy is dependent on the traditional idea of a 'family wage' (Beechey, 1987=1993; Beechey and Perkins, 1987). This is an important study that has opened up new horizons in the study of part-time labour. Unfortunately, Beechey fell ill and could not pursue her case studies.

20 Cockburn accumulated further case studies that paid attention to technological innovation and changes in gender relations in the workplace (1985; 1991; and 1993).

21 There was reason enough for the labour process debate to go unnoticed. It is necessary to remember the lack of interest in this debate within mainstream labour research in Japan. This was because empirical studies from broader viewpoints had already been conducted in Japan in regard to deskilling – one of the major points argued by Braverman. From the mid-1950s to the beginning of the 1960s, many field studies (in building, steel, shipbuilding, coalmining, automotive and chemical industries) were accumulated. They illuminated the overall picture of the issues of deskilling including not only the technological innovation that eliminated the older skills but also the changes in labour relations and labour unions (Rōdō Chōsaron Kenkyūkai (Study Group on Labour Research) 1970, 221–253). When the strength of manufacturing industry in Japan came to international attention after the mid-1980s, mainstream labour research in Japan re-entered the labour process debate through discussions of Taylorism, Fordism and Post-Fordism (Naruse, 1990 and Kyōtani, 1993).

22 Mari Ōsawa calls these Japanese features the ultimate case of 'disintegrated wage labour' (1993b, 172). The theory of the 'marginalisation of wage labour' propounded by Claudia von Werlhof, along with the theory of the 'housewife-isation of labour', is one of the important key words in connecting the fortunes of both women in the economically advanced countries and men and women in the developing countries from a global perspective (Mies, et. al., 1991). However, since it is such a broad concept, it seems to be necessary to build subordinate analytical categories in order for it to be used in empirical analyses.

23 For a discussion of statistical discrimination Kōshi Endō (2002) is instructive.

24 Case studies introduced earlier in this book, mainly from the United Kingdom, had in mind the analysis of job segregation between the genders using the macro-data analysis of Catherine Hakim (Hakim, 1979). Their aim was to transcend the limitations of macro-data. It is necessary to look for a way to establish full-scale case studies in conjunction with studies in gender statistics (Itō, 1994 and Sugihashi, 1997).

Notes

25 Examples of these include Yōko Kawashima Horn (1995), Kimiko Kimoto (1995b; 1999), Masumi Mori (1997), Tomoko Komagawa (1998; 2000), Saori Miyashita (2000), Kazuko Fukasawa (2000c), Harumi Sasatani (2000) and Aiba and Wharton (2001). Although not a case study, Maki Ōmori 's 1995 work is instructive on women's labour in white-collar jobs. This area was not sufficiently covered by labour research on men in the past. A case study by Eiko Shinotsuka on in-hospital assistant carers can be appraised as a pioneering work in the study of care work (1995). There are a number of other case studies that deal with women's labour but this chapter does not refer to them, as they are not studies in which issues are identified from a gender perspective.

26 Finally, although it is beyond the scope of this book, I would like to raise an issue related to the historical research survey in this chapter. When conducting a gender analysis of the labour process, we must initially analyse how lines of segregation are drawn intrinsically between the genders within the labour process. The point I would like to raise is that we must broaden our view as far as possible and consider the various conditions in the environment surrounding the labour process. In particular, we must consider independently owned businesses of the self-employed and family workers to be important external factors regulating the labour relationship in paid work. When we look at the position that independently owned businesses of the self-employed have occupied in the structure of work in Japan, and consider the fact that many women have worked as family workers, we realise that it is essential to conduct a gender analysis of management and labour in independently-owned businesses of the self-employed. This is because it seems that labour practices and gender relations within independently owned businesses of the self-employed have built up a mutually regulating relationship with the regional development of employed labour. Increasing the number of empirical studies of family workers in order to make an in-depth search for the point where employed labour meets intra-familial labour is an essential task. A study by Etsuko Chiba (2000), centred on agriculture, is important in this regard.

Chapter 2

1 The translated term 'job segregation by sex' (*seibetsu shokumu bunri*) has, up until now, been imposed on women's labour studies in Japan. In this book I have decided to stress a gender research stance which draws a distinction between the concepts of sex and gender and, accordingly, use the term 'job segregation by gender'. The term 'job' in this book is different from the strict meaning of 'job', as in trade. Other writers may use 'occupation' (*shokugyō*)

or 'occupational field' (*shokuiki*). Mari Ōsawa's use of 'gender-based segregation of occupational fields' (*seibetsu shokuiki bunri*), synthesising industry, enterprise structure, occupation and jobs (1992a and 1992b), is widely seen as appropriate. However, 'jobs' is used in a qualified way in this book, in order to give central consideration to the distribution of jobs and the labour relations between male and female regular employees, part-timers and dispatched sales employees in sales occupations in joint workplaces in the retail industry. Either the term segregation of occupations or segregation of jobs may be used, according to the context of the discussion.

2 Takehiko Matsudo provided suggestions regarding the possibilities of using an ethno-methodological perspective in analysing the workplace (1994). Matsudo, points out that this perspective is not effective in gaining a structural understanding for the purpose of solving practical social problems (1994, 188) but that it can be used, in combination with a structural approach, as a method of exploring the possibilities for gender equality.

3 Looking at work organisations in this way is not new. In Taylorism, organisations are seen as mechanical and 'rational' and the members of organisations as being influenced purely by economic motives. In contrast to this, Mayo and others have detected emotional and irrational acts by people in their Hawthorne experiments and stressed the group sentiment and informal ties between members of an organisation as the human aspect of organisations (Mayo, 1933=1951and Roethlisberger, 1941=1954). However, Acker and others commented that Mayo and others did not use a gender perspective to analyse the group of female workers, who contributed to maximum productivity. They also made fundamental criticisms of the premise, in previous debates about organisations, of the centrality of organisations to gender (Acker and Houten, 1974). The 1980s inherited this type of research and ultimately a recognition developed of the importance of research introducing gender and sexuality into organisational analysis (Witz, 1997). Amongst these works an important attempt to theorise, through the medium of empirical research, is to be found in Hearn's documents (Hearn and Parkin, 1987 and Hearn et al., 1989). More elaborate empirical research was being published in the 1990s, with the ambitious co-operative research undertaken by Halford and others being the most representative (Halford et al., 1997). According to Mats Alvesson, a gender perspective became the focus of debates on organisation in the middle of the 1990s (Alvesson and Billing, 1997, 8). There are constantly more books being published on the achievements of research into work organisations and gender (Halford and Leonard, 2001 and Wilson, 2001).

4 I am indebted to Halford and Leonard's research for this understanding. They examined existing concepts of organisational culture, emphasised the endless process of building and rebuilding and stipulated that organisational culture

arises from the mutual social actions and negotiations between members of organisations. Particularly important is their understanding of the fact that individuals interpret organisational culture on the basis of their diversity and that there are a variety of ways of relating to and of resisting and bringing about change to the organisational culture. This is because organisational culture has a fluid base (Halford and Leonard, 2001). See also Elizabeth R. Wilson (Wilson, 2001).

5 Under the status ranking system, although wages – called *shokunōkyū*, literally 'evaluation-based wages' 'status pay' would be a more acurate translation. This is a method of paying wages in which payment is made according to 'the attributes of employees', seen as 'the capacities (of employees) regarding unspecified functions'. At first sight, the definition of 'evaluation-based wages' could readily lead to an understanding of the 'evaluation' component as being short hand for the capacity to perform one's functions, with the payment of wages being contingent on this manifest capacity. However, this first glance definition easily leads to misunderstanding. The concept of function embodied in evaluation-based wages is not that of a specific function: it connotes, instead, a function which is abstractly conceived and which is versatile enough to enable it to change. It would, indeed, be preferable to say that there is no concept of function in evaluation-based wages. Further, because 'the capacity (of employees) regarding unspecified functions' does not exist in any clear form, one could this the 'latent capacity' of employees'. This explanation is the reason why we should use the netral 'status pay' when discussing the status ranking system.

6 Takeo Kikkawa says that chain store supermarkets, which displayed rapid growth following the period of high growth, contributed to the 'westernisation of the diet'. In other words, the rapid spread of processed foods drove this westernisation of the diet. At the same time, however, because Japan's traditional structure of food consumption, which values freshness, remained strong in the period of high economic growth, Japanese supermarkets followed a different development process from supermarkets in the West (Kikkawa, 1998). The development of food supermarkets did not occur until the 1980s.

7 Yoshifumi Abe (1993, 44) and Seigo Imoto (1993, 353) make the same observations.

8 Kansai Supermarket is particularly familiar with this historical process.

9 In the research for *Census of Commerce*, which forms the basis for this, there are frequent changes to the classifications of business formats and scale, making comparisons over time difficult. I have re-combined classifications of business formats so as to be able to use them, as far as possible, in making comparisons in the tables and figures in this book. The indicators for large-scale department stores and large-scale supermarkets change dramatically

Compare, for example, indicators for floor space which were over 1,500m^2 (3,000m^2 in special wards of Tokyo and in legally designated cities) in the 1980s and 3,000m^2 and 6,000m^2 respectively for the 1990s. Because of the existence of these discrepancies and the lack of possibility of compensating for them, I decided to use the data as it is, despite the big gap between 1988 and 1991. Incidentally, there is no data by business formats available before 1982. Items classified according to gender and types of employment are not available to the public in the data in the *Census of Commerce* for 1991 and 1994 but I was able to use this original data on the basis of an application for uses outside the aims of the Statistics Law. I would like to express my appreciation to those in the relevant government offices for their assistance in providing this data.

10 Surveys with a gender component were carried out as part of *Census of Commerce* after 1988 but because the Ministry of Economy, Trade and Industry have not kept data for 1988 I did not have any for this year. Also, because a simplified version of the survey was conducted in 1999, there was no data on gender distinctions. I look forward to the advent of surveys containing a gender perspective and for these to be available to the public.

11 Incidentally, 1991 is the only year of *Census of Commerce* in which differences in the use of men and women as a non-regular work force were surveyed. On the basis of this data, we can confirm the overwhelming tendency for the retail industry as a whole to use women as a non-regular work force. Large-scale department stores and supermarkets, in particular, make up a high proportion of retailers with women in the non-regular work force – 80.6 per cent and 89.6 per cent respectively.

12 However, one cannot make simple comparisons with supermarkets in the West because of the considerable differences in the environments of western and Japanese general merchandise supermarkets. As mentioned earlier, for example, the introduction of POS into the United States contributed directly to reductions in the number of staff whereas it did not have this effect in Japan because any surplus time was employed in the intense competition over customer service – by reducing customer waiting time at checkout counters or setting up even better displays (Dateki, 1990, 6). There are some major differences between the United Kingdom and the United States, on the one hand, and Japan on the other. Firstly, whilst store managers in Japan have generally worked their way up on the basis of store experience, even if they are university graduates; in the United Kingdom and the United States, store managers, after graduating from university, undergo a short special programme training them for the position. Secondly, in the United Kingdom and the United States employees without titles (like 'manager') – the mainstay of store labour – are paid by the hour, irrespective of whether

they are full or part-time. In Japan even rank-and-file regular employees get a monthly salary, setting them apart from part-timers who are payed by the hour. I would also like to note that my own work was significantly influenced by the research of Paul du Gay (du Gay, 1996) who tackled the question of the identity of labour subjects through empirical research into the retail industry in Britain.
13 See Masako Mitsuyama (1990) for case studies of part-timers in the supermarket industry.

Chapter 3

1 This research was carried out with Grants-in-Aid for Scientific Research from the Ministry of Education, Science and Culture for 1992 and 1993 (General Research (C): Kimiko Kimoto). There are few full-scale research surveys of department store labour. In Chapter Two I touched on the fact that Alice Lam's case study (1992) of Seibu Department Store, unlike the survey subject in this chapter, does not focus on job segregation by gender.
2 However, the numbers re-employed under this system were limited to fourteen between 1978 and 1988. As for child rearing leave, introduced in 1971, 350 women made use of it in the period until 1988. (Women and Youth 85 (1988).
3 According to Alice Lam, women are increasingly being appointed as buyers in the United States and the United Kingdom, highlighting the tardiness of Japan in this area (Lam, 1992, 164).
4 This survey was conducted between October 1993 and March 1994 with Mutsumi Furuta (Nagano University).
5 In these interviews I analyse female university graduates aged 23 to 32. The interview subjects were: 1 apprentice, 4 at Grade two, 1at Grade three, 2 assistant buyers, 1 buyer and 1 store manager.
6 This is going over something I touched on earlier but the department store industry has been increasing its proportion of part-timers and casual employees. However, in terms of the full-scale mobilisation of the powers of these employees, department stores lag behind supermarkets. Efforts in this direction were only beginning in the 1990s and at the time of this survey, department stores remained unable to see this group as the major force in sales. From 1988, Company A also started a new system aimed at making positive use of part-timers, with particular efforts to implement these practices fully in newly-opened suburban shops. However, in the workplace where this survey was conducted they amounted to no more than assistant roles for women regular employees, in areas such as receptionists in delivery and repairs, and affected only three employees (two males and one female).

7   In 1973, the Fair Trade Commission issued a notice abolishing the dispatching of salespeople in the department store industry, rendering this an illegal practice under the 'Anti-Monopoly Law'. There was, however, an exemptions clause in this notice permitting the use of dispatched salespeople in a limited number of cases requiring specialist skills or knowledge and thus enabling the dispatched salespeople system to survive (Okuda, 1991, 117, 118).
8   There is to date no clear picture of the actual numbers of dispatched salespeople. Not even the Department Stores Association has any accurate statistics on this. All that has been published is extremely partial data, under the category of 'support staff', in a 1989 survey (1991) conducted by the Tokyo Metropolitan Labour Institute. On the basis of my own survey, dispatched salespeople can be divided into two types. One type is made up of salespeople dispatched to shops on a temporary basis when businesses are under pressure. The other is made up of employees who are dispatched to the same shop on an ongoing basis. In the shop where this survey was conducted there were approximately 50 dispatched salespeople of both types but even if we narrow our consideration to the second type, the numbers are as high as 38, compared with 27 regular employees. Excluding a small number of exceptions, all shop floors of this type in women's clothing sections generally have from 1.4 to 2.6 times more dispatched salespeople than regular employees.

Chapter 4

1   The empirical studies that form the basis of the findings in Chapters 4 and 5 were funded by Grants-in-Aid for Scientific Research (C) (2) (1997–99) from the Ministry of Education, Culture, Sports, Science and Technology, and also by a grant from the Research Fund of the Japan Economic Research Foundation (1998). Part of the survey data used here is from the research funded by Grants-in-Aid for Scientific Research (C) (2) (2001–2003), from the Ministry of Education, Culture, Sports, Science and Technology. The discussions in Chapters 4 and 5 are primarily based on the findings of interviews with staff members at Headquarters, including the Personnel and Merchandise Departments, and also at the Area Business Operations Department of Company X. The survey period was between 1997 and 2002. Unless otherwise noted, the data and interviews used in this chapter were collected between the end of the 1990s and the year 2000. I have supplied the year in which the information was collected, as necessary. In discussing the interview data in Chapters 4 and 5, personal details are supplied in a way that does not allow the identification of individuals.
2   The official terms used in Company X for these different career paths are 'national employees', 'regional employees' and 'local employees', respectively.

However, the preferred terms in this book – 'nation-wide', 'area-specific' and 'store-specific' paths – have been adopted to help visualise the career path arrangements. Different career paths offer slightly different base wages. For example, the difference in annual wages at Grade level 5 is about ¥260,000 between the area-specific path and the store-specific path. These wages are based on the status grade. The basic salary for Grade 5, for example, is made up of wages, status wages and expertise wages, which represent 50, 5 and 45 per cent respectively of a monthly total salary of about ¥240,000. For Grade 6, the composition is 40, 15 and 45 per cent respectively of the total monthly salary of about ¥320,000. The proportions of the status wages and expertise wages for this level are higher. Those on or above Grade 7 receive performance evaluation wages in addition. A Grade 7 employee's monthly salary of about ¥420,000 is made up of base wages, status wages, expertise wages and performance evaluation wages in the proportion of 32, 15, 45 and 8 per cent respectively (1998).

3 An executive in the labour union at the time, who was involved in the negotiations on this system as one of the chief negotiators, stated: 'we did not have women in mind at all'.

4 Promotion to the position of chief clerk normally takes two to three years after joining the company for a male university graduate. It is about three years for a female university graduate and employees who have graduated from a vocational college. On the other hand, for a female high school leaver, it takes much longer to become a chief clerk. According to the interview findings in Store A, which will be discussed later (see Table 4.2), Female Chief Clerk 1, a high school leaver in the apparel section, became a chief clerk in her twenties, before she had a baby. This was her fourth year after joining the company. However, for Female Chief Clerk 2, twelve years passed before her promotion. It took sixteen years for Female Chief Clerk 3 (a vocational college graduate in the apparel section) and seventeen years for Female Chief Clerk 4 (a high school graduate in the apparel section). There are, in fact, some male high school graduates who repeatedly fail the Grade 5 examination, for example Rank-and-file Regular Employee 5. He joined the company after having worked for another company, but he keeps failing the examination to go up to Grade 5. However, his case is highly exceptional. As a whole, the length of time required before becoming a chief clerk depends clearly on gender and educational background. Those who had worked for other similar companies before joining Company X tended to become chief clerks on joining the company.

5 Two types of employees are excluded from this study. They are the employees in the General Affairs Department, which gives administrative behind-the-scenes support to the sales floors, and the casual workers, who work for a short

term and for short hours. Quotations made from the interviews will identify the interviewees as 'Section Head 1' or 'Chief Clerk 1', in keeping with the positions and numbers in Table 4.2.

6   The questionnaires were hand-delivered by the store manager. After they were filled in, the envelopes were sealed and put into a box specifically set up inside the store or posted to the Personnel Department in their Area Business Operations Department. The store manager was entrusted with the task of choosing the subjects for the survey but was asked to sample as evenly as possible from different strata of employees. However, it was later discovered that the overwhelming proportion of part-time respondents were actually longer-serving part-time workers. This may have been because, when the chief clerks were giving out questionnaires, it was easier to ask the longer-serving part-time employees to help with the survey. Accordingly, the data must be seen as coming from the longer-serving part-time workers.

7   I cannot say that the second and the third questionnaire surveys listed here are based on sampling which is strictly quantifiable. It is possible, however, to extract some tendencies from them.

8   As mentioned earlier, the rank-and-file regulars are divided into 'leaders' and 'clerks'. Each chief clerk has his or her own sales area but not all chief clerks have a leader assigned under them. In practice, there is not much difference between 'leaders' and 'clerks' in terms of the duties they perform. Accordingly, in the following discussion I will talk of them only as rank-and-file regulars, without making a distinction between the two.

9   This feature is not unique to Company X. Similar job segregation by gender can be observed in other food supermarkets (Tatsuuma and Kimoto, 1999).

10 As studies in the past were focused only on men, the Japanese translation used for 'them and us' was '*yatsura* and *oretachi*' (Naitō, 1975), words used in male speech. To reflect the differences in the gender of the subject in this work, the terms used in the Japanese version of this book are '*ano hitotachi* and *watashitachi*', which are the female equivalents.

11 According to the findings of the supplementary interviews conducted in September 2001, male rank-and-file regular employees do not share this type of sense of 'us'. This is because most of the male rank-and-file regular employees are young men who have not been working for the company for very long. The older male rank-and-file regular employees who have served longer form a minority group in the store. Both younger and older male rank-and-file regular employees belong to the category of 'them'. They are both transient and do not stay in one store for very long.

12 As the question invited open answers, the contents of the responses were varied. The responses were analysed according to their contents and put into groups. Twelve male rank-and-file regular employees, 42 female rank-and-file

regular employees and 191 part-time employees responded to this question. The responses are broad ranging and they are all considered and counted separately. Figure 4.9 shows the percentage of the responses given for each type of occasion, divided by the number of respondents in each group of employees.

13 This sense of reward and achievement, however, is always on the brink of being eroded by staff shortages. Those who answered that they 'don't feel a sense of reward and achievement' are 5 male rank-and-file regular employees, 15 female rank-and-file regular employees and 22 part-time employees. They are a minority, but their voices are prominent in pointing out this problem. Some of these comments are, 'there are not enough people. We might have to leave a job unfinished and this doesn't give me a sense of achievement. I want to have a bit more time so that I don't feel so pressured' (47 year old female rank-and-file regular employee in the apparel section with nine years of service). 'It is necessary to build up a culture in which it is taken for granted that we must try to shorten our working hours. By doing so, the burden currently on individuals might be dispersed and then I think we will be able to enjoy a sense of reward and achievement both physically and psychologically' (27 year old male rank-and-file regular employee in the food section with three years of service). The following are the same concerns strongly expressed among the part-time employees. 'Because there are not enough workers, we always feel we are pressed with work and the job is left undone. Really, we don't have enough employees. I want to have a bit more time at hand' (45 year old in the apparel section with six years of service). 'Everyday is busy. We have such a lot to do everyday. I do as much work as I can in four hours. If I had more time, then I think I would find it rewarding (55 year old in the food section with ten years of service). It should be noted that it is only possible for employees to work in a way that enables them to feel a sense of reward and achievement when there are appropriate levels of staffing.

14 In addition to these factors, we must keep the historical background in mind. In the food section, it was initially male tradespeople who handled fresh produce such as fish and meat. Although the technological innovations that enabled pre-packaging gradually expelled the gruff world of tradesmen, its image as a 'masculine' workplace lingered, with the consequence that it was a place to which women were not assigned. Azuchi [1987] is instructive in regard to the expulsion of the tradesmen.

15 In additon to this book, Ogasawara in her book [1998] paid attention to 'resistance' (*rejisutansu*) by female rank-and-file regular employees. However, the implication of 'resistance' in her book is completely different from that in this book. What Ogasawara examined is resistance by female office

workers (*OL's*) who have no authority or responsibility within an organisation. Such resistance is offered when they 'take reverse advantage of their weak position' and is made possible by their 'abandonment of responsibility as professional workers' [1998, 138]. The acts of resistance described there include long private telephone calls, chatting during working hours and killing time by developing tactics for giving presents of chocolates to their superiors on Valentine's Day. The possibilities for bringing about change in work organisations would be aided by the development of arguments going to the heart of the actual content of work duties and labour relations.

Chapter 5

1. On the question of male store managers, I interviewed eight men working as store managers (at the time of the 1999 survey) and two who had previously been store managers before moving on to the Staff Department of the Area Operations Division of Head Office. I endeavoured to interview a wide variety of store managers, following the advice of the Personnel Department in Head Office regarding management styles. In the case of the latter two, I conducted the interviews by getting them to talk retrospectively about their experiences as store managers. For the sake of convenience, in this chapter I have not referred to their present managerial positions but simply call them 'male store managers'. In the following discussion I also make use of interviews with people in Head Office and in positions related to the Area Operations Division of Company X. The interview period is the same as set out in Chapter Four, from 1997 until 2000, but I also make some use of interviews conducted in 2001–2002. Given the length of the survey period, I have decided to indicate the year in parentheses for major quotations.
2. If we consider that those who have joined the company halfway through their careers make up no more than 14.5 per cent of store managers, we see that mainstream promotion to store manager is largely open to people who joined Company X immediately after graduating from university.
3. As with Table 5.5, I exclude those who joined the company halfway through their careers. I also exclude cases of people who went on to become section heads after becoming store managers. Usually, in Company X people who have become store managers move between stores nearly once every three years – moving progressively from a small-scale, low-ranking store to a large-scale, higher-ranking store – but in their midst are also some people who are on a career path, which at a glance might appear to be a 'demotion'. These are cases, for example, in which one serves as a section head in a considerably larger store after having been a store manager of an extremely small store – on a par with a convenience store – and is then promoted to the

position of store manager. This is not, however, strictly a 'demotion'. This is because although the managerial position in the initial posting carried the title of store manager, the store handled a limited product group, one essentially requiring the skill level of a chief clerk. In no sense, however, would this store manager be free of financial responsibilities as a result of the tentative store manager position. These are, however, exceptional cases and I have excluded them from Figure 5.1 as they create complications when represented in graph form.

4 We can detect amongst women not only a tendency to remain at the one status grade but also a tendency to stay in the one store. We should not overlook the fact that this is the result of the 'consideration' shown by superiors towards female employees. Female Store Manager 5, who joined the company in 1983, worked in the one store for eight years after passing the manager's exam. She says, 'I suppose this was because the store manager was considerate regarding my pregnancy and childbirth. In short, he enabled me to avoid being transferred (to another store) because he said to the Personnel Department, "I would like to take her under my wing because I would like to nurture her". I think that was clearly a case of him showing consideration for me after the birth.' She also adds that 'Company X also had a considerate side, which it showed by not transferring women. This was the type of consideration which said that [women] generally made their home in one store.' The treatment experienced by Female Store Manager 5 is not at all exceptional. Not transferring female employees and consequently not urging them on towards the challenge of improving their status grades is a 'consideration' shown to women by male superiors. This is a very clear example of the paternalistic attitude towards female employees in Company X. At the same time this is also both a factor giving rise to the body of rank-and-file female employees who remain at the bottom of the store and evidence of the generalisation of practices which do not regard women as candidates for the nurturing of talent.

5 In addition to this, the correspondence of store customers was also important. Numerous regional newspapers carried the 'event' of the appearance of female store managers as a news item. According to Female Store Manager 2, 'There were two newspapers covering the story, with female customers reported as giving me varying levels of support. There were some letters from male customers saying, "You ought not to employ female store managers. Please stop this immediately!"' In general, female customers spoke to female store managers, giving them their support as they walked around the store. Furthermore, the problem of subordinates making a fool of the female store manager as a result of the 'intensive work pattern' of Male Store Manager 6, whom we encountered earlier, is caught up with questions regarding

whether female store managers are capable of enduring long working hours. According to the survey interviews, both male and female store managers were in the store for at least eleven hours, and in some cases for over twelve hours a day. The majority of these, in addition to leaving the store late, continue to deal with money matters after leaving the office. Alternatively, it is possible for some store managers to go home, leaving this to subordinates. It is, however, a fact that many store managers stay at work until the store closes: their comments include, 'I cannot bring myself to go home while the store is still open' and 'It is not in my nature to leave things to others'. Most store managers take the whole eight days leave per month to which they are entitled but there are some store managers who have practically no days off because they give priority to their subordinates being able to use up their leave. There are also store managers who bear in mind the guidance given to them by superiors that 'You should leave for home early because if the store manager stays at work until store closing, this makes it difficult for his subordinates to go home'. There is no doubt that long working hours are a significant problem for both male and female store managers. In these days of a tendency towards a lengthening of store opening hours, surely we ought to surmount this problem by means of appropriate personnel and operating systems.

6 In order to avoid any misunderstanding I should add that the bottom up management style, which draws close to the 'us' group, does not imply listening to all and any of the women's opinions. The majority of the 'us' group in small-scale stores are part time workers but they tend to act according to what they learnt when they first joined the company. As also mentioned earlier, small-scale stores have a pronounced 'trainee store' character, appointing rookie chief clerks and rookie section heads and sometimes even rookie store managers. Consequently, because of the difficulty of practising firm leadership power it is easy for part time workers to continue behaving without change to what they first learnt. Moreover, these women feel a strong sense of pride in having come along together with this store and they are also endowed with a resolve of the kind that means that they will not act unless convinced. Given their respect for this point, making them acquire new ways of behaving and new knowledge could be a considerable management problem. Also, if this were not the case, it would not be possible to make these women realise the sense of achievement that accompanies numerical results.

7 I think that the value of this type of bottom up management style will become clear to the extent that each general merchandise supermarket, under conditions of increasing globalisation, considers its company strategy and decides to elaborate a work strategy. If the company strengthens centralisation under Head Office and each store calculates that it will be sufficient merely

for it to continue mechanically following Head Office's stocking practices, then store work will be able to be provided by workers rather than sales people. The significance of the bottom up type of management comes to be valued highly if a store adopts the strategy of apportioning a combination of a transfer of power to the store and centralisation. The benefits become apparent from the perspective of emphasising the physical location conditions, the individual status of each store in its business sphere and its individual character. Valuing bottom up management leads to an acknowledgement of just what an important resource increasing the skill levels and enthusiasm of the 'us' group can be.

References

Abe, Yoshifumi 1993 "Hyakkaten – kakushin ni idomu."(Department Stores – Striving for Reform) In *Rytsū gendaishi: nihon-gata keizai fūdo to kigyōka seishin* (Modern History of Distribution: Japanese Economic Climate and Entrepreneurial Spirit), edited by Nihon Ryūtsū Shinbun: Tokyo, Nihon Keizai Shinbunsha.

Acker, J. and V. Houten 1974 "Differential Recruitment and Control: The Sex Structuring of Organizations." *Administrative Science Quarterly* Volume19 Number 2

Adkins, Lisa 1995 *Gendered Work: Sexuality, Family and the Labour Market*: Bristol, Open University Press.

Aiba, Keiko, and Amy S. Wharton 2001 "Job-level Sex Composition and the Sex Pay Gap in a Large Japanese Firm." *Sociological Perspectives: Official Journal of the Pacific Sociological Association* Volume 44 Number 1.

Alvesson, Mats, and Yvonne D. Billing 1997 *Understanding Gender and Organizations*: London, SAGE Publications.

Asakura, Mutsuko 1999 *Kintōhō no shinsekai: nijū kijun kara kyōtsū kijun e* (The New World of the Equal Employment Opportunity Law: From Double Standard to Common Standard): Tokyo, Yūhikaku.

Azuchi, Satoshi 1987 *Nihon sūpāmāketto genron* (The Principles of Japanese Supermarkets): Tokyo, Parusu Shuppan.

―――― 1995 *'Yasuuri' raisan ni igi ari* (Objections to Praise for 'Cut-Price Sales'): Tokyo, Tōyō Keizai Shinpōsha.

Barrett, Michèle 1980 *Women's Oppression Today: Problems in Marxist Feminist Analysis*: London, Verso.

Beechey, Veronica 1978 "Women and Production: A Critical Analysis of Some Sociological Theories of Women's Work." In *Feminism and Materialism: Women and Modes of Production*. Edited by A. Kuhn and A. M. Wolpe: London, Routledge & Kegan Paul.

―――― 1987 *Unequal Work*: London, Verso. (Translated in 1993 as *Gendai feminizumu to rōdō: josei rōdō to sabetsu* by M. Takashima and E. Yasukawa: Tokyo, Chūō Daigaku Shuppankai.)

Beechey, Veronica, and Tessa Perkins 1987 *A Matter of Hours: Women, Part-time Work and the Labour Market*: Cambridge, Polity Press.

References

Benston, Margaret "The Political Economy of Women's Liberation." *Monthly Review* Volume 21 Number 4.

Bradley, Harriet *Gender and Power in the Workplace: Analyzing the Impact of Economic Change*: London & New York, Macmillan.

Braverman, Harry 1974 *Labor and Monopoly Capital: The Degradation of Work in the Twentieth Century*, New York, Monthly Review Press (Translated in 1978 as Rōdō to dokusen shihon: 20 seiki ni okeru rōdō no suitai by K. Tomisawa: Tokyo, Iwanami Shoten.)

Broadbridge, Adelina 1998 "Barriers in the Career Progression of Retail Managers." *The International Review of Retail, Distribution and Consumer Research* Volume 8 Number1.

———— 1999a "A Profile of Female Managers: Some Insights." *The Service Industries Journal* Volume 19 Number 3.

———— 1999b "Retail Managers: Stress and the Work-Family Relationship." *International Journal of Retail and Distribution Management* Volume 27 Numbers 8 and 9.

Brockbank, Anne, and Joanne Traves 1996 "Career Aspirations: Women Managers in Retailing." In *Women in Organizations: Challenging Gender Politics*. Edited by S. Ledwith and F. Colgan: London, Macmillan.

Chiba, Etsuko 2000 Nōka josei rōdō no saikentō (A Re-examination of Women's Labour on Farms). In *Gendai nihon no josei rōdō to jendā: aratana shikaku karano sekkin* (Gender and Women's Labour in Modern Japan: An Approach From a New Perspective), edited by K. Kimoto and K. Fukasawa: Kyoto, Mineruva Shobō.

Cockburn, Cynthia 1983 *Brothers: Male Dominance and Technological Change*: London, Pluto Press.

———— 1985 *Machinery of Dominance, Women, Men and Technical Know how*: London, Pluto Press.

———— 1988 "The Gendering of Jobs: Workplace Relations and the Reproduction of Sex Segregation." In *Gender Segregation at Work*, Edited by S. Walby: Milton Keynes, Open University Press.

———— 1991 *In the Way of Women: Men's Resistance of Sex Equality in Organizations*: Basingstoke, Macmillan.

Cockburn, Cynthia, and Susan Ormrod 1993 *Gender and Technology in the Making*: SAGE Publications.

Collins, Patricia H. 1998 "The Social Construction of Black Feminist Thought." In *Feminist Foundations*, edited by K.A. Myers, C.D. Anderson, and B.A. Risman: Thousand Oaks, London & New Delhi, SAGE Publications.

Collinson, David, and David Knights 1986 "Men Only: Theory and Practices of Job Segregation in Insurance." In *Gender and the Labour Process*, edited by D. Knights and H. Willmot: Aldershot, Gower Publishing Company.

Connel, Robert W. 1987 *Gender and Power: Society, the Person and Sexual Politics*: Cambridge, Polity Press. (Translated in 1993 as *Jendā to kenryoku: sekushuariti no shakaigaku* by S. Mori, E. Kikuchi, T. Katō, and K. Ochi: Tokyo, Sankōsha.)

Dateki, Sei 1990 "Store Automation, Structural Change and Labor in Supermarkets." *Nihon Rōdō Kenkyū Kikō 'Kenkyū Kiyō'* 1 (The Studies of the Japan Institute for Labour, Number 1).

Dawson, John 2000 "Retailing at Century End: Some Challenges for Management and Research." International Review of Retail, Distribution and Consumer Research, 10(2), 119-148.

―――― 1999b "Employment and Competitiveness in European Commerce." In *Working Paper Series*: The University of Edinburgh, Management School.

Devine, Fiona 1992 "Gender Segregation in the Engineering and Science Professions: A Case of Continuity and Change." *Work, Employment and Society* Volume 6 Number 4.

Donovan, Josephine 1985 *Feminist Theory: The Intellectual Traditions of American Feminism*: London, Frederic Ungar Publishing Co., Inc. (Translated in 1987 as *Feminisuto no riron* by K. Koike: Tokyo, Keisō Shobō.)

Duden, B., and Claudia von Werlhof 1986 *Kaji rōdō to shihon shugi* (*Domestic Labour and Capitalism*) Compiled by Maruyama Mahito : Tokyo, Iwanami Gendai Sensho.

du Gay, Paul 1996 *Consumption and Identity at Work*: London, SAGE Publications.

Ehara, Yumiko 2001 *Jendā chitsujo* (Gender Order): Tokyo, Keisō Shobō.

Endō, Koshi 2002 "Nihonka shita kimyōna tōkei sabetsuron" (The Strange Theory of Japanised Statistical Discrimination) *Poritīku* dai 3 go (Politics Number 3): Shinpōsha.

Engels, Friedrich *Der Ursprung der Familie, des Privateigenthums und des States*. (Translated in 1965 as *Kazoku, shiyū zaisan, kokka no kigen* by S. Tohara: Tokyo, Iwanami Bunko.)

Fitzsimons, Annette 2002 Gender as a Verb: Gender Segregation at Work. Aldershot, Ashgate.

Fukasawa, Kazuko 1993 Rōdōryoku no joseika to sōsharu porishī no henyō ni kansuru kenkyū (sono 1)" (A Study in the Feminization of the Labour Force and Changes in Social Policy, Part 1) *Hannan ronshū* dai 29 kan dai 2 go (Collected Essays Volume 29 Number 2.)

―――― 2000a "Nihon no josei rōdō no tokuchō to honsho no bunseki shikaku." (Characteristics of Women's Labour in Japan and the Analytical Perspective of this Book) In *Gendai Nihon no josei rōdō to jendā: aratana shikaku kara no sekkin.* (Gender and Women's Labour in Modern Japan: An Approach From a New Perspective), edited by K. Kimoto and K. Fukasawa: Kyoto, Mineruva Shobō.

――――― 2000b "Josei rōdō to shakai seisaku." (Women's Labour and Social Policy.) In *Gendai Nihon no josei rōdō to jendā: aratana shikaku kara no sekkin.* Gender and Women's Labour in Modern Japan: An Approach From a New Perspective), edited by K. Kimoto and K. Fukasawa: Kyoto, Mineruva Shobō.

――――― 2000c "Hidentōteki shokushu e no josei no shinshutsu: kensetsugyō no sekō kanri rōdō." (Women's Advancement into Non-traditional Jobs: Execution Management in the Construction Industry) In *Gendai nihon no josei rōdō to jendā: aratana shikaku kara no sekkin.* (Gender and Women's Labour in Modern Japan: An Approach From a New Perspective), edited by K. Fukasawa and K. Kimoto: Mineruva Shobō.

――――― 2002 "Fukushi kokka to jendā poritikkusu." (Welfare States and Gender Politics) In *Fukushi kokka saihen no seiji: Kōza fukushi kokka no yukue 1.* (A Series on the Destination of Welfare States, Volume 1: The Politics of Reorganising Welfare States), edited by T. Miyamoto: Kyoto, Mineruva Shobō.

Furuta, Mutsumi 1994 "Josei to shihonshugi: 'Marukusu shugi feminizumu' no rironteki wakugumi." (Women and Capitalism: The Theoretical Framework of 'Marxist Feminism') *Joseigaku* (The Journal of Women's Studies) Volume 2, edited by Nihon joseigakkai gakkaishi henshū iinkai: Tokyo, Shinsuisha.

――――― 1996 "Anpeido wāku gainen to sono hyōka ni kansuru feminizumu shiten kara no kentō." (A Study of the Concept of Unpaid Work and its Evaluation from a Feminist Perspective) *Josei rōdō kenkyū* 30 go (The Bulletin of the Society for the Study of Working Women Number 30.)

――――― "Marukusu shugi feminizumu." (Marxist Feminism) In *Wādo mappu feminizumu* (Word Map Feminism), edited by Y. Ehara and Y. Kanai: Tokyo, Shinyōsha.

Hakim, C. 1979 "Occupational Segregation." In *U.K. Department of Employment Research Paper.*

Halford, Susan, and Pauline Leonard 2001 *Gender, Power and Organizations*: Basingstoke, Palgrave.

Halford, Susan, M. Savage and A. Witz 1997 Gender, Careers and Organisations: Current Developments in Banking, Nursing and Local Government: Basingstoke, Macmillan.

Hartmann, Heidi 1976 "Capitalism, Patriarchy and Job Segregation by Sex." *Signs* Volume 1, Number 3, Part 2.

Hashimoto, Kenji *Kaikyū shakai Nippon* (Japan, A Class Society): Tokyo, Aoki Shoten.

Hashimoto, Kenji *Class structure in Contemporary Japan*, Melbourne: Trans Pacific Press.

Hearn, J., and W. Parkin 1987 *'Sex' at 'Work': The Power and Paradox of Organisation Sexuality*. Brighton, Wheatsheaf Books.

Hearn, J., Sheppard D.L., Tancred-Sheriff, P. and Burrell G. (editors) *The Sexuality of Organization*: London, SAGE Publications.

Himmelweit, Susan 1995 "The discovery of 'unpaid work': the social consequences of the expansion of work." *Feminist Economics* Volume 1, Number 2, Summer.

Hirota, Toshiko 1979 *Gendai joshi rōdō no kenkyū* (A Study of Modern Women's Labour): Tokyo, Rōdō kyōiku sentā.

Honda, Kazunari 2002 *Chēn sutoa no jinzai kaihatsu* (Human Resource Development in Chain Stores): Tokyo, Chikura Shobō.

Horn-Kawashima, Yōko 1995 "Rōdō shijō kōzō, kigyō soshiki bunka ni okeru jendā sayō to josei rōdō." (Women's Labour and the Operation of Gender in the Labour Market Structure, Corporate Organisation and Culture). In *Jendā no nihonshi gekan* (Gender History of Japan Volume 2). Edited by H. Wakita and S. B. Hanley: Tokyo, Tokyo Daigaku Shuppankai.

Ida, Hiroyuki 1995 *Seisabetsu to shihonsei*. (Sexual Discrimination and the Capitalist System): Kyoto, Keibunsha.

Imoto, Shōgo 1993 "Epirōgu." (Epilogue). In *Ryūtsū gendaishi: Nihon-gata keizai fūdo to kigyōka seishin*. (Modern History of Distribution: The Japanese Economic Climate and Entrepreneurial Spirit), edited by Nihon Ryūtsū Shinbun: Tokyo, Nihon Keizai Shinbunsha.

Ishigaki, Ayako 1955 Shufu toiu daini shokugyō ron (Debates on the Second Occupation of Housewife) *Fujin Kōron* Feb. 1955 (Edited by Ueno Chizuko 1982 *Shufu ronsō o yomu* I (Reading the Housewife Debates I): Tokyo Keisō shobō.

Isono, Fujiko "Fujin kaihōron no konmei." *Asahi Jānaru* 10 February 1960 (Edited by Ueno Chizuko 1982 *Shufu ronsō o yomu* II (Reading the Housewife Debates II): Tokyo Keisō shobō.

Itō, Yōichi, (editor) 1994 *Josei to tōkei: jendā tōkeiron josetsu* (Women and Stat-istics: An Introduction to Gender Statistics): Matsudo, Azusa Shuppansha.

Josei no anpeido wāku kenkyūkai 1995 "Josei no anpeido wāku: kokusaiteki chōsa kenkyū to shiryō." (Women's Unpaid Work: International Research and Resources) In *Tokyo josei zaidan kenkyū josei hōkokusho*. (Tokyo Women's Foundation Research Promotion Report)

References

———— 1995 *Josei no anpeido wāku: kokusaiteki chōsa kenkyū bunken risuto*. (Women's Unpaid Work: International Research Bibliography) In *Tokyo josei zaidan kenkyū josei hōkokusho*. (Tokyo Women's Foundation Research Promotion Report)

Kansai sūpā māketto 1985 *Kansai sūpā 25 nen no ayumi* (A Twenty-Five Year History of Kansai Supermarket).

Kanter, R.M. 1977 *Men and Women of the Corporation*: New York, Basic Books. (Translated in 1995 as *Kigyō no naka no otoko to onna* by Y. Takai: Tokyo, Seisansei Shuppan.)

Kawanishi, Hirosuke 2001 *Nihon no rōdō shakaigaku* (Labour Sociology in Japan): Tokyo, Waseda Daigaku Shuppanbu.

Kawasaki, Satoko, and Yōichi Nakamura, editors 2000 *Anpeido wāku towa nanika* (What is Unpaid Work?): Tokyo, Fujiwara Shoten.

Keizai Kikakuchō, (Economic Planning Agency) 1997 *Kokumin seikatsu hakusho* (White Paper on National Life): Tokyo, Ōkurashō Insatsukyoku.

Kikkawa, Takeo 1998 "'Shōhi kakumei' to 'ryūtsū kakumei': shōhi to ryūtsū no amerikanaizēshon to nihonteki juyō." (The 'Revolution in Consumption' and the 'Revolution in Distribution': The Americanisation of Consumption and Distribution and its Acceptance in Japan). In *20 seiki shisutemu 3, keizai seichō II: juyō to teikō* (Twentieth Century System 3, Economic Growth II: Acceptance and Resistance), edited by Tokyo Daigaku Shakai Kagaku Kenkyūjo: Tokyo, Tokyo Daigaku Shuppankai.

Kikkawa, Takeo, and Mika Takaoka 1997a "Sengo Nihon no seikatsu yōshiki no henka to ryūtsū e no inpakuto." (Lifestyle Changes in Post War Japan and Their Impact on Distribution) In *Shakai kagaku kenkyū* (Studies in Social Science) Volume 48, Number 5: Tokyo, Tokyo University.

———— 1997b "Sūpāmāketto shisutemu no kokusai iten to nihonteki henyō." (International Moves in Supermarket Systems and Japanese Transformations) In *Kokusai hikaku, kokusai kankei no keieishi* (International Comparison: History of Management in International Relations), edited by H. Morikawa and T. Yui: Nagoya, Nagoya Daigaku Shuppankai.

Kimoto Kimiko 1995a *Kazoku, Jendā, kigyō shakai* (Family, Gender and Company Society): Kyoto, Mineruva Shobō.

———— 1995b "Seibetsu shokumu bunri to josei rōdōsha: hyakkaten A-sha no shokuba bunseki kara." (Women Workers and Job Segregation by Gender: From a Workplace Analysis of Department Store A). *Nihon rōdō shakaigakkai nenpō* 6 (Annual Review of Labour Sociology Number 6), Tōshindō.

———— 1999 "Onna no shigoto to otoko no shigoto: seibetsu shokumu bunri no mekanizumu." (Women's Work and Men's Work: The Mechanisms

Underlying Job Segregation by Gender) In *Kōza shakaigaku*, dai 14 kan, *jendā* (Kōza Sociology, Volume 14, Gender), edited by T. Kamata, S. Yazawa and K. Kimoto: Tokyo, Tokyo Daigaku Shuppankai.

─────── 2000a "Rōdō to jendā." (Labour and Gender.) *Ōhara shakai mondai kenkyūsho zasshi*. (Journal of the Ōhara Institute for Social Research, Number 500.)

─────── 2000b "Kigyō shakai no henka to kazoku." (The Family and Changes in Company Society). *Kazoku shakaigaku kenkyū*. (Japanese Journal of Family Sociology, Number 12.)

─────── 2000c Josei rōdō kenkyū no tōtatsuten to kadai (Achievements of and Issues in Women's Labour Studies) In *Gendai Nihon no josei rōdō to jendā: aratana shikaku karano sekkin* (Gender and Women's Labour in Modern Japan: An Approach From a New Perspective), edited by K. Kimoto and K. Fukasawa: Kyoto, Mineruva Shobō.

─────── 2002a "Rōdō soshiki to jendā." (Work Organization and Gender) *Shakaigaku Hyōron* (Japanese Sociological Review Volume 52, Number 4).

─────── 2002b "Kigyō shakairon kara no apurōchi: nihongata 'kindai kazoku' moderu no rekishiteki tokushitsu." (An Approach from the Theory of Company Society: Historical Characteristics of the Japanese 'Modern Family' Model). In *Kazoku to shokugyō: kyōgō to chōsei*. (Family and Occupation: Conflict and Adjustment), edited by K. Ishihara: Kyoto, Mineruva Shobō.

Kimoto Kimiko, and Kazuko Fukasawa, editors 2000 *Gendai Nihon no josei rōdō to jendā: aratana shikaku kara no sekkin* (Gender and Women's Labour in Modern Japan: An Approach From a New Perspective): Kyoto, Mineruva Shobō.

Knights, David, and Hugh Willmott, editors 1986 *Gender and the Labour Process*: Aldershot, Gower Publishing Company.

Komagawa, Tomoko 1998 "Ginkō ni okeru jimushoku no seibetsu bunri." (Segregation by Gender in Bank Clerical Jobs) *Rōdō shakai gakkai nenpō* dai 9 go (Annual Review of Labour Sociology Number 9.)

─────── 2000 "Kōsu betsu jinji kanri seido no henyō: toshi ginkō no 'josei katsuyō'." (Changes in the Personnel Management System Based on Career Paths: 'Positive Use of Women' in Major Banks.) In *Gendai Nihon no josei rōdō to jendā: aratana shikaku kara no sekkin* (Gender and Women's Labour in Modern Japan: An Approach From a New Perspective), edited by K. Kimoto and K. Fukasawa: Kyoto, Mineruva Shobō.

Koyama, Shūzō 1993 "Kouri gyōtai no shinka." (The True Value of Retail Operations) In *Ryūtsū gendaishi: Nihon-gata keizai fūdo to kigyōka seishin* (Modern History of Distribution: Japanese Economic Climate and Entrepreneurial Spirit), edited by Nihon Ryūtsū Shinbun: Tokyo, Nihon Keizai Shinbunsha.

References

Kuba, Yoshiko 1979 "Kaji rōdō to shihon: saikin no Yōroppa ni okeru shokenkyū ni tsuite no nōto." (Domestic Labour and Capital: Notes on Recent Studies in Europe) *Tokyo Gakugei Daigaku Kiyō*, 3 bumon, 30 (Journal of Tokyo Gakugei University 30).

────── 2002 "Jendā to 'keizaigaku hihan': feminisuto keizaigaku no tenkai to kakushin." ('Gender and a Critique of Economics': Developments and Innovations in Feminist Economics) In *Keizaigaku to jendā* (Economics and Gender), edited by Y. Kuba: Tokyo, Akashi Shoten.

Kuhn, Annette, and Ann Marie Wolpe, editors 1978 *Feminism and Materialism: Women and Modes of Production* (Translated in 1984 as *Marukusu shugi feminizumu no chōsen*: London, Routledge & Kegan Paul.)

Kumazawa, Makoto 1986 *Shokubashi no shura o ikite: sairon Nihon no rōdōshazō* (Surviving the Pandemonium of Workplace History: Another Discussion of the Images of Japanese Workers): Tokyo, Chikuma Shobō.

────── 1993 "Josei rōdōsha no sengo." (The Post War Era of Female Workers) In *Shinpan: Nihon no rōdōshazō* (New Edition: Images of Japanese Workers): Tokyo, Chikuma Gakugei Bunko.

────── 2000 *Josei rōdō to kigyō shakai* (Women's Labour and Company Society): Tokyo, Iwanami Shinsho.

Kyōtani, Eiji 1993 *Furekishibiriti towa nani ka: gendai Nihon no rōdō katei* (What is Flexibility?: Modern Japanese Labour Processes): Tokyo, Madosha.

Lam, Alice C.L. 1992 *Women and Japanese Management: Discrimination and Reform*: London, Routledge.

Matsudo, Takehiko 1994 "Soshiki wa fudan ni tsukurareru: soshiki to rōdō no esunomesodorojī." (Organisations are Constantly Constructed: The Ethno-methodology of Organisations and Labour) In *Soshiki to nettowāku no shakaigaku* (Sociology of Organisations and Networks), edited by K. Miyamoto, S. Morishita, and D. Kimizuka: Tokyo, Shinyōsha.

Mayo, Elton 1933 *The Human Problems of an Industrial Civilization*: Boston, Harvard University. (Translated as *Sangyō bunmei ni okeru ningen mondai* by E. Muramoto: Tokyo, Nihon Nōritsu Kyōkai, 1951.)

Mies, Maria, Veronika Benholdt-Thomsen, and Claudia von Werlhof 1991 *Women: The Last Colony*: Zed Books. (Translated as *Sekai shisutemu to josei* by M. Furuta and H. Yoshimoto: Tokyo, Fujiwara Shoten, 1995.)

Mitsuyama, Masako 1990 "Sūpāmāketto ni okeru nōryoku shugi kanri to kigyōnai kyōiku." (Ability-Based Personnel Management and In-Company Training). *Hokkaidō Daigaku Kyōikugakubu Kiyō* dai 54 go (Journal of the Faculty of Education, Hokkaido University Number 54).

Miyashita, Saori 2000 "Gijutsu kakushin to jendākan bungyō: insatsugyō to DTP." (Technological Innovation and Job Segregation by Gender: Printing Industry and DTP). In *Gendai Nihon no josei rōdō to jendā: aratana shikaku kara no sekkin* (Gender and Women's Labour in Modern Japan: An Approach From a New Perspective), edited by K. Kimoto and K. Fukasawa: Kyoto, Mineruva Shobō.

Mizuta, Tamae 1980 "Josei kaihō no shiten (7), marukusu shugi to feminizumu." (A Women's Liberation Perspective, No. 7: Marxism and Feminism). *Mirai* dai 170 go (*Future* Number 170).

Molineux, Maxine 1979 "Beyond the Domestic Labour Debate." *New Left Review* Number 116, July-August (Translated as Kaji rōdō ronsō o norikoete in *Keizai Rōdō Kenkyū*, 1987.)

Mori, Masumi 1997 "Shōsha ni miru seisabetu koyō kanri no konnichiteki keitai: 'Shin-nihonteki keiei' to jendā." (The Present Form of Sex-discriminatory Employment Management Seen in Trading Companies: 'New Japanese Style Management' and Gender). *Keizai to shakai* dai 9 go (Economy and Society Number 9).

Naitō, Norikuni 1975 *Igirisu no rōdōsha kaikyū* (The British Working Classes): Tokyo, Tōyō Keizai Shinpōsha.

Nakamura, Megumi 1988 "Ōte sūpā ni okeru josei kanrishoku, senmon-shokusha." (Female managers and specialists in large supermarkets). In *Shokuba no kyaria wūman* (Career Women in the Workplace), edited by K. Koike and Y. Tomita: Tokyo, Tōyō Keizai Shinpōsha.

Naruse, Tatsuo 1990 "Nishi yōroppa ni okeru rōdō katei ronsō no tenkai to sono genjō." (The Development of the Labour Process Debate and its Current State in Western Europe) *Keizai Kagaku Tsūshin* 62 (Journal of Economic Science Number 62).

Nikkeiren, (Japan Federation of Employers' Associations) 1969 *Nōryokushugi kanri: sono riron to jissai* (Ability-based Personnel Management: Its Theory and Practice).

Nikkeiren Kantō Keieisha Kyōkai, (Kantō Employers' Association, Japan Federation of Employers' Associations) 1968 *Rōmu shiryō No. 95: joshi jūgyōin no nōryoku kaihatsu to katsuyō no genjō* (Resource Materials in Labour Management, No. 95: Current Status of Development and Utilization of Female Employees' Abilities).

Nomura, Masami 1993 *Jukuren to bungyō: nihon kigyō to teirā shugi* (Skill and the Division of Labour: Taylorism in Japanese Firms): Tokyo, Ochanomizu Shobō.

Ogasawara, Yūko 1998 *OL tachi no 'rejisutansu'* ('Resistance' by Office Ladies): Tokyo, Chūkō Shinsho.

Okada, Yasushi 1991 *Hyakkaten Gyōkai* (The Department Store Industry): Tokyo, Kyōikusha.

Ōmori, Maki 1995 "Josei howaito karā no genjō to mondaiten" (The Current Status and Issues of Women White-collar Employees) In *Shakai seisaku gakkai nenpō dai 39 shū: gendai nihon no howaito karā* (Annals of the Society for the Study of Social Policy Annual Report, Number 39: White-collar Employees in Modern Japan): Tokyo, Ochanomizu Shobō.

Orihashi, Seisuke 1996 *Sūpā gyōkai* (The Supermarket Industry): Tokyo, Kyōikusha.

Ōsawa, Machiko 1993 Keizai henka to joshi rōdō: nichibei no hikaku kenkyū (Economic Changes and Women's Labour: A Comparative Study of the US and Japan): Tokyo, Nihon Keizai Hyōronsha.

Ōsawa, Mari 1992a "Gendai nihon shakai to josei: rōdō, kazoku, chiiki." (Women and Modern Japanese Society: Labour, Family and Community). In *Gendai nihon shakai* dai 6 kan (Modern Japanese Society Volume 6), edited by Tokyo daigaku shakai kagaku kenkyūjo: Tokyo, Tokyo Daigaku Shuppankai.

———— 1992b "Sangyō kōzō no saihen to 'koyō no joseika': 1973-1985 nen (The Reorganisation of the Industrial Structure and the 'Feminisation of Employment': 1973-1985)." In *Gendai nihon no rōshi kankei: kōritsusei no baransu shīto* (Labour Relations in Modern Japan: Balance Sheet of Efficiency), edited by K. Kurita: Kawasaki, Rōdō Kagaku Kenkyūsho Shuppanbu.

———— 1993a "Nihon ni okeru 'rōdō mondai' kenkyū to josei." (Women and Studies of 'Labour Issues' in Japan). In *Shakai seisaku gakkai nenpō dai 37 shū: gendai no josei rōdō to shakai seisaku* (Annals of the Society for the Study of Social Policy Annual Report, Number 37: present-day women's labour and social policy): Tokyo, Ochanomizu Shobō.

———— 1993b *Kigyō chūshin shakai o koete: gendai nihon o jendā de yomu* (Beyond the Company-Centred Society: Reading Modern Japan Through Gender): Tokyo, Jiji Tsūshinsha.

———— 1995 "Rōdō no jendāka." (The Gendering of Labour) In *Jendā no shakaigaku gendai shakaigaku* dai 11 kan (Sociology of Gender – Modern Sociology Volume 11), edited by S. Inoue, C. Ueno, M. Ōsawa, M. Mita, and S Yoshimi: Tokyo, Iwanami Shoten.

Pei Ekuiti Kenkyūkai (Study Group on Pay Equity) 1997 *Shōsha ni okeru shokumu no bunseki to pei ekuiti* (An Analysis of Work Duties in a Trading Company and Pay Equity).

Perrons, Diane, and Jennifer Hurstfield 1998 "Flexible Working and the Reconciliation of Work and Family Life or a New Form of Precariousness." In *National Report for the UK*, Coordinated by Dianne Perrons, European Commission.

Rōdō Chōsaron Kenkyūkai, (Study Group on Labour Research), editor 1970 *Sengo Nihon no Rōdō Chōsa* (Labour Survey of Post-war Japan): Tokyo, Tokyo Daigaku Shuppankai.

Roethlisberger, F.J. 1941 *Management and Morale*: Cambridge, Harvard University Press. (Translated in 1954 as *Keiei to kinrō iyoku* by K. Noda and K. Kawamura: Tokyo, Daiyamondosha.)

Sainsbury, Diane 1996 *Gender, Equality and Welfare States*: Cambridge, Cambridge University Press.

Sanderson, Kay and Rosemary Crompton, and 1990 *Gendered Jobs and Social Change*: London, Unwin Hyman.

Sargent, Lydia, editor 1981 *The Unhappy Marriage of Marxism and Feminism: A Debate on Class and Patriarchy*: Boston, South End Press.

Sasatani, Harumi 2000 "'Dentōteki joseishoku' no shin hensei: hōmu herupu rōdō no senmonsei." (The new organisation of 'women's traditional jobs': the expertise of home help work). In *Gendai nihon no josei rōdō to jendā: aratana shikaku kara no sekkin* (Gender and Women's Labour in Modern Japan: An Approach From a New Perspective), edited by K. Kimoto and K. Fukasawa: Kyoto Mineruva Shobō.

Scott, Alison M. 1994 "Gender Segregation in the Retail Industry." In *Gender Segregation and Social Change*, edited by A.M. Scott: Oxford, Oxford University Press.

Scott, Joan W. 1988 *Gender and the Politics of History*: New York, Columbia University Press. (Translated in 1992 as *Jendā to rekishigaku* by M. Ogino: Tokyo, Heibonsha.)

Senda, Yukiko 2001 "Kōsu betsu koyō kanri to jendā: tayōsei o ikasu." (Career Path Based Management and Gender: Utilising Diversity) In *Jendā manejimento* (Gender Management) Edited by Y. Sano: Tokyo, Tōyō Keizai Shinpōsha.

Shibayama, Emiko 1993 "Josei rōdōsha: danjo no shokugyō, kazokuteki sekinin to shakai sankaku no ryōritsu chōwa" (Women Workers: Men and Women's balancing of Job and Family Responsibilities and Social Participation). In *Gendai nihon no rōdō mondai: atarashii paradaimu o motomete* (Labour Issues in Modern Japan: In Search of a New Paradigm), edited by H. Totsuka and S. Tokunaga: Kyoto, Mineruva Shobō.

Shibuya, Atsushi 1983 "Saikin no ōbei ni okeru fujin kaihō riron no tenkai ni tsuite no ichikōsatsu." (A Consideration of the Recent Development of Women's Liberation Theories in Europe) *Ritsumeikan Daigaku sangyō shakai ronshū* dai 36 go (Ritsumeikan Review of Industrial Society Number 36).

Shimazu, Chitose 1978 *Fujin rōdō no riron* (Theories of Women's Labour): Tokyo, Aoki Shoten.

References

Shinozuka, Eiko 1995 *Josei ga hataraku shakai* (A Society in Which Women Work): Tokyo, Keisō Shobō.

Sokoloff, Natalie 1980 *Between Money and Love: the Dialectics of Women's Home and Market Work*: New York, Prager Publishers. (Translated in 1987 as *Okane to aijō no aida: marukusu shugi feminizumu no tenkai* by Y. Ehara, H. Fujisaki, T. Iwata, M. Kamiya, and S. Takenaka: Tokyo, Keisō Shobō.)

Sugihashi, Yayoi 1997 "Rōdō tōkei, shihyō no jendāringu: nihon o chūshin ni." (Gendering of labour statistics and indices: focus on Japan) *Tōkeigaku* dai 72 go (The Study of Statistics 72).

Takagi Ikurō and Wakana Shutō, and 1998–1999 "'Danjo kongōshokuka' ni kansuru kenkyū, 1, 2, 3." (A Study of the Shift to Mixed Genders in Jobs, Numbers 1, 2, 3) *Chingin to shakai hoshō* 1244 go, 1247 go, 1248 go (Wages and Social Security Numbers 1244, 1247 and 1248): Rōdōshinposha.

Takagi, Tadao 1960 "Fujin undō ni okeru rōdō fujin to katei fujin." (Working Women and Housewife Women in the Women's Movement) *Shisō* (Thought) December 1960 (Edited by Ueno Chizuko 1982 *Shufu ronsō o yomu* II (Reading the Housewife Debates II): Tokyo, Keisō shobō.

Takahashi, Yūkichi 1992 "Gendai nihon no kigyō shakai to chingin, shōshin kanri." (Company Society in Modern Japan and the Management of Wages and Promotions) In *Shakai seisaku gakkai nenpō* dai 36 shū (Annals of the Society for the Study of Social Policy Number 36: Tokyo, Ochanomizu Shobō.

Takaoka, Mika 1997 "Sengo fukkōki no nihon no hyakkaten to itaku shiire: nihonteki torihiki kankō no keisei katei." (Department Stores During the Post War Reconstruction Period and Consignment Sales: The Formation Process of Japanese Business Practices). *Keieishigaku* dai 32 kan 1 go (Japan Business History Review Volume 32 Number 1).

Takenaka, Emiko 1980 "Rōdōryoku saiseisan no shihon shugiteki seikaku to kaji rōdō." (Domestic Labour and the Capitalistic Nature of the Reproduction of Labour) *Keizaigaku Zasshi* 81 kan 1 go (Journal of Economics Volume 81 Number 1).

———— 1983 *Joshi rōdō ron* (A Theory of Women's Labour): Tokyo, Yūhikaku.

———— 1989a *Sengo joshi rōdōshi ron* (A Theory of the Post War History of Women's Labour): Tokyo, Yūhikaku.

———— 1989b "1980 nendai marukusu shugi feminizumu ni tsuite no jakkan no oboegaki: Patriarchal Capitalism no riron kōsei o megutte." (Some Notes on Marxist Feminism During the 1980s: Concerning the Structure of the Theory of Patriarchal Capitalism) *Keizaigaku Zasshi* 90 kan 2 go (Journal of Economics Volume 90 Number 2).

―――― 1991 *Shin joshi rōdōron* (The New Theory of Women's Labour). Edited by Takenaka Emiko: Tokyo, Yūhikaku.

―――― 1993 "Sōkatsu gendai no joshi rōdō to shakai seisaku: ronten no sābei." (Summation of Contemporary Social Policy and Women's Labour: Survey of the Points at Issue). In *Shakai seisaku gakkai nenpō dai 37 shū: gendai no josei rōdō to shakai seisaku* (Annals of the Society for the Study of Social Policy Number 37: Contemporary Women's Labour and Social Policy): Tokyo, Ochanomizu Shobō.

―――― 1994 "Henbō suru keizai to rōdōryoku no joseika." (The Changing Economy and the Feminisation of the Labour Force) In *Rōdōryoku no joseika: 21 seiki e no paradaimu* (The Feminisation of the Labour Force: Paradigm Towards the 21st Century), edited by E. Takenaka and Y. Kuba: Tokyo, Yūhikaku.

―――― *Joseiron no furontia: byōdō kara kōhei e* (Women's Theories Frontier: From Equality to Equity): Osaka, Sōgensha.

―――― "Shakai seisaku to jendā." (Social Policy and Gender) In *Shakai seisaku gakkai 100 nen* (One Hundred Years of the Society for the Study of Social Policy) Edited by 'Shakai seisaku sōsho' henshū iinkai: Kyoto, Keibunsha.

―――― 2001 "Atarashii rōdō bunseki gainen to shakai shisutemu no saikōchiku: rōdō ni okeru jendā apurōchi no gendankai." (A New Concept of Labour Analysis and the Restructuring of the Social System: The Current Level of the Gender Approach to Labour) In *Rōdō to jendā* (Labour and Gender), edited by E. Takenaka: Tokyo, Akashi Shoten.

―――― 2002 "Kaji rōdōron no gendankai (The Current Level of Domestic Labour Theory) In *Keizaigaku to jendā* (Economics and Gender), edited by Y. Kuba: Tokyo, Akashi Shoten.

Takenaka, Emiko, and Yoshiko Kuba, editors 1994 *Rōdōryoku no joseika: 21 seiki e no paradaimu* (The Feminisation of the Labour Force: A Paradigm Towards the 21st Century): Tokyo, Yūhikaku.

Takeuchi, Keiko 1992 "Koyō rōdōryoku no joseika to kigyō." (The Feminisation of Employed Labour and Corporations) *Seikei Daigaku Bungakubu Kiyō* dai 28 go (Bulletin of the Humanities Faculty, Seikei University Number 28).

Tateno, Katamasa 1994 *Nihon sūpā hattatsushi nenpyō* (Chronology of the Development of Supermarkets in Japan): Tokyo, Sōseisha.

Tatsuma, Nobuo, and Kimiko Kimoto 1999 "Shokuhin sūpā samitto." (Summit of Food Supermarkets) In *Seikyō ni okeru shigoto o tou* (Inquiring Into Work in Co-operatives), edited by Seikyō Sōgō Kenkyūjo (Japan Consumption Co-operative Institute).

Thompson, Paul 1983 *The Nature of Work*: London, Macmillan. (Translated in 1990 as *Rōdō to kanri: gendai rōdō katei ronsō* by T. Naruse and K. Aoki: Kyoto, Keibunsha.)

Tokyo Toritsu Rōdō Kenkyūsho 1991 *Hyakkaten joshi jūgyōin no shūgyō jittai to ishiki* (The Employment Conditions and Consciousness of Female Employees in Department Stores).

Tomisawa, Konomi 1993 "Apareru sangyō." (The Apparel Industry) In *Ryūtsū gendaishi: Nihon-gata keizai fūdo to kigyōka seishin* (Modern History of Distribution: Japanese Economic Climate and Entrepreneurial Spirit), edited by Nihon Ryūtsū Shinbun: Tokyo, Nihon Keizai Shinbunsha.

Tomlinson, F., Anne Brockbank, and Joanne Traves 1997 "The Feminization of Management? Issues of 'Sameness' and 'Difference' in the Roles and Experiences of Female and Male Retail Managers." *Gender, Work and Organization* Volume 4 Number 4, October.

Totsuka, Hideo, and Shigeyoshi Tokunaga, editors 1993 *Gendai Nihon no rōdō mondai: atarashii paradaimu o motomete* (Labour Issues in Modern Japan: In Search of a New Paradigm): Kyoto, Mineruva Shobō.

Ueno, Chizuko 1982 *Shufu ronsō o yomu I, II* (Reading the Housewife Debate Volumes 1 and 2): Tokyo, Keisō Shobō.

——— 1990 *Kafuchōsei to shihonsei* (Patriarchy and Capitalism): Tokyo, Iwanami Shoten.

——— 1995 "'Rōdō' gainen no jendāka." (Gendering of the concept of 'labour'). In *Jendā no nihonshi* (The History of Gender in Japan), edited by H. Wakita and S.B. Hanley: Tokyo, Tokyo Daigaku Shuppankai.

Vogel, Lisa 1981 "Marxism and Feminism: Unhappy Marriage, Trial Separation or Something Else?" In *The Unhappy Marriage of Marxism and Feminism: A Debate on Class and Patriarchy*. Edited by L. Sargent: Boston, South End Press.

Wakisaka, Akira 1986a "Sūpā ni okeru joshi rōdōryoku." (The Female Labour Force in Supermarkets) *Okayama Daigaku Keizaigakkai Zasshi* 17 3/4 *go* (Okayama Economic Review Volume 17 Numbers 3/4).

——— 1986b "Joshi rōdōsha shōshin no kanōsei: sūpā chōsa no jirei kara." (Possibilities for Advancement for Female Workers: Examples From Supermarket Surveys) In *Gendai no jinzai keisei: nōryoku kaihatsu o saguru* (Building Human Resources Today: An Examination of Ability Development), edited by K. Koike: Kyoto, Mineruva Shobō.

Walby, Sylvia 1986 Patriarchy at Work: Patriarchal and Capitalist Relations in Employment: Cambridge, Polity Press.

——— 1989 "Segregation in Employment in Social and Economic Theory." In *Gender Segregation at Work*. Edited by S. Walby: Milton Keynes, Open University Press.

Walby, Sylvia, editor 1989 *Gender Segregation at Work*: Milton Keynes, Open University Press.
────── 1990 *Theorizing Patriarchy*: Oxford, Basil Blackwell.
Walsh, John P. 1993 *Supermarkets Transformed: Understanding Organizational and Technological Innovations*: New Brunswick, Rutgers University Press.
Wilson, Elizabeth M., editor 2001 *Organizational Behavior Reassessed: The Impact of Gender*: London, SAGE Publications.
Witz, Anne 1992 *Profession and Patriarchy*: New York and London, Routledge.
────── 1993 "Women at Work." In *Introducing Women's Studies: Feminist Theory and Practice*, edited by V. Robinson and D. Richardson: London, Macmillan.
────── 1997 "Women at Work." In *Introducing Women's Studies: Feminist Theory and Practice* (Second Edition), edited by V. Robinson and D. Richardson: London, Macmillan.
Yahagi, Toshiyuki 1993 "Ryūtsū chaneru no hendō." (Changes in Distribution Channels) In *Ryūtsū gendaishi: nihon-gata keizai fūdo to kigyōka seishin* (Modern History of Distribution: Japanese Economic Climate and Entrepreneurial Spirit), edited by Nihon Ryūtsū Shinbun: Tokyo, Nihon Keizai Shinbunsha.
────── 1994 *Konbiniensu sutoa shisutemu no kakushinsei* (Innovativeness of the Convenience Store System): Tokyo, Nihon Keizai Shinbunsha.
Yashiro, Atsushi 1984 "Joshi rōdōsha no koyō kanri: ōte hyakkaten no jirei bunseki." (Employment Management of Female Workers: An Analysis of Examples From a Large Department Store) *Mita Shōgaku Kenkyū* 27 kan 5 go (Mita Business Review Volume 27 Number 5).
Yashiro, Atsushi 1992 "Ōte kourigyō ni okeru josei no kanrishoku e no shōshin: jinji bumon no kinō no jittai." (Women's Advancement to Managerial Positions in Large Retail Companies: The Actual State of the Functions of Personnel Departments) *Nihon Rōdō Kenkyū Zasshi* 388 *go* (The Japanese Journal of Labour Studies Number 388).
Young, Iris 1981 "Beyond the Unhappy Marriage: A Critique of Dual Systems Theory." Edited by Lydia Sargent 1981 *Women and the Revolution: The Unhappy Marriage of Marxism and Feminism*: London, Pluto Press.

Postscript

It is a relief to have finally finished writing. About ten years have passed since I began work on the survey of actual conditions in work organisations, the basis of this book. I would like to make some final remarks about the status of this book, on the basis of my research.

From the time of my graduate student days I have found understanding work and life as a whole and gaining a closer understanding of the state of men and women in modern society to be very attractive research themes. Unable to find my way there directly I progressed to these themes via various detours. The 1980s were a truly significant period for me. As part of a research group attempting to elucidate the image of workers at the Toyota Motor Company Limited, I took part in a research survey spanning practically the whole decade. Then, in the latter half of the 1980s, I came across empirical research in the English language field on the subjects of feminism and gender. The 1980s took on an epochal significance for me as this discovery was the birth of my aspiration to see whether it might not be possible to link family and work, from a gender viewpoint.

I was able to publish my first attempt to link Toyota workers' families and their firm as *Family, Gender and Company Society* (Minerva Shobō, 1995). Whilst putting this together I was also busy, from the early 1990s, with a documents survey of women's labour studies and was left feeling that this research field was certainly not complete and that it was of a dubious standard in terms of developing towards an argument connecting the family and the labour process. This was because, as I mentioned in the Introduction, in Japan we were limited to talking about or explaining employed labour using the gender-based division of labour in the family as the starting point. Empirical research into the question of why, and as a result of which major causes, the labour process continues to be organised along gender lines was virtually impossible to find. It will be impossible to get closer to an understanding of the relationship between the family and work if we do not redress this. This is why I decided to attempt to undertake research focussing on the labour field, fundamentally and in my own way. In 1992 I began feeling my way with a fact-finding survey into department stores and also general merchandise supermarkets. Since I had sketched out a research strategy of someday, after the labour analysis, returning to the work of shedding light on the whole picture surrounding the connection between post war work and family lifestyle in Japan, retail industry was a natural subject for my case studies. This was not just because retail industries have a high rate of dependence on female labour but also because retail industries have had a decisive impact on individual and family consumption patterns and, more broadly, on work and lifestyle patterns.

However, I had not originally thought that I would end up spending ten years on an analysis of gender in work organisations. When I stepped into the retail workplace, I felt countless wonderful and fathomless attractions. This was another reason for making various 'detours'. Through the 'Research Group Into the State of Work in Consumer Co-operatives Association' (*Seikyō ni okeru Shigoto no Aarikata Kenkyūkai*) (Tsutomu Hyōdō, Chairman), part of the Consumer Co-operatives Institute of Japan (*Seikyō Sōgō Kenkyūkai*) in which I was able to participate from 1995, I came to learn of one of the food supermarkets, which were constructing excellent operations systems. I have not used the collaborative research data from this project in this book but I do put the knowledge I gained to use in the analysis in this book. I was also able to undertake overseas research at the University of Surrey, Roehampton, and the London School of Economics and Politics (LSE) in 2000, thanks to a grant from the Hitotsubashi Foundation, temporarily putting on hold my research into the Japanese retail industry. In this period, as well as holding frequent discussions with researchers into British women's labour studies, I was able to learn from the accumulation of research into large-scale retail industries. At the same time I undertook questionnaire surveys of part-timers in several British supermarkets and was able to grasp the ways in which the state of work organisations in Britain differs from those in Japan. Whilst 'detours' acted to slow down the pace of work on the original object of the research, they also provided me with considerable stimulus, when I was considering the best way in which to approach the realities of retail work organisations, and also broadened my field of vision. The desire to present the ideas which emerged from my investigation of the case studies has been the most significant source of my energy to keep going these past ten years.

The surveys of department stores and general merchandise supermarkets always provided opportunities for making exciting discoveries and also for meeting people. In particular, the female store managers in the general merchandise supermarket, Company X, whilst being like a generation of younger sisters for me, were also, without a doubt, my 'teachers'. I wrote this book with a strong awareness of wanting to make clear the meaning of their positive challenge. I also came to feel strongly that, firstly, I had to understand the deep layers of the work organisation – the nameless women, starting with the parttimers, who absorbed the tremendous impact of radical statements full of pride and enthusiasm. Secondly, that I had an obligation to elucidate the structures connecting the top and the bottom of the organisation. The organisation of work analysis methodology permeating this book, which I mentioned in the opening paragraphs of Chapter 2, has been refined on the basis of the interview surveys. My efforts in putting together this book have concentrated on giving the most honest and thoughtful interpretation possible of the accumulated survey data.

Various previously published works form the basis of this book but these have been used following extensive corrections, revisions and re-arrangement of material. The following is a list of the main essays upon which this book is based. Chapter 1 contains claims identical to those in Chapter 1 (Kimoto 2000c) of *Gender and Women's Labour in Contemporary Japan* (2000) (*Gendai nihon no josei rōdō to jendā*), which I edited along with Kazuko Fukasawa , but it incorporates subsequently located new documents. Chapter 3 is a revised and corrected version of an article (Kimoto 1995b) which I contributed to a special edition of the journal *Annual Review of Labor Sociology* (*Nihon Rōdō Shakai Gakkai Nenpo)*, and which was based on a report to their symposium (November 1994), 'Female Labour in "Companycentred society"' ('*Kigyō shakai*' *no naka no josei rōdōsha*). From the second half of the 1990s I devoted a considerable amount of time to the research survey of the general merchandise supermarket, Company X, and I was on the verge of drowning in a sea of data but then the prospect of putting together this book arose with a request form the editorial committee of *Japanese Sociological Review* (*Shakaigaku Hyōron)* and in response to which I contributed 'Work Organisations and Gender' (*Rōdō soshiki to jendā)* (2000) to a special issue, 'The Challenges of Micro and Macro Problems' (*'Tokushū: mikuro-makuro mondai e no chōsen*). I determined the basis for part of Chapter 2 and Chapters 4 and 5 in the course of writing this essay but Chapters 4 and 5 were largely re-written to include data analysis. I must await the appraisal of readers regarding the analytical method of case studies and the analytical results but the lengthy period of time spent on the survey enabled me to make repeated visits to the enterprises which were the objects of the survey and also to clarify my own thoughts regarding my analytical viewpoint. Be that as it may, I wrote this book with the purpose of completing part of a long-standing task. However, it seems that I will not be able to halt my research into the retail industry for some time and that I must repeat my search anew for a way of promoting research which will make clear the relationships between work and family.

I received the assistance of a considerable number of people in the writing of this book. I will refrain from naming them all individually but I should like to express my particular gratitude to all the people who tenaciously stuck with me during my interviews. I also record my heart-felt thanks to both the department store, Company A, and the general merchandise supermarket, Company X, who generously provided the site for the surveys. Yuki Aritomi, an assistant in the Graduate School of Social Sciences of Hitotsubashi University, took considerable trouble in consolidating the substantial volume of research data. As is always the case, I learned a tremendous amount from her accurate treatment of data. I am also grateful to Miyoko Machida of Keisō Shobō publishers, who called on me with superb timing as I was coming to the end of putting together this work and who launched the publication of this modest scientific work. My occasional chats with her became invaluable opportunities for questioning and thinking anew about the meaning of my own research.

The research surveys upon which this book is based were carried out thanks to the assistance of Grants-in-Aid for Scientific Research from the Ministry of Education, Culture, Sports, Science and Technology; the Japan Society for the Promotion of Science (1992–1993, 1997–1999, 2001–2003); and the Research Fund of the Japan Economic Research Foundation (1998).

April 2003
Kimiko KIMOTO

Index

ability-based personnel management 41–2
Acker, Joan 238
affirmative action 30
Alvesson, Mats 238, 250
androcentrism 195, 197–9, 200, 203–04, 209, 216–17, 221, 225, 227–8, 230, 232
Azuchi, Satoshi 46, 48–50, 245

Barrett, Michèle 10
Beechey, Veronica 8, 10, 14, 22–4, 33, 233–6
Benston, Margaret 7
bottom up management 164, 206, 207, 208, 210, 211, 214, 215, 248, 249
Braverman, Harry 21, 61, 235–6

capitalism 8, 14, 31
career development 27, 63, 95, 110, 169, 180–3, 186–7, 193–6, 200, 205, 207, 209, 212–13, 216, 226–7
 of men 213
 of women 213
 of store managers 181
 of female store managers 200
case studies 3, 23–5, 27–33, 36–7, 40–1, 60, 108, 223, 236–7, 241, 266–7
Cockburn, Cynthia 25, 236
collective management 41–2

company society 4, 5, 6, 31, 233
creation of female store managers 108, 160–8, 170–1, 186, 192–5, 205, 213–21, 228–9
Crompton, Rosemary 27, 34

decentralisation of operations 61
Department Stores Law 45, 48, 50, 101
desire for promotion 85–7
dispatched salespeople 56, 7–7, 83, 95–102, 104, 107, 225–6, 242
distribution network 44–5, 95–6, 101, 104, 106, 225
division of labour 3, 6, 11–14, 22–4, 29, 35, 80, 235, 265
domestic labour 6–16, 18, 20–2, 28, 234–5
 explanations 21
 debate 7–11, 13–15, 18, 20–2, 28, 234–5
 in Japan 14
 in the West 7, 9–11
 division by gender 13
domestic roles 23, 29, 35
dual closure 26
dual systems theory 14

economic reductionism 59
employment management 31, 43

Equal Employment Opportunity Law between Men and Women 42, 43, 60
  Revised x, 43
evaluation-based wages 239
excessive gendering of work duties 67, 102
exclusion 25–7, 69, 199

'familial' model 24
family 3, 5–6, 8, 10–24, 28–9, 35, 41, 70, 106, 113, 124, 129, 152, 155, 157, 191, 233–7, 265–8
family responsibilities 20, 22, 24, 28, 157
  model 22, 24
family wage 21–2, 235–6
  ideology of a 'family wage' 21–2
female store managers 108, 160–71, 174, 179, 186–7, 189, 192–5, 197, 200–21, 227–31, 247–8, 266
female type management 209
female university graduates 67–8, 70, 78–9, 90–5, 101, 105–07, 116, 130, 191, 196, 199, 226, 241
femininity 217
feminisation of employment 29, 30, 34
feminisation of the labour force 7, 30
food supermarkets 47–51, 53, 55, 239, 244, 266
Fukasawa, Kazuko 7, 30–31, 235, 237, 267
full-timers 19

gender analysis of the labour process 22, 237
gender fairness x, 232
gender perspective xi–xii, 3–5, 7, 15, 21–4, 29, 31–3, 233–40
gender relations xi–xiii, 3, 10, 17, 21–5, 32, 35–7, 88, 95, 102–04, 106, 136, 159–60, 164, 171, 179, 180–1, 195, 200, 204–05, 208–09, 211–17, 224, 229, 230–1, 236–7, 246, 248
gender stereotyping xii, 20
general merchandise supermarkets xiii, 33, 44, 46–55, 58, 108–09, 155–6, 160, 166, 196, 223, 226, 240, 248, 266–8

Halford, Susan 28, 238–9, 253
Hartmann, Heidi 14–15, 21–2, 25–6
Hashimoto, Kenji 234
Hearn, Jeff 238
hegemonic masculinity 204
hidden curriculum 82
Himmelweit, Susan 15
Honda, Kazunari 175
horizontal segregation 34
housewives 8–10, 18–20, 106, 121, 235–6
  housewife debate 8, 9
  housewife labour 9

Ida, Hiroyuki 14
in-company welfare 5, 18
in-house slavery 12
Ishigaki, Ayako 9

Isono, Fujiko 9

Japan's labour practices ix–x, 60
job allocation 44, 79, 122, 142
job segregation by gender xiii, 5, 11, 22–5, 28, 30–8, 59, 62, 67, 76, 88, 94, 95, 97, 102, 104, 108, 114, 118, 123, 135, 154, 237, 241, 244

Kanter, Rosabeth M. 200–01, 207
Kikkawa, Takeo 45, 49, 50, 155, 239
Kimoto, Kimiko 18, 233–7, 241, 244, 267
Komagawa, Tomoko 237
Kuba, Yoshiko 10–11, 17, 233–4

labour market 3, 6, 8, 10–14, 17–23, 27–9, 32, 34, 36, 41, 235
labour practices 60, 237
labour process 3, 14, 18, 21–4, 28–33, 36–7, 223, 235–7, 265
labour process debate 21, 23, 28, 235–6
labour relations 4, 31–2, 35–8, 41, 44, 77, 108, 123, 236, 238, 246
labour sociology 5
labour studies 3–7, 11, 16–17, 19, 24, 28–9, 31, 33–4, 43, 223, 237, 265–6
Lam, Alice C. L. 60, 241
large-scale retail industry x, 44, 63
Large-Scale Retail Stores Law 47, 50–1, 58

large companies 5, 18–19, 30
large general merchandise supermarkets 51–5, 58

male type management 209
management 18, 23, 27, 30–8, 39, 40–3, 47, 50, 52, 59–63, 67–72, 76, 79, 80–2, 89, 91–3, 98, 102, 104, 106–08, 110, 113–14, 125–8, 136, 149–51, 154–64, 168–73, 176–81, 186, 192, 195–217, 220–1, 224–31, 237, 246, 248, 249
bottom up style 164, 206, 207, 208, 210, 211, 214, 215, 248, 249
of targets 98
style of male store managers 208
managerial positions 41, 67, 70, 73–6, 85, 86–7, 93, 103, 105, 108, 114, 124, 151, 168, 188, 191, 195, 203, 215, 218, 224–5, 227–8, 246
Marxist Economics 7, 9
Marxist feminists 10, 22
masculine conception 24
Mayo, G. E. 238
methodology 7, 11, 13–14, 19–23, 31, 33, 223, 267
modern family 11–12
model 18–19

organisation 22, 25, 31–2, 37–40, 44, 47, 50, 61–3, 76, 81, 83, 88, 90, 95, 102, 104, 107–08, 113–14, 123, 139, 149–54, 156–65, 170, 178,

192, 199, 200–01, 204, 209–32, 238, 245–6, 265–7
organisational challenge xi, xiii, 160–1, 164, 213, 223, 227–9
organisational culture xiii, 28, 39–40, 82, 86–8, 94, 103, 156–8, 192, 195, 197, 200, 203, 205–06, 209, 212–14, 216, 221–2, 224–7, 229–32, 238–9
organisational efficiency 121, 123, 232
organisational innovators 229
organisation analysis 63, 223, 225
Ōsawa. Machiko 30
Ōsawa, Mari 13, 16, 29, 30, 236, 238

paid work 3–4, 7, 8–18, 21, 29–31, 234, 237
part-timers ix, xi, 17, 19, 30, 55–6, 58, 60, 76–7, 153, 231, 238, 240–1, 266–7
patriarchy 14, 21
performance 219, 221, 229–30, 243
personnel assessments 41, 43, 110–13, 189
personnel management 30, 31, 35, 41–3, 67–70, 113, 158, 169, 196–7, 199–200, 225–7
  based on career paths 43
  based on the status ranking system 43
  system 30–1, 35, 42–3, 67–70, 113, 196–7, 199, 227
point of sales/control of information 50
positive use of women 40–3, 60, 63, 67–8, 72–3, 88–9, 108, 116, 123, 160–1, 164–9, 218, 226–7
proletarian marriage 12

qualifications 26–7, 34, 41, 110, 125
  lever 27

rank-and-file regular employees xi, 102, 125, 133, 136, 176–7, 214, 218, 231, 240, 244–5
reductionist method 21
regular employees ix–x, 4–5, 43, 53–59, 70, 72, 76–90, 94–104, 107, 109–10, 113–18, 120–6, 130, 133–4, 136, 140, 148, 150–2, 154, 159, 174, 176–7, 183, 191, 197, 214, 218, 225–6, 231, 238, 240–5
reproduction 6, 8, 36
resistance xiii, 19, 26–7, 39, 62, 120, 141, 150, 158, 177, 200, 204, 223, 225, 245–6
response-negotiation relations xiii, 38, 91, 106, 108, 158, 225
retail industry 33, 44, 48, 55, 60, 63, 176, 238, 240–1, 266, 268
Revised Equal Employment Opportunity Law between Men and Women 43

'special theory' approach 33
sales formats 47, 48, 50, 51
sales jobs 60, 80, 101
Sanderson, Kay 27, 34
Scott, Alison M. 35, 59
Scott, Joan W. xii
second wave of feminism 12, 15

segregation xiii, 5, 11, 22–38, 44, 59, 62, 67, 76–9, 88, 94–7, 101–04, 108–09, 113–16, 120–3, 135, 139, 149–51, 154, 156–60, 223–30, 233–38, 241, 244
  in the organisation 154
  in the workplace xiii, 37
segregation line 108
seniority 18, 42, 69, 71
  seniority-based wages ix, 18, 42
Shibuya, Atsushi 10, 260
shift to a service economy 30
Shimazu, Chitose 12, 233–4
short cycle labour force ix
Shutō, Wakana 17
special theory 7, 11–13, 16, 19, 20, 28, 33
status grade 42, 69, 72, 74, 78, 81, 110–11, 157, 169, 172, 189–191, 199–200, 204, 219, 243, 247
status pay 69
status ranking system xi, 41–4, 67–71, 106, 110, 113–14, 125, 156, 166, 189, 191, 223, 239
store managers 61, 108, 111–12, 114, 116–17, 119–20, 123–4, 126, 131, 132, 135, 136, 137, 138, 139, 141, 149, 160–221, 228–31, 240–1, 244, 246–8, 266
strategy 8, 26, 35, 37, 49, 61, 106–07, 217, 226, 229–30, 235, 248–9, 266
structure of Japanese food consumption 48, 52

Takagi, Ikurō 17
Takagi, Tadao 9

Takenaka, Emiko 7, 10–16, 29, 233–5
Taylorism 236, 238
technological innovations 25, 27, 30, 32, 36, 50, 236, 245
them and us 135, 139, 149, 158, 244
theory of statistical discrimination 30
trade unions 235

Ueno, Chizuko 10, 14, 16–18, 233
unified theory 14–15
unpaid work 8, 15–17, 234–5

vertical segregation 27, 34
Vogel, Lisa 10, 233

Walby, Sylvia 14, 36
Walsh, John P. 61–2
Witz, Anne 22, 26, 28, 238
women's labour studies ix, xii, 3–7, 11, 17, 19, 24, 28–9, 31, 33–4, 43, 223, 237, 265–6
women's latent potential 40–2
women's liberation 8–9, 12
working class families 12, 22
working hours 70, 76, 84–8, 91–4, 102–05, 109, 130–1, 152, 157, 245–8
work organisations ix–xiii, 31–2, 37–40, 44, 62–3, 76, 83, 90, 102, 104, 108, 113–14, 123, 139, 149, 151–2, 154, 156, 159, 170, 200, 209, 215, 223–5, 227, 229–30, 231–2, 238, 246, 265–7

Yahagi, Toshiyuki 47, 49, 50
Young, Iris 14